PHOTO: RAY LUSTIG

CHARLES KRAUTHAMMER was educated at McGill, Oxford and Harvard universities. He is a graduate of the Harvard Medical School and was Chief Resident in Psychiatry at Massachusetts General Hospital. In 1978 he came to Washington to direct planning in psychiatric research for the Carter administration, and began contributing articles to *The New Republic*. He served as a speechwriter to Vice President Walter Mondale during the 1980 campaign, then joined *The New Republic* as a writer and editor. In 1983 he became a contributing essayist for *Time* magazine and in 1984 began a weekly column, now nationally syndicated, for the Washington *Post*. In 1984 he received the National Magazine Award for Essays and Criticism. He lives in Washington, D.C., with his wife Robyn, an artist, and his son Daniel.

Cutting Edges

CUTTING EDGES

Making Sense of the Eighties

Charles Krauthammer

87 - 678

Random House New York

Portions of this work first appeared in *Commentary*, and *The Washington Post.* Grateful acknowledgment is also made to the following
for permission to reprint previously published material:
   The New Republic: various articles by Charles Krauthammer.
Reprinted by permission of *The New Republic,* © 1979, 1980,
    1981, 1982, 1983, 1984, 1985, The New Republic, Inc.
   Time magazine: various articles by Charles Krauthammer. Copyright © 1983, 1984, 1985, Time Inc. All rights reserved. Reprinted
               by permission from TIME.

Library of Congress Cataloging in Publication Data

Krauthammer, Charles, 1950—
Cutting edges.

   1. United States—Civilization—20th century—Addresses, essays, lectures. 2. United States—Popular culture—History—20th
century—Addresses, essays, lectures. 1. United States—Politics and
government—20th century—Addresses, essays, lectures. I. Title.
      E169.1.K6883   1985   973.926   85-8334
          ISBN 0-394-54801-9

Manufactured in the United States of America
Typography and binding design by J. K. Lambert
             98765432
             First Edition

TO MY PARENTS

Shulim and Thea Krauthammer

Acknowledgments

MOST OF THESE ESSAYS FIRST APPEARED IN *The New Republic*. OTHERS appeared in *Time* and the Washington *Post*. I thank these publications for granting permission to republish my essays in this collection.

All acknowledgments begin with Martin Peretz, whose example of political courage inspired me to become a political writer, and to whose patience, encouragement and generosity of spirit I owe my writing career.

My colleagues at *The New Republic* have been particularly helpful in shaping and criticizing my ideas. Many thanks to Michael Kinsley, Rick Hertzberg, Morton Kondracke, James Glassman, Jefferson Morley, Marc Granetz, Ann Hulbert, Jack Beatty and Dorothy Wickenden. I have been very lucky to have editors as gifted as Meg Greenfield at The Washington *Post*, and Ross Kriss and Ray Cave at *Time*, I thank them for their encouragement and help. And many thanks to Peter Osnos, my editor for this collection. It was his energy and devotion that turned an idea into a book, and his thoughtfulness and patience that made the process far less difficult than it should have been. David Seideman has contributed most generously of his scholarship and quick intelligence as my research assistant. His help has been invaluable, as has the tireless research of Anne Hopkins at *Time*. Thanks to Joan Shaffer, Jeanie Booros, and Beth Toridis for typing many an incoherent early draft.

To Dr. Hermann Lisco and Dr. Gerald Klerman, my mentors and advisers at Harvard Medical School, I owe much, for their wisdom and guidance throughout my medical career and beyond.

This book is dedicated to my parents, whose example of piety, learning and duty is the rarest gift that any parent can make to a child.

And finally a word about my wife, Robyn. Changing professions in midlife is not easy. Without encouragement and support, it is impossible. I had the extraordinary good fortune to have a wife who urged me to follow my heart, who endured the journey with me, and whose wit and courage has made the journey a joy. My deepest thanks to her, without whom not a word of this would ever have been written.

Contents

Introduction

WHEN I WAS STUDYING POLITICAL THEORY AT OXFORD, ONE OF MY FRIENDS WAS a physiology student on leave from Harvard Medical School. I was studying John Stuart Mill. He was studying sheep's hearts. Since I had seriously considered going into medicine, I kept trying to gauge his work against mine, and both against some impossible standard of what was the worthwhile thing to do in life. Young people like to talk about such matters, and Brown and I talked about it more than most. In his room was a bookshelf that fascinated me. It contained a set of neatly bound, three-ring notebooks. Each, in turn, contained a complete set of med-school lecture notes: anatomy, histology, cardiology and so on. I imagined that all one had to do was to know—memorize, perhaps—everything on this single shelf, and one would command a certain irrefutable reality. Medicine promised not only moral certainty (is anything as unarguably good as healing?), but intellectual certainty, a hardness to the truth, something not found in the universe of politics.

The bookshelf exerted a siren effect on me. As I found my own studies becoming increasingly abstract (my thesis was on the tension between Mill's politics and esthetics), I kept coming back to it. One day, midway through my thesis and deep into a black hole of circular speculation, I picked up the phone and called the registrar at Harvard Medical School. I asked if the place they had offered me a year before was still open. It was. Two weeks later I found myself in Boston listening to the opening lecture on enzymes. I began my own set of three-ring notebooks.

They are in storage now.

When one makes as circuitous a journey as I have from political study to medicine to psychiatry to writing, one is expected to offer some explanation. When interns at *The New Republic* ask me for advice on how to become a columnist, I am tempted to say, "First, go to medical school." That is not a terribly bad idea. I suspect some of the habits of thought I absorbed in medicine have influenced my writing. I hope so, since modern, scientific medicine is perhaps the most sophisticated engine ever devised for systematically organizing vastly different orders of knowledge.

But I didn't go into medicine to learn to organize. Why then? There are undoubtedly deeper reasons of class, family, history, and accident that make up one's destiny. But I think always of Brown's notebooks, and of the intellectual and moral shelter they promised—like the magical catalogue of catalogues in Borges' "The Library of Babel," which men imagine will conquer the darkness of an unintelligible universe.

In Borges, such a thing was a fiction within a fiction, as, of course, it turned out to be in real life. I am astonished now at my naïveté (I still remember my surprise when I discovered that the *New England Journal of Medicine* contained editorials) but not particularly regretful. Medicine taught me science, a crucial form of literacy without which one misses the singularity of this century. Doctoring taught me about real suffering, which I can now readily distinguish from the more literary forms of anguish. And life in the shadow- and mirror-world of psychiatry cured me finally of a young man's need for hardness to truth. Very valuable lessons all.

But as far greater writers before me have discovered, the life of medicine, noble and narrow, is confining. I never lost my love of politics. What made me especially restless was that I could hear its disputations through the clinic walls. After seven years, I decided that there was no shortage of hands to take up my work in medicine, but there was a shortage of hands, voices actually, advancing the things I believed in outside. So outside I went.

I went to *The New Republic,* then, as now, engaged in a struggle for the soul of the Democratic party. Uniquely among intellectual organs, *The New Republic* was trying to rescue liberalism from its drift toward defeatist isolationism, and from its growing confusion as to American purpose. This is not the neoliberalism with which *The New Republic* is often credited, and which is concerned with matters domestic, primarily with fine-tuning the democratic machinery. Nor is it neoconservatism, of which *The New Republic* is often accused, and which has given up on both the Great Society and liberalism (in the Millian sense). *The New Republic* was engaged in something different: a robust, self-confident defense of liberal values at home and abroad. A fight I wanted to join, and so (after a detour or two) I joined *The New Republic.* The rest of the story is this book.

The view it presents of political and social life in America in the eighties is hardly systematic. But it is informed by several purposes. The first of these is to offer a skeptical survey of the myths and fads which periodically wash over our culture in waves of enthusiasm, leaving confusion, and some amusement, in their wake. A second is to conduct a critical—clinical, perhaps—inquiry into those political and moral questions of inescapable ambiguity (like abortion or human experimentation) which demand illumination rather than solution, and which divide us far more bitterly than they should. The last is to apply to much of the rest of the political universe, where the questions are, in my view, decidely unambiguous, a political philosophy of liberal internationalism. That tradition, whose pedigree stretches from Harry Truman through Henry Jackson and, alas, no further, is rather a political orphan nowadays. My fondest hope is that this book might provide it with something of a home.

I am, however, not a theorist. I find criticism easier, and safer. Marx, for example, was the greatest social theorist of the modern era, and the wreckage of human lives that his theories have occasioned might have appalled even him. It certainly appalls me. My mission is modest. Not to change the world, but to understand a little of it. And perhaps, every once in a while, as Tom Stoppard puts it, to give a bit of a nudge.

Washington, July 1985

I

MYTHS

Likeness

THE MIRROR-IMAGE FALLACY

"AS IS EVIDENT JUST FROM THE LOOK ON HIS FACE," OBSERVES, *The New Yorker* in a recent reflection on the Lincoln Memorial, "[Lincoln] would have liked to live out a long life surrounded by old friends and good food." Good food? *New Yorker* readers have an interest in successful soufflés, but it is hard to recall the most melancholy and spiritual of Presidents giving them much thought. *New Yorker* editors no doubt dream of living out their days grazing in gourmet pastures. But did Lincoln really long to retire to a table at Lutèce?

Solipsism is the belief that the whole world is me, and as Mathematician Martin Gardner points out, its authentic version is not to be found outside mental institutions. What is to be found outside the asylum is its philosophic cousin, the belief that the whole world is *like* me. This species of solipsism—plural solipsism, if you like—is far more common because it is far less lonely. Indeed, it yields a very congenial world populated exclusively by creatures of one's own likeness, a world in which Lincoln pines for his dinner with André or, more consequentially, where KGB chiefs and Iranian ayatollahs are, well, folks just like us.

The mirror-image fantasy is not as crazy as it seems. Fundamentally, it is a radical denial of the otherness of others. Or to put it another way, a blinding belief in "common humanity," in the triumph of human commonality over human differences. It is a creed rarely fully embraced (it has a disquieting affinity with martyrdom), but in a culture tired of such ancient distinctions as that between children and adults (in contemporary movies the kids are, if anything, wiser than their parents) or men and women ("I was a better man as a woman with a woman than I've ever been as a man with a woman," says Tootsie), it can acquire considerable force.

Its central axiom is that if one burrows deep enough beneath the Mao jacket, the *shapka* or the chador, one discovers that people everywhere are essentially the same. American anthropologist Samantha Smith, age eleven, was invited to Moscow by Yuri Andropov for firsthand confirmation of just that proposition (a rare Soviet concession to the principle of on-site inspection). After a well-photographed sojourn during which she took in a children's festival at a Young Pioneer camp (but was spared the paramilitary training), she got the message: "They're just . . . almost . . . just like us," she announced at her last Moscow press conference. Her mother, who is no longer eleven but makes up for it in open-mindedness, supplied the corollary: "They're just like us . . . they prefer to work at their jobs than to work at war."

That completes the syllogism. We all have "eyes, hands, organs, dimensions, senses, affections, passions." We are all "fed with the same food, hurt with the same weapons, subject to the same diseases, healed by the same means, warmed and cooled by the same winter and summer." It follows, does it not, that we must all want the same things? According to Harvard cardiologist Bernard Lown, president of International Physicians for the Prevention of Nuclear War, that's not just Shakespeare, it's a scientific fact: "Our aim is to promote the simple medical insight," he writes, "that Russian and American hearts are indistinguishable, that both ache for peace and survival."

Such breathtaking non sequiturs, cardiological or otherwise, are characteristic of plural solipsism. For it is more than just another happy vision. It is meant to have practical consequences. If people everywhere, from Savannah to Sevastopol, share the same hopes and dreams and fears and love of children (and good food), they should get along. And if they don't, then there must be some misunderstanding, some misperception, some problem of communication. As one news report of the recent conference of Soviet and American peace activists in Minneapolis put it, "The issue of human rights sparked a heated discussion . . . and provided participants with a firsthand view of the obstacles to communication which so often characterize U.S.–Soviet relations." (The sadistic sheriff in *Cool Hand Luke* was more succinct: pointing to the rebellious prisoner he had just brutalized, he explained, "What we've got here is failure to communicate.") It is the broken-telephone theory of international conflict, and it suggests a solution: repair service by the expert "facilitator," the Harvard negotiations professor. Hence the vogue for peace academies, the mania for mediators, the belief that the world's conundrums would yield to the right intermediary, the right presidential envoy, the right socialist international delegation. Yet Iraq's Saddam Hussein and Iran's Ayatollah Khomeini, to take just two candidates for the Roger Fisher school of conflict resolution, have perfectly adequate phone service. They need only an operator to make the connection. Their problem is that they have very little to say to each other.

There are other consequences. If the whole world is like me, then certain conflicts become incomprehensible; the very notion of intractability becomes paradoxical. When the U.S. embassy in Tehran is taken over, Americans are bewildered. What does the Ayatollah want? The U.S. Government sends envoys to find out what token or signal or symbolic gesture might satisfy Iran. It is impossible to believe that the Ayatollah wants exactly what he says he wants: the head of the Shah. Things are not done that way any more in the West. (Even the Soviet bloc has now taken to pensioning off deposed leaders.) It took a long time for Americans to get the message.

Other messages from exotic cultures are never received at all. The more virulent pronouncements of Third World countries are dismissed as mere rhetoric. The more alien the sentiment, the less seriously it is taken. Diplomatic fiascoes follow, like Secretary Shultz's recent humiliation in Damascus. He persisted in going there despite the fact that President Assad had made it utterly plain that he rejected efforts by the U.S. (the "permanent enemy") to obtain withdrawal of Syrian forces from Lebanon. Or consider the chronic American frustration with Saudi Arabia. The Saudis consistently declare their refusal to accept the legitimacy of a Jewish state in the Middle East, a position so at variance with the Western view that it is simply discounted. Thus successive American governments continue to count on Saudi support for U.S. peace plans, only to be rudely let down. When the Saudis finally make it unmistakably clear that they will support neither Camp David nor the Reagan plan nor the Lebanon accord, the U.S. reacts with consternation. It might have spared itself the surprise if it had not in the first place imagined that underneath those kaffiyehs are folks just like us, sharing our aims and views.

"The wise man shows his wisdom in separation, in gradation, and his scale of creatures and of merits is as wide as nature," writes Emerson. "The foolish have no range in their scale, but suppose every man is as every other man." Ultimately to say that people all share the same hopes and fears, are all born and love and suffer and die alike, is to say very little. For it is after commonalities are accounted for that politics becomes necessary. It is only when values, ideologies, cultures and interests clash that politics even begins. At only the most trivial level can it be said that people want the same things. Take peace. The North Vietnamese want it, but apparently they wanted to conquer all of Indochina first. The Salvadoran right and left both want it, but only after making a desert of the other. The Reagan administration wants it, but not if it has to pay for it with pieces of Central America.

And even if one admits universal ends, one still has said nothing about means, about what people will risk, will permit, will commit in order to banish their fears and pursue their hopes. One would think that after the experience of this century the belief that a harmony must prevail between peoples who share a love of children and small dogs would be considered evidence of a most grotesque historical amnesia.

From where does the idea of a world of likes come? In part from a belief in universal brotherhood (a belief that is parodied, however, when one pretends that the ideal already exists). In part from a trendy ecological pantheism with its misty notions of the oneness of those sharing this lonely planet. In part from the Enlightenment belief in a universal human nature, a slippery modern creation that for all its universality manages in every age to take on a decidedly middle-class look. For the mirror-image fantasy derives above all from the coziness of middle-class life. The more settled and ordered one's life—and in particular one's communal life—the easier it becomes for one's imagination to fail. In Scarsdale, destitution and desperation, cruelty and zeal are the stuff of headlines, not life. Thus a single murder can create a sensation; in Beirut it is a statistic. When the comfortable encounter the unimaginable, the result is not only emotional but cognitive refusal. Brutality and fanaticism beyond one's ken must be made to remain there; thus, for example, when evidence mounts of biological warfare in faraway places, the most fanciful theories may be produced to banish the possibility.

To gloss over contradictory interests, incompatible ideologies and opposing cultures as sources of conflict is more than antipolitical. It is dangerous. Those who have long held a mirror to the world and seen only themselves are apt to be shocked and panicked when the mirror is removed, as inevitably it must be. On the other hand, to accept the reality of otherness is not to be condemned to a war of all against all. We are not then compelled to see in others the focus of evil in the world. We are still enjoined to love our neighbors as ourselves; only it no longer becomes an exercise in narcissism.

But empathy that is more than self-love does not come easily. Particularly not to culture so fixed on its own image that it can look at Lincoln, gaunt and grave, and see a man ready to que up at the pâté counter at Zabar's.

Time, August 15, 1983

Survivorship

COURAGE

THE IDEA OF HEROISM HAS FALLEN ON HARD TIMES LATELY. ITS NADIR occurred almost exactly one year ago, when the Iranian hostages (remember them?) were welcomed home as heroes. Perhaps it was only a designation by default, since we didn't quite know what other word to use and it seemed impolite to call them what they obviously were—victims. Their ordeal had all the markings of victimhood: they entered into it through no choice of their own; they were thoroughly passive throughout (as we were); and their release, like their capture, occurred independently of any action on their part. To be sure, they merited our support and sympathy for their suffering. But hardly twenty-one-gun salutes for their heroism.

The universal celebration of their courage could only have occurred in an era of survivor chic, when the idea is in vogue that there is no higher human achievement than making it through life. From Southampton to Malibu, radical chic, like wide ties, has come and gone. Survivor chic is in. We have such a heavy schedule of crises to be gotten through nowadays —identity, midlife and so on—that only a select few can manage the time, the energy (the courage!) to work through them all. But those who make it through ("through" is the operative word in survivorship) a couple of broken marriages, a mud slide on the beachhouse and perhaps a facelift or two, earn the title of survivor and the general acclaim that goes with it.

Now, to those who would object that the autobiographical hot-tub set has trivialized the notion of survival, I would reply that the idea of survival as an achievement, rather than a mere condition, is a trivialization to begin with. I suspect it derives, at least in part, from the popularized Darwinian notion that survival is a reward for fitness and thus a token of achievement. When applied to human affairs, that idea is either pernicious (since it implies that those who perish somehow deserve it) or silly. And the silliness is evident not only when an aged starlet triumphantly tells Merv Griffin that she is a survivor, but also when a country, in its relief, mistakes hostages for heroes. A year later, and perhaps shamed by the example of Sakharov and Walesa, we know better.

I don't mean to be unfair. The hostages themselves are quite innocent of the charge of survivor chic. First, their suffering was more than merely existential. There is a world of difference between sitting blindfolded in a room listening to a million marchers chant for your death and, say, struggling to get in touch with your feelings in wood-paneled twice-a-week therapy. Furthermore, the hostages, for the most part, seemed genuinely bewildered by the notion that merely pulling through had made them heroes. That was last year, however. They may come to share our general confusion on the subject of heroism. After all, a country that confers the Presidential Medal of Freedom on one actor (John Wayne) who played the role of hero for the cameras and confers the Presidency on another, betrays a certain inability to distinguish real from counterfeit heroes.

We also have trouble distinguishing courage, which requires choice, from tenacity, which doesn't. In the wide acclaim accorded such recent stage and film productions as *The Elephant Man, Whose Life Is It, Anyway?, Inside Moves,* and the DeBolts documentaries, an unlikely series of protagonists have invariably been characterized as courageous. I think that's a mistake. For those from whom unkind fate has taken almost everything, necessity does the work of courage, to use George Eliot's phrase. This is not to deny the perseverance and determination and nobility of these characters, but it is to question the current fashion that being is in itself an act of courage. Courage is different. It is, simply understood, the willingness to risk one's self for someone or something other—for example, to pledge one's life, fortune and sacred honor for the independence of one's country. I am, admittedly, insisting on a small distinction. But an important one, I think. I revere courage, and I would like to reserve the word for people like Thomas Jefferson and Lenny Skutnick.

Lenny Skutnick is not one of the original signers of the Declaration of Independence. And when he jumped into the freezing Potomac River to save a drowning survivor of the Air Florida crash, he risked neither his fortune nor his sacred honor. But he did risk his life. After saving the woman, Skutnick had to be taken to the hospital because he had exposed himself dangerously in the icy water. After a short spell he went home— and this time we got the word right—a hero.

Beyond characterizing him correctly, however, we didn't quite know what to do with Lenny Skutnick. Most of us, after all, are too young to have seen a hero before.

The two park rangers who hovered above the wreckage in a helicopter and plucked survivors out of the water were induced on the evening of the crash to reenact for the cameras their initial dash to the helicopter. Here they were, within hours, *acting* the role of heroes. I fear that someone is already working on a script for the "Fourteenth Street Bridge Disaster," and when they ask Lenny Skutnick to play himself, it will be hard for him to say no. Jumping into a freezing river is one thing, but resisting the embrace of the age is another.*

The New Republic, February 3, 1982

* Postscript: they did make the movie and Lenny did say no. A real hero.

Revolution

GRENADA AND THE END OF

REVOLUTION

REVOLUTION IS A LARGE IDEA, AND GRENADA A SMALL ISLAND. OF SUCH incongruities comedy is made. In Grenada, of course, it turned out not to be all comedy. As the bloody fratricidal denouement showed, even comedy staged on small islands can end in tragedy when the actors are jealous ideologues. And when they use live ammunition. We now have the memory of Maurice Bishop to remind us that even in parody the revolution eats its children.

That the Grenadian revolution was a parody is evident from its only remaining legacy, its documents. These have been largely ignored because they are not portentous enough. True, there are secret treaties with North Korea, Cuba and the Soviet Union; close ties with East Germany and Libya; and the airport, whose military uses were amply demonstrated by the U.S. Army. But Grenada was not exactly an active threat to world peace. Geopolitically, its documents are as uninteresting as the island itself. But as historical artifacts, as the unselfconscious autobiography of a revolution, they are fascinating. Their interest lies principally in their texture, in the tone of high seriousness with which they render the story of what happened when revolution came to Grenada. They tell us something about what happened to Grenada, and much about what has happened to revolution.

First, and always, there is the problem of scale. The memos addressed to Yuri Andropov, then chief of the KGB, and Defense Minister Dimitri

Ustinov are from "Hudson Austin, General of the Army." The Soviets did not take kindly to such strutting. When Soviet Chief of Staff Ogarkov was pressed by his Grenadian counterpart, Chief of Staff Major Einstein Louison (in Moscow for military training), for slightly more aid than the Soviets had agreed to in writing, the somewhat nervous Grenadian report of the meeting records that "Marshal Ogarkov replied rather jokingly that students should be concerned with their studies."

Then there was Cde. (Comrade) Ian Jacobs's one month, eight-city tour of the United States to raise American consciousness and American money. His report on the trip judges both goals to have been accomplished. Media coverage was good, and the fundraising a success. What exactly does that mean? Usually when third world officials come to the United States to raise money, they have in mind, say, a new air defense system or an ambitious industrial project. Jacobs came for a word processor. He didn't quite get it. He reports with satisfaction, "We should be able to raise between three to five thousand U.S. dollars—a figure that should allow us to purchase a word processor within the next three to six months." Inflated figures, it turns out. By his own account, though he shilled for the "word processor project" at every stop from Sacramento to Philadelphia, it was not until he got to Miami that he found a contributor willing to donate "between $1,000 and $2,000"—but only on the condition that it be laundered to get him a tax exemption.

And it is not hard to see why historians won't linger long over the secret agreement between the Communist Party of Cuba and the ruling party of Grenada, the New Jewel Movement. The protocol begins with the invocation, "Brotherly united by the same ideals of struggle in their respective countries, as well as of active solidarity in favor of the peoples that struggle for national liberation, and likewise, sharing the same convictions against imperialism, colonialism, neocolonialism, Zionism and racism," etc., etc. Accordingly, Cuba agrees to send Grenada, among other things, "two technicians in billboards and posters," "two technicians in sound equipment for public meetings," a "specialist in the work of the religious people," and a press cartoonist. In another document, Bishop urges that someone be sent to Cuba or Nicaragua to learn how to keep a phony set of books for the IMF.

Armed with a chief of staff, a word processor and a press cartoonist (no record about whether it found a crooked accountant), Grenada was ready to do battle with imperialism.

What the revolution lacked in scale, it made up for in volume. The American invasion force turned up tons of documents, boxes upon boxes of reports, minutes, diaries—a sort of gigantic *Reflections on the Revolu-*

tion. The report of a meeting of the Party's Central Committee in mid-September 1983 runs to more than twenty thousand words. It begins by calling to the attention of the Central Committee sixteen previous and available reports from "1. Minutes of the last emergency Central Committee [meeting]" to "16. Workers' Committee analysis of the Working Class for the Month of August." Things move quickly in a month.

Before his death Lenin said, "We have become a bureaucratic utopia." Grenada aspired to that—the number of meetings, reports, reports on meetings, and meetings on reports, is staggering—but, unfortunately, the bureaucratic revolution appears to have occurred very early in the literacy campaign. One example: Cde. Hazel-Ann (no last name given), in Moscow for ideological training, reports that one of her fellow Grenadian students is ill. "The doctor's report is that he has high pertension [sic] and is sick with his heart."

Back home high pretension was epidemic. Heart sickness followed. For there is poignancy in the idealism shown by ordinary people caught up in the enthusiasm of revolution, committed to its promise, utterly and sincerely devoted to making it work—whatever it is. Hazel-Ann, for example, had apparently heard of the party strife of mid-September 1983 that was ultimately to lead to the final massacre and collapse of the revolution. Her fourteen-page, painfully neat, handwritten report from Moscow detailing the progress she and the other Grenadian comrades in her cell had made ends thus:

We take this opportunity to express our deep concern about the situation as analyzed by the C.C. [Central Committee]; and our confidence in the Party's leadership and our collective ability to avert the situation through hard, organised, systematic, self-critical Leninist-type work. The C.P.S.U. [Communist Party of the Soviet Union] International Leninist Party School N.J.M. [New Jewel Movement] Party Cell repledges our commitment to the Party; to building a strong Party on Marxist-Leninist principles and to the defence and building of the Revolution, along the lines that would bring us to achieving SOCIALISM. Long Live Our Party!

The several features of this citation characterize much of the party's internal communication: (1) an earnestness born of an intense will to believe; (2) an ambiguity bordering on confusion as to what exactly one is believing in; all expressed in (3) the most rigid Marxist-Leninist language, a jargon so jarring that it lends a touch of irony to Grenada's boast to having been the first Marxist revolution in the English-speaking world. Interestingly, this Marxist-Leninist mumbo jumbo appears less in the

Party's public discourse—after all, Bishop's speeches had to be understood by ordinary people—than in the private communications of the leadership. Unlike Orwell's cynical O'Brien, in Grenada the big brothers and sisters were not too worldly to believe what they made others believe.

At its crucial final meeting, the Central Committee recognizes that the country, the "material base" as Bishop puts it, is falling apart. Major Louison (Einstein, back from Moscow), observes that the roads are the worst he's ever seen, and the Central Committee falls into a fierce debate over defects in party structure and ideology that can account for this state of affairs. (With the island's productive energies being poured into meetings, reports and note-taking, it isn't surprising that there was little left to devote to the material base. Louison did observe that "while we are losing links with the masses, the middle-class types have been coming to the revolution for jobs." That clue is quickly ignored.) The minutes are full of criticism and self-criticism of "right opportunism," "petit bourgeois deviationism," "economism." They all agree on the antidote, "firm Leninism," but they're stuck on exactly what that means. A comrade called on to explain his vote against a two-man leadership for the party replies that "He is not clear how the dialectics will unfold. He said that he has not seen it anywhere in the science." People who talk like that in the Kremlin surely are referred (to the KGB perhaps) for psychiatric evaluation.

In Grenada they rise to the Central Committee. At its penultimate meeting of August 26, 1983, the consensus is that the party is in deep crisis and the revolution in danger of collapsing. Bishop speaks last. His summary remarks include the recommendation to "research the history of the Party during the last five or six years, minutes and conclusions will be useful to look at," "study the history of the Communist Party of the Soviet Union," and "reread *Standards of Party Life* by Pronin [sic]." At a 1981 rally Bishop had called on the masses to "Unionise! Mobilise! Educate! Democratise!" In the privacy of the Central Committee, his final advice is plagiarize.

In the end, plagiarism, jargon and ideological study are not enough. Even Bishop admits that the mood of the "masses" is very low and the revolution falling apart; the consensus estimate is that it has no more than three to six months left. What could save it? What is missing? For that the Central Committee, by all accounts, had no answer. But the revolution did.

"General Rule: no social revolution without terror," said Napoleon. Bishop may have been grandiose, but he was not cruel. He may have been a dictator (hundreds, perhaps thousands, passed through his prisons), but he was not a terrorist.

Bulletin From The Main Political Department, October 19, 1983. Revolutionary soldiers and men of the People's Revolutionary Armed Forces: Today our People's Revolutionary Army has gain [sic] victory over the right opportunist and reactionary forces which attacked the Headquarters of our Ministry of Defense. These anti-worker elements using the working people as a shield entered Fort Rupert. . . . [T]he counter-revolutionary elements, headed by Maurice Bishop . . . [and comprised of] only businessmen, nuns, nurses and lumpen elements. . . .

Bishop and many lumpen were killed in the final massacre. But even the last tragic act could not escape the revolution's parodic destiny. The final communiqué of the new junta concludes with a stirring invocation of the memory of those who had just died fighting against Bishop and for the newest revolution:

Comrades, the death of OC Conrad Mayers, W02 Raphael Mason, Sgt Dorset Peters, and L/Cpl Martin Simon have not gone in vain, but have further manured [sic] the struggle of our Grenadian people. Long live the Memory of our fallen comrades. Long live the Grenada Revolution. Forward Ever, Backward Never. Death to Imperialism.

The hero as fertilizer. The curtain falls.

I started by suggesting that revolution is a large idea. Perhaps one should say *was* a large idea. Decades of trying to shoehorn it into the Grenadas of this world has diminished it greatly. It still has legitimacy: the first act of any gang of thugs that can seize a radio station and an airport is to proclaim itself a revolutionary junta, usually of national salvation. But it is precisely because every gang of thugs, or posturers, or dreamers, claims its honor that it has become so debased. Like other newly internationalized Western concepts ("rights" as defined by the U.N., for example), it has been emptied of meaning. And empty of meaning it acquires power.

Michael X, the Trinidadian hanged in his native country for (simple) murder after a career in London as a salon revolutionist, declared that "the only politics I ever understood is the politics of revolution." To which V.S. Naipaul, also a Trinidadian, answers, "London words, London abstractions, capable of supporting any meaning . . . [he] chose to give them." Maurice Bishop, who like Michael X had been through both London and the West Indian Black Power Movement of the early 1970s, was adept at the political use of empty abstractions. In 1981 he gave a speech on "freedom of the press" to explain why he shut down the last remaining independent newspaper in Grenada: "[The] most important reason of all: This is revolution, we live in revolutionary Grenada, this is a revolutionary condition, and there is a revolutionary legality, and they will have to abide by the law of the revolution. When the revolution speaks, it must be heard, listened to. Whatever the revolution decrees, it must be obeyed; when the revolution commands, it must be carried out; when the revolution talks, no parasite must bark in their corner."

Any word that grants automatic legitimacy and at the same time is capable of supporting any meaning becomes a source of great power. The circle is vicious: as "revolution" becomes more ubiquitous, it becomes more empty of meaning, more powerful a tool, and thus more attractive to the next gang of thugs, posturers and dreamers.

The idea of revolution is debased first by overuse. Yet revolution is not a serious idea everywhere. In the Eastern bloc it evokes only cynicism; in the West, where it is considered a safe form of play for the young, nostalgia. People who want to believe in revolution have now to believe in third-world revolution. The idea of revolution has devolved of necessity upon that part of the world to which it is least suited. For what, in a post-colonial world, with the wars of independence won, can revolution mean? Almost invariably—from Tanzania to Cambodia to Grenada—it is said to mean socialism. That makes for problems of scale, or to state it more broadly, of culture and development, as the Grenada documents show. After all, what can socialism mean in a place where there is no working class? What can working class mean where there is no industry? To speak of revolution in such circumstances is either an act of deception or a form of false consciousness.

But there is a deeper, older reason for the fallen state of the revolutionary idea. It is not cultural, but ideological; not a function of revolution's current entrapment in the developing world, but a function of its entrapment in nineteenth-century Marxism. For it was not just London-talk that Maurice Bishop spoke, but Marx-talk; not just an alien idea he brought to his island, but a socialist one—and of a particular kind: scientific socialism. By "scientific" Marx intended to distinguish his historicist socialism from the "utopian" variety, on which he could not heap enough ridicule. The folly of the utopian socialists, like Proudhon, was to betray an interest in what post-revolutionary society would look like. Marx denounced as infantile the idea of detailing the society of the future. The working class has "no ideals to realize," he said, "but to set free the elements of the new society with which old collapsing bourgeois society itself is pregnant." The purpose of revolution is to allow "the solution to the riddle of history" (communism) to unfold; to guess at the answer in advance is to misunderstand the entire revolutionary process.

"In Marx you will find no trace of utopianism in the sense of inventing the 'new' society and constructing it out of fantasies," said Lenin. The end of Marxist revolution—i.e., what socialism is to be—is explicitly, inherently, purposely left open and undefined. In a word, empty. As Melvin Lasky points out, this indeterminateness of the revolutionary idea, this sundering of utopia from revolution, of ends from means, is the great legacy of Marx's overthrow a century ago of the utopian socialists.

Since the preferred form even of national revolutions today is Marxist, the modern revolutionary idea necessarily is capable of supporting any meaning. (It is no accident that the only authentically transforming revolution of our time was the Iranian revolution, a decidedly non-, indeed, anti-Marxist affair.) The triumph of anti-utopian revolutionism has bequeathed to us a generation of revolutionaries with no idea of the kind of society they wish to construct (again, the Ayatollah knows precisely what he wants the world to look like—Qum) and, most importantly, with no hesitation about pursuing revolution in the absence of such an idea. A century ago an Irish Chartist leader denounced such negative revolutionaries as "mere speculators in anarchy." Today they are not only a majority at the U.N., they are custodians of the revolutionary idea itself.

"What socialism will look like when it takes on its final forms we do not know and cannot say," said Lenin. Little wonder that neither could the Central Committeemen in Grenada, so desperate to build socialism, so bereft of any idea what that meant. They not only suffered from the smallness of their island; they suffered from the emptiness of their guiding ideology. It is a cardinal feature of this age—indeed it is what makes this the age of revolution—that they should have decided to carry on regardless. The result is instructive.

The New Republic, January 30, 1984

On Moral Equivalence

"IF HE DOES REALLY THINK THAT THERE IS NO DISTINCTION BETWEEN virtue and vice," warns Dr. Samuel Johnson, "why, sir, when he leaves our house let us count our spoons." Judging by the recent pronouncements of some of our leaders, it is time to start husbanding spoons. Not that anyone in public life denies that there are moral distinctions to be made; but there seems to be a growing unwillingness—or is it an inability?—to make them, even the most simple.

Consider the case of another wise and respected doctor, Dr. Seuss. His latest epic, *The Butter Battle Book,* is a parable of the nuclear age. Two peoples, the Yooks and the Zooks, find themselves in such fierce—and pointless—confrontation that each is ready to drop the fatal Bitsy Big-Boy Bomberoo on the other. They are very similar, these Yooks and Zooks. They seem to differ in only one way: one side takes its bread butter-side up, the other butter-side down.

Yooks, Zooks. East, West. Butter-side up, butter-side down. What's the difference? cries the good Dr. Seuss in a plea predictably hailed for its sanity by everyone from Art Buchwald ("must reading") to Ralph Nader ("a bundle of wisdom in a small package"). Now is it really necessary to observe that in this world, as opposed to Dr. Seuss's cuddly creation, what divides Yooks and Zooks is democracy and constitutional government, among other conventions? The principal reason Yooks insist on arming themselves is that the Zooks of this planet have the unfortunate tendency to build gulags (for export too) and to stockpile those nasty intercontinental ballistic Bomberoos.

The allergy to elementary distinctions is not confined to child educators and their admirers. It also turns up on the political front, even among presidential candidates. For example, when Louis Farrakhan publicly threatened the life of the Washington *Post* reporter who had disclosed Jesse Jackson's "Hymie" slur, Jackson characterized the episode as a "conflict" between "two very able professionals caught in a cycle that could be damaging to their careers."

This is the language of moral equivalence. "Two professionals"—each guy just doing his job—cleverly places the two men on the same moral plane. "Caught"—passive victims, both men done to and not doing—neatly removes any notion of guilt or responsibility. "In a cycle"—no beginning and no end—insinuates an indeterminateness in the relationship between the two men: Someone may have started this, but who can tell and what does it matter? (Nor is this the first time Jackson has pressed the cycle image into dubious service. Remember his "cycle of pain" in Lebanon, as if Navy Lieut. Robert Goodman, the flyer for the American peace-keeping force that had lost more than 250 men to terrorist attack, and President Hafez Assad, who had at least acquiesced in that attack, were equal partners in crime?) Having framed the issue in these terms, Jackson proceeded to the logical conclusion: he proposed a meeting between Farrakhan and the reporter, offering himself as mediator.

What was most disturbing about this affair was not the excesses of an extremist, but how his candidate parsed the problem, and worse, how uncritically that rendering was received. That Jackson's peculiar moral logic should have gone virtually unchallenged among his Democratic rivals (they criticized Farrakhan's death threats instead—a victory of discretion over valor) is an index of just how unserious about moral distinctions we have become. As conservative economist Thomas Sowell put it, the inability to make moral distinctions is the AIDS of the intellectuals: an acquired immune deficiency syndrome. It certainly is not inborn. Children can make elementary distinctions between, say, threatener and threatened. Moral blindness of this caliber requires practice. It has to be learned.

We learn it in several ways. One arrives at much of the currently fashionable agnosticism about the cold war (the inability to tell Yooks from Zooks because of nukes) through world-weariness. After forty years of long twilight struggle, one feels one has had enough. And when the easy distinctions become too much, the hard ones, like choosing one group of guerrillas over another in a murky Third World struggle, become intolerable. Thus, that facile evasion now elevated to the status of wisdom, that one man's terrorist is another man's freedom fighter. "Who goes there, friend or foe?" asks Uncle Sam of a Central American revolutionary in a recent cartoon. "I am a rebel trying to overthrow my government through murder, mayhem and terrorism," he replies. "That doesn't answer my question," responds Uncle Sam, the implication being that there is something arbitrary about supporting one set of guerrillas (Nicaragua) and not another (El Salvador).

Is there? Pol Pot, Jonas Savimbi, Edén Pastora Gómez and an assortment of Salvadoran Marxist-Leninists have taken up arms against their respective governments. Is there nothing to choose between them? If one is serious about the issue, one has to ask how they fight: Bombs on school buses? Mines in harbors? Or attacks on the other side's military? They all differ qualitatively and—forgive the piety—morally. One is also obliged to ask about goals: to sort out the totalitarians from the democrats, and when one really encounters them (Grenada, for example), to call thugs, thugs. The pox-on-all-their-houses sentiment is not just traditional American isolationism making a comeback. It is moral exhaustion, an abdication of the responsibility to distinguish between shades of gray. The usual excuse is that the light has grown pale; the real problem is a glaze in the eye of the beholder.

Another mode of unlearning moral distinctions is through an excess of empathy. The claim is that we must not judge before we fully understand. "Context," protested Jackson, arguing that one must first put Farrakhan's threats in the context of the Black Muslim's apocalyptic language and his history (like his good deeds combating drug abuse). But this is to confuse moral analysis with psychotheraphy. Treating people seriously, that is, as adults—whatever their history, their culture, their unconscious drives— means judging what people do and say, not what they intend or feel. To defer judgment pending full understanding is to ensure that we will make no judgments at all.

Not that psychological insight and moral judgment are mutually exclusive. John le Carré is extraordinarily skillful at showing the psychological affinity between the British master spy Smiley and his KGB nemesis Karla. But in the end, there is no mistaking Le Carré's view of the worthiness of their respective enterprises. One can understand and still judge, so long as one is not tempted to understand everything.

Finally, perhaps the deepest cause of moral confusion is the state of language itself, language that has been bleached of its moral distinctions, turned neutral, value-free, "nonjudgmental." When that happens, moral discourse becomes difficult, moral distinctions impossible and moral debate incomprehensible. If abortion is simply "termination of pregnancy," the moral equivalent of, say, removing a tumor, how to account for a movement of serious people dedicated to its abolition? If homosexuality is merely a "sexual preference"—if a lover's sex is as much a matter of taste as say, haircolor (or having it butter-side up or butter-side down)—then why the to-do over two men dancing together at Disneyland? But there is a fuss, because there is a difference. One can understand neither with language that refuses to make distinctions.

Why, after all, say "single-parent family" when we mean fatherless home? (Single, male-headed households are a small minority of the single-parent family group.) The descriptive, and sympathetic, "fatherless" acknowledges that something is missing; the ostentatiously neutral "single-parent family" would have us believe that the distinction between a single- and a double- —why not a triple?—parent household is entirely statistical.

Using unflattened, living language does not commit one to an anti-abortion, anti-gay or anti-welfare position. One can argue forcefully for free choice in abortion, rights for homosexuals and aid to fatherless families without pretending that the issues here are merely clinical, aesthetic or statistical. They are moral too. But to make, or even follow, moral arguments, we need language that has not yet obliterated any trace of distinctions.

And yet the language of moral equivalence has become routine. Calling something the moral equivalent of war, for example, is a favorite Presidential technique for summoning the nation to a cause. That metaphor, coined by William James, was last pressed into service by Jimmy Carter to gird us for the energy crisis. Before that, we have had wars on poverty, crime, cancer and even war itself (World War I). Now, Mr. Carter knew that turning down thermostats and risking lives in combat make vastly different claims on the citizenry. Indeed, he sought to exploit that disproportion to rally the nation to the unglamorous task of conserving energy. The idea was to make the notion of conserving energy more important. What went unconsidered was what that kind of linguistic maneuver does to the idea of going to war. The problem with summoning a great moral theme in the service of a minor one—the problem with declaring moral equivalence when it does not exist—is what that does to the *great* idea. In a dangerous world Americans might some day be called upon to go to war, and if that happens, the difference between reaching for a thermostat and reaching for a gun will become painfully apparent.

The trouble with blurring moral distinctions, even for the best of causes, is that it can become a habit. It is a habit we can ill afford, since the modern tolerance for such distinctions is already in decline. Some serious ideas are used so promiscuously in the service of so many causes that they have lost all their power. Genocide, for example, has been used to describe almost every kind of perceived injustice, from Vietnam to pornography to Third World birth control. A new word, holocaust, has to be brought in as a substitute. But its life before ultimate trivialization will not be long. Only recently a financial commentator on PBS, referring to a stock-market drop, spoke of the holocaust year of 1981. The host did not blink.

Counted your spoons lately?

Time, July 9, 1984

Apocalypse

THE END OF THE WORLD

"THIS MAY HURT THE CEMETERY BUSINESS, BUT I DON'T OWN A PLOT," declared a smiling Jerry Falwell in a recent Sunday television sermon. The faithful hardly needed to be told why, but for the benefit of those who hadn't heard the good news, he explained that, like others who had been saved, he was going not down but up—into the clouds to meet the returning Christ in what is known to evangelicals as the Rapture. That is to be followed by the torments of the seven years of the Tribulation, and ultimately by the Millennium, a thousand years of bliss. Reverend Falwell was smiling because he was sure that when Jesus said, "This generation shall not pass, till all these things be fulfilled (Matthew 24:34)," he meant *this* generation. As proof, Falwell went on to list the eleven signs, from the restoration of the Jews in Israel to "the absence of dynamic leadership in the world," that characterized the final premillennial stage. Or as Reverend Tim LaHaye put it, "the countdown to Armageddon has begun."

Falwell and LaHaye are among dozens preaching this message, and millions (eight million in the United States alone is a conservative estimate) who believe it. The imminence of the millennium is the common, if not the dominant, theme of the many enthusiasms on display in evangelical broadcasting and publishing. From TV prime-timers like Billy Graham, Rex Humbard, Pat Robertson, Oral Roberts and Falwell, to the most obscure preacher on local radio, hardly a fundraising plea passes without some reference to the coming of the new age. One interim development has been the emergence of an entire new publishing industry featuring titles like *The Beginning of the End* ("Invasion of Afghanistan. Upheaval in Iran. Annexation of Jerusalem. Shortage of Oil in Russia. The result? An invasion of Israel by Russia . . . an invasion which will trigger the end of the world) and *Christians Will Go Through the Tribulation: And How to Prepare for It* (the how-to book to end all how-to books, with chapters like "Preparing to survive nuclear war," "Protecting your food supply," "Wind power generation of electricity," and "Preparing for supernatural warfare," with recommendations by Brother McKeever on where to buy supplies).

Though these books do not get reviewed in *The New Republic,* their popularity is immense. The number-one nonfiction best seller of the 1970s —in its first twenty-six months it went through twenty-one printings—was Hal Lindsey's *The Late Great Planet Earth,* a step-by-step history of the immediate future. The millennial subculture supporting these publications is vast and committed, but submerged. It tends to be noticed only when a believer who happens to be in the public eye inadvertently permits a glimpse of the iceberg, as when James Watt told the House Interior Committee, "I don't know how many future generations we can count on before the Lord returns."

Since Watt's job is to see that Yellowstone Park is around when this generation has indeed passed, his slip of faith evoked some congressional concern. But it mainly evoked amusement as the slightly eccentric beliefs of an already eccentric man. In religious ages, however, such views were taken, and dealt with, more seriously. The recurrent millennial enthusiasms of the late Middle Ages were almost invariably suppressed brutally. Yet the tradition survived. "America in the early nineteenth century was drunk on the millennium," writes Ernest Sandeen in *The Roots of Fundamentalism.* It gave rise to many eschatological sects, the most successful of which were the Mormons. The most famous at the time, however, were the Millerites, who survive today as the Adventists, and whose founder, William Miller, predicted the Second Coming in 1843. That was a mistake. As Sandeen observes, "It took a long time for Americans to forget William Miller." Dwight Wilson, another chronicler of these sects, adds, "His error produced a general disillusionment with premillennial teachings, and even made the faithful thereafter a bit shy of date-setting."

The shyness began wearing off after 1917, the year of the Bolshevik Revolution and the Balfour Declaration, which prefigured the rise of Russia (the leader of the "Armies of the North") and Israel. These events spurred a revival of millennial belief that grew more intense with World War II and the subsequent emergence of the Soviet Union as a superpower and Israel as a state. Israel's capture of Jerusalem, the development of global arsenals of extinction, the social dislocations of modern industrial society, and now the looming presence of the magical year 2000 have made the visions more fevered and the visionaries more expectant than ever.

Evangelicals are not the only ones to feel the tremors. For the first time, the pollsters report, most Americans are pessimistic about the future. That pessimism, no doubt related to recent American economic and geopolitical defeats, has been harnessed to the traditional messianism of the American civil religion (as Robert Bellah calls it), to produce a sense of apocalyptic apprehension among the nonreligious. New York *Times* columnist, Flora Lewis, was, I think, the first to sense these rumblings. Last year she made at least two allusions to the feeling of fundamental change in the world prefigured by the advent of the year 2000. She went so far as to attribute the "feeling of dangerous weakness" in the West to "a deeper bewilderment as societies move into the third millennium and sense change coming without knowing how to direct it." This, mind you, in 1982, with eighteen years to go. But Lewis merely picked up these subterranean fears; a new class of secular prophets has arisen to give them shape and content. As a result, in the last decade, apocalyptic visions have burst spectacularly into popular consciousness. There are a thousand variations on the theme, though most fall into one of three categories, in descending order of finality and current popularity: nuclear, ecological and economic.

It hardly bears mentioning that the anti-nuclear movement is based on an apocalyptic premise. But what is so remarkable about this crusade is the degree to which it insists on the ritual re-enactment and reiteration of that premise. It exhibits a fascination with the precise details of the Final Days that can only be called religious. The most imaginative Christian millennialist can hardly match the passion for extravagant detail of the Ground Zero activist. And it is doubtful that even James Watt is as sure of the inevitability of man's doom as is Jonathan Schell. In fact, the urgency of Schell's tone would lead one to set a date much earlier than Watt's.

Nuclear eschatology appeals so powerfully to the imagination that it has temporarily eclipsed its rival, the eco-catastrophe school. There are a hundred variations on that subtheme—overpopulation, resource depletion, ozone stripping, carbon dioxide poisoning, nuclear meltdowns, toxic waste, acid rain, pesticides, even supersonic transport—and a book to go with each. It is easy to forget how much currency was accorded these highly perishable, ever-changing themes. As recently as 1970, recalls John Silber in *Bostonia* magazine, *Life* reported that there was a probability that by 1980 urban dwellers would have to wear gas masks to breathe, by the early 1980s a smog inversion would kill thousands of people in some major city, and by 1985 the amount of sunlight reaching the earth would be reduced by half and new diseases that man could not resist would reach plague proportions. The Club of Rome's highly influential report, *The Limits to Growth*, based on a sophisticated computer study, predicted in 1972 that the combined effects of pollution, population growth, resource depletion and industrialization would drive the "world system" to the limits of the earth and ultimate collapse." A later version, Willy Brandt's "North-South Report," warned that the immiseration of the third world (the theory that supplants Marx's now defunct prophecy of the immiseration of the industrial working classes) would lead to catastrophic global war. And so on. The bibliography on the subject is so vast as to make one fear, at least, for our forests.

A third though minor and more mundane form of the genre is economic: catastrophe by mismanagement. It is not only the premise of such popular entertainments as *The Crash of '79, Rollover,* and *How to Prepare for the Coming Depression;* it is the nightmare behind the paroxysmal panics—over hyperinflation, depression, collapse of the international banking system—that occasionally seize the financial markets. Nonetheless, visions of economic collapse do not seem to have the same hold on the popular imagination as their nuclear and ecological counterparts. A Great Crash would lead only to poverty, riots and despair, not to extinction, and thus fails to fill our deepest apocalyptic needs.

Though the various doomsday schools tend to produce radically different scenarios, they all demonstrate a strikingly similar, fundamentalist habit of thought. It is characterized chiefly by a deadly literalness. Of course, their texts differ. The evangelicals read the future primarily in the Books of Daniel and Revelations. Their secular counterparts read it in the charts and graphs of the most recent past human behavior (population doubling times, resource consumption patterns, warhead production rates, etc.), extrapolated directly into the future to the inevitable catastrophic discontinuity where the line falls off the chart. An instructive example can be found in biologist Paul Ehrlich's *The Population Bomb*, first published in 1968. It gives a scenario for the future set precisely in 1983: because of pollution, overpopulation and pesticides, American harvests have declined precipitously. The wheat crop is less than 25 million metric tons (1982's actual crop was 76.4 million tons), "steak has become a memory," only children are allowed to eat "special low-mercury cod," and food rationing has begun. This is after "almost a billion human beings starved to death in the last decade," and after the "population control laws . . . aimed at blacks and the poor" led to years of urban rioting. The President decides to save the blighted crop with a dangerous chemical that had been banned by a solemn U.N. treaty. This causes a "starvation-wracked Japan," now gone nuclear, to join a Sino-Soviet axis against the United States, which prompts the President to launch a preemptive nuclear attack on them all. ("The idea of preventive war has been popular with our military for decades," writes Ehrlich, or, as Randy Newman sings, "They don't love us anyhow/So let's drop the big one now.")

What is so remarkable about this scenario is not that every element is so wildly wrong (after all, everyone makes mistakes), but that each is so clearly a precise, linear extrapolation into the future of trends occurring at the time the book was written. Apocalypticists, of course, tend to choose only negative factors to project into the future, but the literal transposition of past into future is a common feature of all futurology: it is what makes science fiction movies and world's fair "future" exhibits, for example, so easy to date, regardless of what future they are ostensibly portraying. (Buster Crabbe's Flash Gordon spaceship was a Packard with fins, as were the art deco flying machines of the 1933–1934 Chicago World's Fair.)

The same fundamentalist habit of thought responsible for this scriptural and historical literalism produces a rigid view of human nature, and consequently a constricted view of human possibility. The millennial preacher derives his view of human fixity from the doctrine of original sin. His secular counterpart simply assumes it to keep his model simple: he omits from his calculations man's capacity for adaptation—what economists call elasticity—because that quality is so hard to program into a computer. Take the Club of Rome's complex calculations of resource depletion, based on existing world reserves and rates of world consumption. It concluded, in 1972, that the world would run out of gold in nine years; silver, mercury and tin within fifteen years; and oil in twenty. Now, let's see. Gold is still with us; no silver, mercury or tin shortage is in sight; and if we were to repeat today the same calculations for oil, we'd have to conclude that the world has another thirty years' supply left. When the first calculations were made for oil, the world seemed to have only a nine-year supply left. That was in 1936. The problem with these exercises is that neither numerator nor denominator is fixed. Our horizon keeps receding as we approach it because both demand and supply—which in turn derive from taste, knowledge, technology and substitution—are elastic, a property not found in the world view of computers or their catastrophist masters.

Aside from a fundamentalist view of history, and human nature, secular and religious apocalypticists share a certain moralism, as unmistakable beneath the Hollywood slickness of *The China Syndrome* as in the homiletics of a Falwell sermon. The two camps agree that we are doomed by our sins, though each has a different favorite: the evangelicals are partial to moral depravity (pornography, abortion, divorce); the secularists, to pride (plundering nature, disturbing the ecosphere, seeking strategic superiority).

This reflects in part the class and cultural difference between the two groups. Religious millennialists have always been drawn from socially and economically marginal classes. In the Middle Ages they often formed the fanatical, mystical fringe of revolts of the dispossessed. Today they form the fringe of the newly mobilized moral majoritarians, whose grievances against the modern liberal state run very deep. They are quite distinct from their secular counterparts, who tend to be urban, educated, and middle class. You don't see many "Jesus is coming, ready or not" bumperstickers at a Diablo Canyon lie-in.

These social differences shape their outlook. The evangelicals, displeased as they are with the modern world and with their lot in it, are so positively enthusiastic about the End that they welcome the signs of global deterioration that signal its approach. Pat Robertson counsels no weeping over the great calamities of our time: "We are not to wring our hands and say, 'Isn't that awful?' That isn't awful at all. It is good . . . a token of our salvation." This optimism is hard to find among the nonreligious. For them, the End is simply the end. It is followed not by bliss but by silence. They are not really millennialists at all, but true apocalypticists. And that makes them understandably pessimistic. (An interesting exception is Steven Spielberg, whose films are hopeful, even joyful, a fact that is intimately connected with their quasi-religious quality. *Close Encounters of the Third Kind,* for example, is a study of apostolic calling and redemption—coming literally from on high—though Brother McKeever might find Spielberg's rendition somewhat revisionist.)

But the belief in a postapocalyptic future affects more than the mood of the believer. It profoundly influences his actions. The true millennialist tends to be socially passive. The appropriate response to the imminent End and subsequent Redemption is to prepare—principally by means of a deeply personal religious commitment (an act of acceptance) to ensure individual salvation and a place in the millennium. For the secularist who lacks a deus ex machina, the apocalyptic vision calls not for preparation but prevention. And that means politics, but politics of a peculiar kind: an all-encompassing single-issue politics. Practitioners of traditional single-issue politics don't expect their concerns to be universally shared: blacks fight for civil rights, Jews for Israel, Catholics against abortion, knowing —and accepting the fact—that other groups may have contrary interests and beliefs. Not so in apocalyptic politics. Those who believe that the end of the world is coming and that they hold the key to preventing it, tend to believe that their program is good—indeed, absolutely necessary—for all. They become convinced of their moral obligation to carry out their mission, and impatient with those standing in their way. Germany's Greens promise extraparliamentary "direct action" if democratic means to not keep nuclear weapons off their soil. Paul Ehrlich called (in 1968!) for population control "by compulsion if voluntary methods fail." And why not? History hangs in the balance.

What is most disturbing about this kind of politics, however, is not the moral bullying of a militant fringe. The more subtle and pernicious danger is the intellectual style of its leading ideologues, a style marked by a profound intolerance, which not only rigs the terms of the debate (as when they imply that only *they* are in favor of children and other living things), but often abolishes debate altogether. In all sincerity they can't understand opponents who choose death over life. So rather than engage opponents on the facts, they diagnose them. The antinuclear psychiatrist and Hiroshima expert, Robert J. Lifton, has written a book in which he explains that those who hold views contrary to his suffer from "nuclearism," a kind of addiction to nuclear weapons. This is a medical update: Lifton's previous diagnosis had been "psychic numbing," a pathological denial of impending doom so crippling that one loses the capacity for rational action and thought, and spends one's time rearranging the deck chairs on the *Titanic.*

The problem with the intellectual style of those who are convinced that we are all on the *Titanic* is that the whole purpose of democratic politics is to rearrange ("authoritatively allocate") deck chairs and other social goods. Its method is to accommodate the push and pull of competing interests and weigh competing values. As Isaiah Berlin argues in "John Stuart Mill and the Ends of Life," the genius—and tolerance—of liberalism derives from its refusal to declare any single value supreme. The nature of apocalyptic politics is to do just the opposite: to declare that one value, and the program to achieve it, is uniquely important. It then follows that all others are insignificant, if not dangerous distractions. Jonathan Schell is so insistent on that point that I am inclined to agree with Otto Friedrich's wry observation that "the end of the world is, in a way, a pun." Or, to state the problem another way: apocalyptic politics demand a declaration of emergency. But democracy never coexists well with emergency, a lesson we have always learned during wartime. We also learned it from McCarthyites and other right-wing hysterics, who found the normal democratic processes insufficient to meet their self-declared emergency.

But, it is said, how can we worry about intellectual styles, democratic processes, and deck chairs when the world is about to end? For God's sake, we're on the *Titanic!* Well, are we? Like all unanswerable questions, this one is best left for last. No one knows, or can pretend to know, and those who are seized with the certainty that they do know deserve to be treated with some skepticism. They take insufficient account of the elasticity of human nature and the adaptability of human societies. They conveniently ignore what Professor Joseph Nye calls the "crystal ball effect," the fact that leaders today, unlike Kaiser Wilhelm and Asquith in 1914, know precisely what the world will look like after the next world war, a fact that accounts for the remarkable caution with which the superpowers treat one another. The doomsayers also have a credibility problem. Their historical record is not particularly good. In 1962 Bertrand Russell predicted nuclear war within months. C. P. Snow made a similar prediction, adding that his view was not a matter of opinion or speculation, but scientific certainty. Hardly anyone recalls now the pronouncements of the Club of Rome and its imitators, made with equal scientific certainty, that by now industrial civilization would be wracked by scarcity, overpopulation and uncontrollable pollution.

Nevertheless, the fact that new Millerites rise and fall every few years doesn't prove that today's Millerites may not in fact be right. Does that mean that we are in an emergency? Yes, but no more than other civilizations, since all are susceptible to destruction. That possibility exists, always, everywhere. Numberless societies have been destroyed by natural disaster, war and internal collapse. There is a certain hubris in believing that ours is the first to face the prospect. But more than hubris, danger too. Not from the true millennialists, who are passively, and joyously, making their devotions and stocking up on biscuits and distilled water. But from the fretful apocalypticists, whose declarations of emergency—of an ever-changing succession of emergencies—make political claims on all of us. Sidney Hook once said that those who make survival the supreme value are declaring that there is nothing they will not betray. The same holds for those who use the threat of apocalypse as an instrument of political blackmail. That is reason enough to resist the sirens calling us to the moral equivalent of war, and go on with our daily business.

The New Republic, March 28, 1983

Privacy

PSEUDO-PRIVATE LIVES

POLITICAL IMAGERY DERIVES MAINLY FROM PUBLIC ACTIONS. BUT PUBLIC actions are suspect, precisely because they are undertaken in the knowledge that they will be observed. A glimpse of private life can shape a public image far more powerfully, not just because the private revelation is more titillating, but because it has what public action can never have: the air of unself-consciousness, and thus the stamp of sincerity. The paradox, of course, is that the truly private is inaccessible, and thus immune to political exploitation. The solution is the creation of a new category of experience, the pseudo-private: ostensibly private action designed exclusively for public consumption.

We encounter the phenomenon every time a high government official who has been saying one thing for weeks is reported to believe "privately" the opposite. This private confession, of course, appears on the front page of the New York *Times.* Here the word private is emptied of its conventional meaning ("not public, or open to or shared with or known to the public"); it is meant to be taken as a substitute for "genuine." But since these revelations are not the inadvertent slips of a tongue loosened by fatigue or a double martini—they are public utterances wrapped in the aura of truthfulness that surrounds privacy—the whole maneuver is a fraud. But it works.

It works even in less subtle forms, like political advertising, where simulated intimacy is a staple. One technique is to give the impression that the camera has stumbled on a characteristic domestic scene, like the Tom Hayden ad in which we chance upon him packing his kids off to school, or the Nancy Kassebaum ad in which Nancy and her dad, Alf Landon, sit around the den chatting about leadership. In general, the idea is to let the microphone into the confessional for selected excerpts; or to use 35mm Technicolor to produce the effect of a Super-8 home movie. The purest form of the art is simple fabrication. That is a specialty of hagiographers, like our own Parson Weems. He knew the power of anecdote, its ability to shape perceptions of character; and unlike his subject, George Washington, he did not feel himself to be constrained by the requirements of truth. It wasn't until the fifth edition of his *Life and Memorable Actions of George Washington* that he came up with the cherry tree episode, yet for the last 150 years it has set the standard for the genre. As *Newsweek* said of Hitler's "secret diaries," "genuine or not, it almost doesn't matter in the end." Weems would have understood. As long as a revelation is believed, it will have its effect.

The effect is not always positive. Jimmy Carter learned this when a chance encounter with an aquatic rabbit turned into a metaphor for the ineptness of his Presidency. (Carter, mistakenly assuming that documentary evidence could attenuate the power of such parables, produced a fuzzy photo designed to show that his disposition toward the rabbit was both manly and pacific, but the damage was done.) Richard Nixon learned the same lesson when he released a few tapes, thinking they would exonerate him. And God only knows what Lyndon Johnson was thinking when he showed his gallbladder scar to the press; had he known it would create an image of almost grotesque crassness, he might have kept his shirt tucked in.

The greatest political consultant of them all thought that leaders should always keep their shirts tucked in. Machiavelli advised princes to cultivate a calculated aloofness to protect the mystique of power. In an age of revolving Borgias, that was good advice. But today the powerful national leader feels the opposite need: to humanize himself by judicious curtain-lifting that allows selected glimpses of the man as he really is—that is, as he is meant to be seen. The process goes on all the time, but lately there have been three particularly elegant examples of the political use of intimacy.

King Hussein of Jordan, working through Karen Elliott House and the *Wall Street Journal,* has produced a classic of the pseudo-private confession. It illustrates quite brilliantly the dual purpose of the genre: to rewrite history and to reshape character. For Hussein, giving the world his own version of events (what in another context is known as an alibi) is very important. Consider the problem posed for him by President Reagan's 1982 peace plan. He is a king in a region of the world where everyone is at war. A peace plan is proposed that hinges on him. He faces the most difficult negotiations of his life. At the end of these weeks of negotiations he will have to make a decision which, one way or the other, will enrage powerful friends and enemies. What to do? Hussein, who makes up in craftiness what he lacks in courage, invited a sympathetic reporter—and only one reporter—to tag along after him through the weeks of decision, and, most important, to share his "private" thoughts. These thoughts included his own account of his private communications with President Reagan and other world leaders, and of the course and content of his private negotiations with Yasir Arafat. The net effect of this personal history was to demonstrate how Hussein had been let down by Reagan, King Fahd, Menachem Begin and Yasir Arafat (everyone, it seems, but the pregnant Queen Noor) and thus simply could not be expected to join the peace process. Most observers, including Ms. House herself, were sophisticated enough to discount many of Hussein's claims. Nevertheless, the sensational private revelations had their effect. In a subsequent editorial-page piece, Ms. House followed Hussein closely in apportioning blame for the current Middle East stalemate. And NBC's John Chancellor, cloaked regardless of season in hand-me-down opinions, cited the House articles as evidence that the Reagan plan had been done in—by George Shultz.

The pseudo-confessional aims to rewrite history, but its subtler purpose is to reshape image. Hussein had another problem. With the Middle East falling apart and himself immobile as usual, his friends and admirers in the West were getting tired, even skeptical, of his image as a plucky, courageous little king cruelly constrained by circumstance. Well, after reading about his troubled sleep, his anxieties and his nightmares, interspersed with private shows of attentiveness to son and family (all duly reported on the front page), one is tempted to nominate him for 4-H Club Father of the Year. He may be a king, but he is human. Doth not a king fret? After all, his grandfather was assassinated. And the bullet that was meant for Hussein was deflected by a medal on his chest. Wouldn't that make you a lifelong equivocator?

We're all human, of course, but you and I are not responsible for the fate of a nation. Leaders who are must be judged by different standards. The fact that F.D.R. was sick at Yalta may make interesting history, but it doesn't lower the standards by which we must judge his decisions there. Menachem Begin broke his hip and now walks with a cane, but statesmen cannot lean on such infirmities as excuses. Hussein's disability is the lack of courage. Winston Churchill once wrote that "nothing in life is as exhilarating as to be shot at without result." For Hussein nothing in life is as debilitating. And to judge by his pseudo-confession, he hopes that nothing will be quite as exonerating. As soon as the human, private side of him can be seen, the world will understand why he cannot act. (President Mubarak was grazed by a bullet in the Sadat assassination; Begin has narrowly escaped death many times. But only of Hussein is it said, and always said, that he *cannot* act, when what is meant is that he *will* not act.) The Middle East burns. Other leaders are properly excoriated for lacking the courage to act. But not Hussein. He has nightmares.

Yuri Andropov is not quite as expansive as Hussein, but his contribution to the literature of political pseudo-intimacy is far more imaginative. When Samantha Smith, age eleven, from Manchester, Maine, wrote to him expressing her worries about nuclear war, and asking, by the way, why he wanted "to conquer the world or at least the United States," Yuri wrote back. First he told her that she was "a courageous and honest girl, resembling in some way Becky, Tom Sawyer's friend from the well-known book by your compatriot Mark Twain." (We finally know what Andropov reads when he is not listening to jazz.) "Yes, Samantha," he continued, "we in the Soviet Union are endeavoring and doing everything so that there will be no war between our two countries. . . . That's what we were taught to do by Vladimir Lenin, the great founder of our state." Good stuff, especially when read on national television by little Samantha herself. (The Soviet Embassy called her a couple of days ahead of time to alert her, and whoever else might be interested in her private correspondence, of the letter's arrival.) The sight of this sweet-looking eleven-year-old on TV, reading a little passage from her Russian pen pal (as the former KGB chief was jauntily referred to) made me wonder if perhaps it wasn't time to send David Garth, Jerry Rafshoon and the rest to Moscow for training. But then again, the Soviets are still relative pikers at this sort of thing. The world leader in the technology of spurious intimacy remains the White House and its mechanical monster, the autopen, a machine that wields a real pen to actually write the President's signature on letters so that birthday greetings to hundred-year-olds do not have the appearance of having been artificially produced. It's a forger's dream. Which brings us to Hitler's diaries.

Unlike the Hussein confessions and the Andropov letter, the Hitler diaries spare us the problem of deciding how much is from the heart and how much is ulterior motive. They represent pseudo-intimacy in its rarest form: a pure culture created, literally, under laboratory conditions.

Imagine that you want to change history. There are two ways of doing it. You can change the future by becoming a world-historical figure. Your chances of doing that are four billion to, say, ten. Or you could change the past by rewriting history. How? By harnessing the most powerful political tool of all: people's utter fascination with the private acts of the great, and their habit of confusing the private with the true. Forge a diary, and the world will proclaim that history now has to be rewritten to accommodate it.

The problem with the Hitler scam is that from the start it was as phony as a three-mark bill.* It was too theatrical (found in a hayloft? come on, guys), too clumsily conceived (do even people of Kantian discipline—which Hitler was not—keep thirteen years of diaries in identical note-books?), and too circumstantially implausible (can anyone running an empire and a world war keep a diary for thirteen years, and have none of his hundreds of associates ever make mention of it?).

So who did it? We don't know who the author is, but we can guess at his intent. Consider the evidence: the implication that Hitler did send Hess on his peace mission to Britain; second thoughts about whether to crush the British at Dunkirk, or let them go; no reference to the Holocaust; an expression of regret about the amount of destruction on *Kristallnacht;* a thoughtful reference to Eva Braun. One senses here the hand of keepers of the flame working into the night to rehabilitate their old boss, to make him human.

Whoever they are, and however clumsy, the forgers had the right idea. Their task was awesome. Humanizing Hitler is the ultimate feat of political jujitsu. Archimedes thought he needed a lever to move the world. In politics, a diary will do.

The New Republic, May 23, 1983

---

* Ed.'s note: Four days after this essay went to press, the West German Interior Ministry declared the diaries a hoax, and arrested those responsible.

II

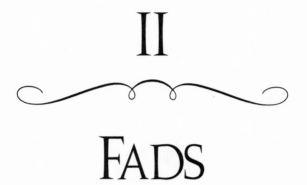

FADS

Confession

THE CULT OF CONFESSION

CAMUS ONCE OBSERVED THAT "TO ACHIEVE NOTORIETY IT IS ENOUGH, after all, to kill one's concierge, but unhappily this is usually an ephemeral reputation, so many concierges are there who deserve and receive the knife." Camus was pessimistic about the possibility of fame on a mass scale. He might not have been had he lived to see the TV talk show, the instant autobiography, Barbara Walters or any of the other confessional gadgetry of our age.

The 1970s are considered a period of introspection. They were also a period of self-revelatory chic. It became fashionable and profitable to parlay one's fifteen minutes of fame into a ghost-written autobiography (cf. Linda Lovelace). Radicals retreating from the barricades to the navel took refuge in hotel ballrooms for the therapeutic self-criticism of est. Jerry Rubin kept us constantly informed of his conversions from radicalism to feminism to stockbroker's capitalism. For the older set, Betty Ford set the pace. Her forthright admission of drug and alcohol addiction was so successful that it created a confessional epidemic. Joan Kennedy was quick to follow suit, and before long every aspiring starlet and harlot was frantically pulling skeletons out of the closet and throwing them on the public stage. Addictions, obsessions, phobias and depressions; perversions, diversions, even the occasional felony were churned out to meet the insatiable demand. Those who had spent a fortune baring their souls to Beverly Hills psychiatrists recouped their losses with a spread in *People* magazine. And those who a generation ago would have knelt and whispered furtively in the ears of a benign father confessor, now call on that devout anti-Catholic, master of the autobiographical arts, television's Phil Donahue.

There is no crime against man or nature that Donahue will not explore. His parade of cross-dressers, PCP-smokers, and child-beaters would have made P. T. Barnum proud. But Donahue has outdone even Barnum. In the old days, one merely gawked at these unfortunates. Donahue's genius is to get them to talk. And they speak in the self-assured tones of the recently shriven. The flasher contritely explains his appearance on the show as a means of "working through" his problem, helping others, and warning those who might be tempted to follow in his path. But of course he is merely pulling the ultimate flash—lowering his psychic knickers to millions in one shot. What he says has the form of confession, but it is, in fact, a narcissistic celebration of what we've come to call his lifestyle.

Out of this mass of self-revelation has evolved a new and growing subspecies: the political confession. It is a form of political theater highly developed in the communist world—where public confessions are unusually well rehearsed—but, until recently, greatly undervalued in this country. We've had our share of confessed political sinners, but the genre has never been so popular and so profitable as it is today. In fact it has become so specialized that it has spawned two distinct sub-types.

The first was perfected by the people who brought us Watergate. We think of Watergate as having created a new class of criminals, but it also gave us a new form of confession, the maximalist confession. Until that time (in the McCarthy era, for example) public disclosure of your errors and those of your friends were designed to get you off the hook. The Watergate confessions were designed to make you a star. The technique was to tell all and to embellish if need be. The lure was the book contract and the college lecture circuit. And the result was a clattering of jail-cell typewriters not heard since the heyday of the Moscow show trials. John Dean became a *Rolling Stone* correspondent and the subject of a TV movie. Haldeman and Ehrlichman became writers of note. Smaller fish had to be content with making the rounds of the talk shows, where they plied their trade as full-time penitents.

There was one problem with the maximalist confession. It could get you on the "Dinah Shore Show," but it couldn't get you back in the White House. The price of celebrityhood was to be barred from politics for life. Something better had to be found. Enter the minimalist confession.

West of the Elbe, the minimalist confession has traditionally held sway. Its purpose is to salvage the confessor's future. The technique is to admit as little as possible. Ted Kennedy's televised address to the people of

Massachusetts after Chappaquiddick was in the classic minimalist tradition. Its hallmark was the forthright statement that he accepted full responsibility for his actions. Since that statement was empty of content and since the purpose of his confession was to enable him to carry on exactly as before, the acceptance of full responsibility was a hollow gesture. It reminded me of the lawyer in the *New Yorker* cartoon who says, "Your Honor, my client would like to plead responsibility but not guilt." The politician, on the other hand, pleads guilt but not responsibility. The misdeed carries no adverse consequences; the only real penalty is the humiliation of the confession itself.

Mastery of the minimalist confession has become essential in presidential campaigns. Here what must be atoned for is not a crime but a linguistic misdemeanor. The press hungrily casts about for a gaffe, and won't let go when it lands one. Jimmy Carter learned that lesson well in the 1976 campaign when he was almost destroyed by the "ethnic purity" remark. At first he tried to pass it off as a slip of the tongue or a meaningless idiosyncratic expression. But that brought only more criticism. Ethnic purity obliterated all other campaign news and left Carter politically defenseless until, in a ritualized ceremony of recantation and redemption, Martin Luther King, Sr., gave him absolution on network television. Within days the issue was dead. In 1980 it happened to Carter again. In October, during the period of his recovery in the polls, he was accused of "meanness," a charge which monopolized campaign coverage for days. It became clear that the only way to stop the hemorrhage was to confess. He did the obvious. He sent for America's preeminent mother confessor, Barbara Walters, and on the first question of the interview pled guilty to the charge. His sentence was reduced to time served with Barbara and he was able to get on with his campaign. (In their campaigns, Ed Muskie and Jerry Ford learned that crying in public and misplacing Poland are more serious political crimes since they do not lend themselves to confession. They are literally unpardonable.)

But the ultimate minimalist confession was created by one of the cleverest and most able members of Congress, the former president of the American Conservative Union, Robert Bauman. In the middle of his reelection campaign he was arrested for soliciting sex from a sixteen-year-old boy. After a week's regrouping, he emerged flanked by family and minister to give a remarkable press conference. It is the classic text of the minimalist confession. First, it acknowledges not the act itself, but instead some character flaw ("homosexual tendencies"). Second, in the best Kennedy tradition, responsibility is accepted but the blame is placed elsewhere—this time on alcoholism. Third, what is promised is not a change of heart but a new dose of therapy. Fourth, and most important, the confessor declares absolution for himself ("I've made peace with my God") and announces that from now on the subject is closed.

This typology of confessions enables us to understand the otherwise inexplicable Rita Jenrette. Ms. Jenrette, wife of one of the convicted Abscam congressmen, caused a stir and much confusion last year when she published "Diary of a Mad Congresswife" in the Washington *Post.* Readers were puzzled because she had a reputation for standing by her husband and for never missing a chance to be photographed walking arm in arm with him to the courthouse. Yet this piece, which she claimed to be writing in his defense, was very damaging to him, with its tales of sexual and alcoholic indiscretion. What was she doing? She had simply realized that her husband's original minimalist defense—the confession based on alcohol that puts it all behind you—had failed, and their careers in politics were finished. All that was left was show biz. And if she was ever to get her career as a singer off the ground, she had to deliver the maximalist celebrity confession. If the Watergate crowd could do it, why couldn't she? Why not. Watch for her on Donahue.

The art of confession has become such a standard part of the political repertoire that any refusal to play the game is met now with consternation. The most dramatic example occurred at the recent confirmation hearings for Alexander Haig. After days of trying and failing to uncover any Haig wrongdoing in Watergate, Senator Paul Tsongas said plaintively to him: "On several occasions there has been an obvious way for you to say it was wrong, it will not happen again. But we don't get that. . . . We are almost beseeching you for that reassurance, somehow like unrequited love. We are not getting reassurance. It is our one shot, and if we don't get it now, I don't know when we are going to get it." The senator's love went unrequited. "The kinds of *mea culpas* . . . you want I just can't give because I don't feel that," said Haig. Frustrated but persistent, his suitors kept begging him for just one tiny, perfunctory confession of guilt: Haig refused. He could barely contain himself. "What is it you are after?" he demanded of Senator Paul Sarbanes, "something that you want me to say that you have been unable to get from somebody else?"

That somebody, of course, is Richard Nixon. What Tsongas and Sarbanes longed to hear was that final sorrowful "I done wrong" from the mouth of Richard Nixon. Despite an orgy of lower-level recantation and repentance, the hope for the consummate Watergate confession by the king himself had been frustrated by the Ford pardon. Not even David Frost's $650,000 could buy it (although we were willing to pay that price just for the *chance* to hear Nixon say it). I think Haig was right. What the unrequited lovers knew they could never get from the master, they tried to get from the servant. And Haig infuriated them by spurning their affections.

Nixon and Haig may not have much appreciation for the notion of public trust, but they do appear to have a firm grasp of the nature and purpose of confession. Haig's assertion that where there is no wrongdoing and no guilt there should be no confession is self-evident. For confession to be real and not just a sham, it cannot be, as Tsongas implied it was, a one-shot deal. It must involve not only the admission of guilt for wrongdoing committed, but remorse and genuine resolution not to repeat (contrition), and willingness to accept the consequences of one's actions (penance). And there are public figures, like John Profumo and Eldridge Cleaver, who have taken confession seriously. Their fates are sad, perhaps, but they do have a touch of nobility. The fact that they, and not the real charlatans, are frequent objects of derision testifies to our current preference for counterfeit over real confession.

How do we account for this epidemic of confession? It is not just confined to politics and popular culture. Alfred Kazin says of contemporary literature: "There is so much confessional poetry and fiction, that I ask myself . . . what the spell is on all of us." His answer is that nowadays we have more to confess. "The open lust for political advantage over human rights and belief in our American superpowers have made breakdown and confession, Vietnam, Watergate, and investigation a part of our time."

Kazin is certainly right that we feel guiltier than we ever have (though one may reject his implication that we've earned it). But our appetite for confession signals something more—a need for reassurance that our values are indeed worth upholding. The example of the show trial is instructive.

The extraordinary lengths to which communist regimes have gone to produce public confessions is, on the face of it, puzzling. Surely, if their only function is to create scapegoats or public diversions, or to eliminate enemies, there are easier ways. Why the need for a bureaucracy of interrogators, torturers and courtroom choreographers? As the trial of Xiang Jing and the Chinese Gang of Four remind us, the real purpose of the show trial is to confer legitimacy on regimes that lack firm constitutional, religious or historical sanction. There is little that can reinforce the prevailing values better than a parade of enemies-of-the-state turned penitent sinners, admitting their guilt in open court to open microphones and asking for just retribution. In 1952, when the verdict was read at the Slansky show trials in Prague, the gallery, which included many West European communist journalists, stood and cheered. One of those who parroted a scripted confession was Eugen Loebel, deputy foreign trade minister. When he was sentenced to life imprisonment his fellow workers at the ministry were moved to stage a protest. They demanded the death penalty.

Xiang Jing, no stranger to show trials herself, understood their function perfectly well. She knew that her trial had nothing to do with the return of legality to China. It was an instrument for conferring legitimacy on the new ruling group. By refusing to confess she denied that to her opponents and subverted the purpose of the trial.

In this country we don't torture people into show-trial confessions. We just turn on the television lights and let the penitents wander onto the stage in search of fame or just plain political survival. And the market accommodates the confessor because the demand is high. More is at work here than the need for entertainment or exorcism. Vietnam, Watergate and the decline of traditional values have placed much of what we used to believe in question. The spectacle of public repentance by corrupt public officials or exposed homosexuals is one of our sad, last ways of shoring up the old values. And it seems to matter little to us if the confession is worth no more than Eugen Loebel's.

The New Republic, February 21, 1981

Exercise

STRETCH MARX

LIKE ALL CLASSICS THAT HARMONIZE FORM AND CONTENT, A book about food, and how to burn it off, *Jane Fonda's Workout Book*, comes in the form of a sandwich. The bulky middle consists of stacks of good, lean meat: page upon page of beautiful women, stretched out in various athletic poses to illustrate The Workout. The meat is packed between two whole-wheat slices of politics Fondue: at the beginning a long, autobiographical confessional in which Jane Fonda explains her long ascent from bulimia and *Barbarella* to exercise and activism; and, at the end, a disquisition on how The Workout alone cannot bring true fitness until pollution, job stress and corporate growth ("concentration means inflation") are stopped, or, alternatively put, until economic democracy reigns. Heretofore, economic democracy (Tom Hayden's term for a kind of grass-roots democratic socialism) was justified on the grounds of equality or social justice. Now The Workout provides an entirely new rationale: it purifies the pores. And who knows? Given the phenomenal success of this book and the current fitness craze, it could be that Mrs. Hayden has finally found the basis for an authentic American socialism: body worship.

But Jane could use a better scriptwriter. The three-part coda reads like leftover background research from her recent movies. One chapter is devoted to the villainy of food moguls (*The Electric Horseman*), another to the arrogance of industrial polluters (*The China Syndrome*), and the third to the stress-inducing perils of office work (*Nine to Five*). The agitprop homilies suffer in translation from the screen. They turn a book with otherwise excellent chapters on "Beginner's Abdominals" and "Advanced Buttocks" into a Big Mac of trendy Hollywood politics, stuffed with every radical cliché of the last fifteen years. *Hayden Meets Holism* would have been a better title. Those who missed out on limited editions of *Pumping Iron with Engels* or *In Sneakers: Michael Harrington Speaks* will appreciate this book. It manages the acrobatic feat of linking every woolly trend imaginable: acupuncture, "natural" medicine, anti-corporatism, chiropractic, nutrition, a new feminism ("our right to physical as well as economic, political and social equality"), cancer phobia, economic democracy, lean thighs, community control and an aversion to sugar. The only thing missing is a call for nuclear disarmament. Not to worry. The Workout came out just before that wave crested. Look for it in the revised edition.

The opening slice of whole wheat, "Lessons Learned: A Body Abused," is Jane's story. It is literally her oral history, a chronicle of all the things —foods, drugs, ideas—she has stuffed into herself. Her theme is that since the day she was born she has internalized (her favorite word) things from the outside; her refrain, an ironic twist on Adam's complaint, is that others —usually men—made her eat it. "Like many young girls, I internalized this message [that women are judged by their looks] and, in an effort to conform to the sought-after female image, I abused my health, starved my body and ingested heaven-knows-what chemical drugs." She certainly did some weird things. In boarding school she went on eating-vomiting binges, a condition called bulimia, though to Jane's credit she did so long before it became fashionable. Jane's complaint is that her school never taught her not to; it crammed her instead with a "tedious general science course." She later graduated to pep pills and diuretics, and for that she is very sore at doctors. Until she met her "wonderful naturopathic" doctor, "no one had ever explained that there were other ways of losing weight besides starvation diets, Dexedrine and diuretics." Apparently, it never occurred to her to try eating less and exercising more. "Looking back, I realize that to a large extent I was a victim of medical malpractice."

One could almost feel sorry for her were it not for her whiny tone and perpetual claim to the status of victim. And if it weren't for her portrayal of herself as a fearless crusader for the idea of taking responsibility for one's own life. It seems that her every choice was foisted on her by . . . society. Why was she so obsessively worried about her looks, a universal anxiety for which she might at least be a bit grateful since it accounts for the sales of her book? "I was so conditioned to thinking of myself as fat that later, when I was really thin, I could never convince myself that I was thin enough." And how does the now-liberated Fonda explain floating naked through the film *Barbarella*? "I was completely unaware of the extent to which I had internalized the cultural pressures that associate a woman's success with sex. . . ." She must have missed the film.

Is it too impolite to suggest that her current "activist" incarnation is yet another internalization? Does this woman never stop eating? Having ingested the values first of Roger Vadim and now of Tom Hayden, she delivers with mind-numbing seriousness the startling message that one should never take one's values from others and, in particular, that women should never accept sexual stereotypes that make them appendages to men. A curious message for a book that peddles Tom Hayden's ideas wrapped in Jane Fonda's body.

The *Workout* has turned into more than just a number-one best seller. It has become a fitness industry. There is a Workout record album, a Workout videocassette and a string of Workout salons. On the whole, it is a remarkable piece of entrepreneurship: the right idea at the right time in the right package. It is a pity that Jane doesn't just take the money and run. We admire people who can turn an idea into a bundle. But to call Fonda a capitalist success story is to embarrass her. For one thing, it then becomes hard to distinguish her from other profit-makers (who play the villain in her political fables). For another, having gone holistic, she feels compelled to demonstrate that everything she does is interrelated and in the service of the highest ideals. She goes to great lengths to plead that her interest in fitness is but another expression of her humanistic politics. That is what lifts the *Workout* from the level of just another best seller (like *Garfield Gains Weight*), or profits-from-vanity industry (like Estée Lauder's) to the level of historical artifact. Where else can one find a straight-faced attempt to give fitness an ideology, to tie exercise to progressive politics?

I do not claim that a strong, healthy woman is automatically going to be a progressive, decent sort of person. Obviously other factors are involved in that. But I am sure that one's innate intelligence and instinct for good can be enhanced through fitness.

One would ordinarily pass over this nugget as just another sign of Fonda's loopy thinking, if it didn't point up a singular irony of holistic Haydenism. Body worship is traditionally the province of the political right. This is not the first time we have had a fitness craze. In *The Healthy Body and Victorian Culture*, Bruce Haley describes a similar "national mania" for athletics and fitness that engulfed Britain in the second half of the last century and coincided with the birth of social Darwinism and the rise of British jingoism. In our century, fascism took the idea of physical purity, yoked it to racist fantasies and pressed them both into the service of fanatic nationalism. On the face of it, the new notion that fitness makes for goodness is as absurd as the old one that fitness justifies survival. If I follow Fonda's defense of the new dispensation, and it isn't always easy, it seems that physical self-development is necessary for women to liberate themselves from (you guessed it) internalized sexual stereotypes and become whole persons. But surely any sentient observer can see that the fitness craze has little to do with gender and much to do with class. Exercise is the new middle-class hobby—working people get their exercise on the job —supplanting meditation and sex, the principal diversions of the 1970s. My theory is that meditation and sex are simply not narcissistic enough for the 1980s. Meditation is solipsistic, to be sure, but it is directed toward some higher consciousness and thus contains some element of relatedness. And sex ordinarily requires at least two people. Exercise, on the other hand, is uniquely self-absorbing and asocial. None of this, of course, is to argue against deep knee-bends. Exercise doesn't need social justification. It is fun, it makes your heart race and it even may help you live longer. To pretend that it is more than that is to travel beyond silliness into cynicism.

In *The Road to Wigan Pier* George Orwell noted dourly,

the horrible—the really disquieting—prevalence of cranks wherever Socialists are gathered together. One sometimes gets the impression that the mere words "Socialism" and "Communism" draw towards them with magnetic force every fruit-juice drinker, nudist, sandal-wearer, sex-maniac, Quaker, "Nature Cure" quack, pacifist and feminist in England.

He took pains to make clear that he was "arguing *for* Socialism, not *against* it." But he added, "as with the Christian religion, the worst advertisement for Socialism is its adherents."

Economic democrats, beware Adidas socialism.

The New Republic, August 16–23, 1982

Futurespeak

NINETEEN EIGHTY-FOUR, WHICH PROMISED TO BE THE YEAR OF
realignment politics, turned instead into the start of something quite
different: generational politics. That usually means the young trying to
seize power from the old. Nothing very original here. In 1960 John
Kennedy, congratulating his own youthfulness, hailed the passing of the
torch from Eisenhower's generation to his, forward-looking enough to be
born in this century. In 1974, Gary Hart campaigned for the Senate on
the slogan, "Now it's our turn."

By 1984 the message had been rendered more subtle. Any power
struggle can stand some mystification as a fight over substance. This
year's struggle was therefore portrayed as not just a fight between young
and old, but between young and old ideas. According to Hart's formulation, the distinctions between left and right, liberal and conservative,
now obsolete, were hereby superseded: the real choice was between past
and future.

It was a clever campaign theme, one that might have been expected to
enjoy the normal—i.e., brief—half-life of all such themes. Instead it has
turned into conventional wisdom. Futurespeak is everywhere. Democrats
seem to agree on little except that they must seize the future if they are
ever to rule again. Political consultant Robert Squier spoke for the post-
landslide consensus when he recently wrote that the crucial choice facing
Democrats is indeed not "left vs. right" but "past vs. future." Bruce

Babbitt, governor of Arizona and rising young star, entitled a recent speech "1984 is not 1934." Its theme: shedding "the dogmas of the past."

Nor is futurespeak an exclusively Democratic phenomenon. It is now the refrain of the Young Turk Republicans. Newt Gingrich, leading "conservative revolutionary"—an oxymoron that satirizes the very idea of left-right distinctions—put it the same way to David Stockman, leading *contra:* the real debate is now "future or past."

What are they talking about? If everyone is rushing to lay claim to the politics of the future, can the word have any meaning?

I count at least four.

1. **Nothing.** The idea of the future can be the perfect political vessel precisely when it is empty. During election years, a time of traditionally sanctioned political inanity, this is the preferred usage. Politicians are constantly promising to "take us into the future," as if we might not get there on our own. (John Glenn, in fact, argued haplessly that he was best prepared to do so since he had already been there.) More traditional empty vessels are no longer quite so serviceable. Motherhood sounds presumptively antifeminist, apple pie excessively caloric. The future— bright, streamlined and progressive—is irresistibly *now.* A favorite for political consultants, who must invent.

2. **Pragmatism.** In this usage, service to the future is code for freedom from ideology. Here, the future is used not vacuously but negatively: it means rejection of the past, the past being congenitally doctrinaire, ideology-bound and rigid. Servants of the future, free from "the dogmas of the past," are open-minded and innovative. They have no fixed ideas, no program, perhaps not even principles. Whatever works they'll try. They know one thing: We have seen the past, and it no longer works. A natural for governors, who must improvise.

3. **Laissez-faire.** For some, the future does have a positive shape, and they like what they see. In any case, the future is coming and resistance is futile. A wise politics will accept the inevitable and not put up foolish resistance. It will let the future unfold, as opposed to those tied to the past who will try to inhibit its natural tendencies. Of course, our ideas of the future are invariably based on linear projections of present trends, according to which winners can be expected to become bigger winners and losers bigger losers. In effect, favoring the future means preferring winners. High-tech good, smokestack bad. Atari Democrats won't let sentiment or attachment to "special interests," the barnacles of past-consciousness, slow things down. Abroad, revolution is another discerned "tide of history" (explained Senator Christopher Dodd in his

national address on Central America) to be ridden, not resisted. This brand of futurism is in fact a cover for a profoundly conservative quietism, a kind of Darwinism for pacifists. It is also a staple of neoliberals of the non-interventionist persuasion.

4. **Social revolution.** The activist variant of 3. Some are not content to let history unfold. They want to help. Like all vanguards, their mission is to get on the right side of history and push. Some corporatist liberals, for example, look admiringly to Japan Inc., where the fabled Ministry of Industry and Technology picks up-and-coming winners, then makes sure they win. "Conservative revolutionaries" see a decidedly different future, but are in an equal hurry to get there. Gingrich's manifesto to Stockman chides him for playing the old "Liberal Welfare State" games while the "Opportunity Society" waits to be born. Change is coming, change is necessary, say the social revolutionaries. Moreover, it is good. Let's get there, quick. A natural sort of futurism for what used to be called liberals in a hurry.

Now, this Babel of futures is simply too confusing. I say we can't have one word serving four masters. What to do? I propose awarding exclusive copyright to school 1. On several grounds. Since for them the metaphor is wholly empty, this arrangement is perhaps least likely to do any harm. Also they need it most. Types 2, 3 and 4 have perfectly usable—and more honest—substitutes. Americans know where you stand if you advocate pragmatism, laissez-faire or social revolution. Call it the future, and they cannot tell you apart without a scorecard. And besides, in a country that annually borrows $200 billion from posterity to pay for the present, it seems proper that rights to the future be reserved for those who, when they use the word, mean nothing at all.

The Washington Post, December 21, 1984

Travel

LIVING ON A RETURN TICKET

AUGUST IS HOLIDAY TIME. FRANCE HEADS FOR THE BEACH, CONGRESS for home and psychiatry for the asylum of Truro on Cape Cod. What makes for a holiday? Not time off from work. That happens on weekends, and no one calls that a holiday. Nor merely leaving home. That happens on business trips. Ask Willy Loman. On holiday one escapes more than work or home. One leaves oneself behind. The idea of holiday is a change of person, the remaking of oneself in one's own image. The baseball camp for adults, for example, where the bulky stockbroker, facing an aged Whitey Ford, can imagine himself the slugger he never was: that's a holiday.

On holiday one seeks to be what one is not. The accountant turns into a woodsman, the farmer into a city slicker. And when they all go overseas, they insist that their tourist spot be tourist-free, the better to experience the simulated authenticity of another way of life. To holiday is to go native, to *be* native—temporarily, of course.

Reversibility is crucial. One wants to be native only for a time. The true holiday requires metamorphosis, but, even more important, return to normality. Return is what distinguishes excursion from exile. If the change of persona becomes irreversible—if the Mardi Gras mask becomes permanently, grotesquely stuck—holiday turns to horror. One must be able to go home.

There are many ways, besides a Cook's tour, to travel: One cheap, popular alternative these days is the psychic holiday: the cosmos on $5 a day. The preferred mode of travel is drugs, the destination lotus land. Madness is exotic. True, it is no longer celebrated, as it was in the heyday of R. D. Laing and the "politics of experience," as the only real sanity in this world of (nuclear, capitalist, fill-in-the-blanks) insanity. But it retains a mystique, a reputation for authenticity and depth of vision. We know that the mentally ill inhabit a terrible place, literally a place of terrors. But that makes madness, like its two-dimensional facsimile, the horror film, all the more titillating.

For some, therefore, the ideal is to go there on a visit, a trip. The most widely used drugs, in fact, promise to re-create the experience of a major mental illness. Marijuana lets you circumnavigate the land of schizophrenia; LSD parachutes you in for the day. Quaaludes and downers promise a languid overnight stay in the Lethean land of depression, cocaine in the energized hothouse of mania.

As in any holiday, however, there must be an exit. For a drug to be widely popular it must be thought to be nonaddictive. That was cocaine's early, and false, claim to fame: the perfect high, it gets you there and back. (It is only those living in utter despair who choose a drug like heroin that takes you there for good: they are seeking not to holiday, but to emigrate.) The spirit of the psychic holiday was uncannily captured by Steven Spielberg, when he called Michael Jackson's peculiar child fantasy world (Disney dolls, cartoons, asexuality) a place where "I wish we could all spend some time." Living there, like living in New York, being another matter altogether.

For others there is the thrill of the political holiday, which offers not personal but social upheaval. It is a favorite recreation of what V. S. Naipaul calls the "return-ticket revolutionary," the comfortable Westerner who craves a whiff of social chaos and will travel to find it. First we had the Venceremos Brigade, eager to swing a sickle at people's cane. Now we have the European and American kids who hang around Managua wearing combat boots and T-shirts that read NICARAGUA LIBRE. In the '70s it was Gale Benson, the bored white English divorcée, who followed the cult of Black Power Militant Michael X to Trinidad to play at a revolution. Now it is the carpenter from South Shields, England, wearing a kaffiyeh and an AK-47, who is evacuated from Tripoli after five weeks with the PLO, and tells a reporter aboard his Yemen-bound ship that he plans to fight Israel for a year or two more, then go home to England.

They will always be with us, these political truants, and you shall know them by the return tickets in their pockets. Strife, preferably war, is for them fun, or at least a relief from the boredom of civilization. And for them, though not for the natives they patronize, when things get hot there will always be England.

Foreign correspondents, who commute to war by day, then return for drinks at the Hilton, know something of the thrill the traveling revolutionary seeks. Journalists, however, remain observers. They do not pretend to have remade themselves from a gringo into a Sandino, precisely the conceit of the return-ticket revolutionary.

Finally, there is the cheapest vacation of all: the moral holiday, when the rules are suspended and one is transformed into anything one wants. There are two ways to achieve this happy condition. One is to stay home and wait for an official suspension of the rules, an official "letting go" (that is what the Russian word for vacation means) like the *Fasching* in Germany or Mardi Gras in the Americas. The other way is to travel to a place where one can make up one's own rules. Some go to Club Med to shed pinstripes for swim trunks, a billfold for beads and a metropolitan persona for any laid-back one they choose to invent. Some, like Billy Graham or the latest tour from the National Council of Churches, go to the Soviet Union and make up entirely new meanings for words like freedom. "We believe they are free," said N.C.C. Tour Leader Bruce Rigdon of the McCormick Theological Seminary, referring to Soviet demonstrators thrown out of Moscow's Baptist Church. And some go to the Middle East, on which they pronounce solemn, chin-tugging judgment full of right and wrong and anguished ambivalence, to make up rules—for others. There are so many of these travelers that the Middle East has become, in Saul Bellow's words, the "moral resort area" of the West: "What Switzerland is to winter holidays and the Dalmatian coast to summer tourists, Israel and the Palestinians are to the West's need for justice." The West Bank alone offers the moral tourist a sandbox full of paradoxes, ironies and ambiguities too neat, and cheap, to refuse. For the Israeli these are questions of life and death; for the traveling moralist (Anthony Lewis makes the hajj at least twice a year), they are an occasion for indignation and advice, the consequences of which are to be observed safely from overseas.

In the end, it is the two-way ticket that makes the holiday of whatever type at once so safe, so pleasurable, and, literally, so irresponsible. It is a walk on the wild side, but a walking tour only; a desire to see and feel and even judge, and then leave. To stay—i.e., to be serious—is to miss the point. "A perpetual holiday," said George Bernard Shaw, "is a good working definition of hell." Getting home isn't half the fun. It's all of it.

Time, August 27, 1984

Football

THE TROUBLE WITH FOOTBALL

THE FIRST THING—THE ONLY THING, AS VINCE LOMBARDI WOULD SAY
—the puzzled anthropologist needs to note about the Super Bowl is the
Roman numeral. Sunday was XIX. Born in a fit of NFL portentousness,
the numeral is nicely revealing of an event (and a sport, as this polemic
is intended to demonstrate) Roman in more ways than one. A cross
between a Roman circus and a Roman orgy, the Super Bowl is America's
closest brush with Colosseum life—a fine name, by the way, for a football
magazine.

Rome had gladiators bash each other up until one died. Football does
not go quite so far. A concussion or a crushed knee is enough to earn a
player a moment's lie-down and a ceremonious carting off to the cheers
of the assembled. The American spectacle, it must be admitted, includes
a ball. But the football is something of a distraction. The heart of the game,
as the connoisseur knows and the isolated camera reveals, is "line play" in
all its glorious mano-a-mano intimacy.

As for orgies, well, delicacy prevents me. . . . I remind you only of Joe
Namath's demure claim that sex the night before improved his game.
There may be a certain logic to that, but it remains unclear why Super
Bowl patrons, bounding off their corporate jets, feel they need the same
preparation to improve their spectating.

Don't misunderstand. It is not that football is decadent. To say that in
the age of Twisted Sister and low-cal dog food would be unfair. The

problem with football is that it is imperial. Where *did* it pick up all that absurd Augustan ritual—the oversized flag, the color guard, the presidential coin toss—urged on by platoons of highly energetic vestal virgins? We used to make do with a recorded rendition of "The Star-Spangled Banner," a nicely alliterative tune, not too solemn, perfect for slight foreshortening with joyful cries of "play ball." Now without a fly-by by the Blue Angels and invocations by ministers of all denominations, one can hardly get the game off the ground.

Like all empires, football is no respecter of place. The Super Bowl can be staged anywhere, and is. The site is annually auctioned off to the highest-bidding city. It would be played in Cracow, if the Cracow Bowl had enough sky boxes.

Football has even less respect for time. In fine imperial fashion, it decrees its own calendar, with its own Year One. To make matters worse, football tried to abolish the seasons. Bad enough helmets knocking about through fall and winter; the USFL had the audacity to invade spring and summer. It might have taken a constitutional amendment to restore the natural order, had not the invisible hand, acting through the agency of the market (low TV ratings), intervened. God bless Adam Smith. Beginning next year, the USFL will be consigned, like Proserpina in the Underworld, to fall and winter. Spring will be left to the happier sound of ball meeting bat.

That sound—what the President calls the American sound—makes the final, fatal case against football. If baseball exists, why football?

Baseball is so modestly republican. The World Series is a continuation of the season by other means. Played in real towns, it is awarded, democratically, to the city with the most wins, not the best caterers. And the players are built to human, yeoman scale. Footballers wear uniforms designed to make them mammoth and interchangeable, like products of an oversized assembly line. Baseball outfits are meant to betray the real body underneath. In baseball's perfectly American balance of anarchy and order, uniforms *are* worn. But republican flannels, for God's sake, not the pads and helmets of a Nixonian Swiss guard.

In all fairness, though, I dissent from the most common charge against football: that its ritualized violence is a seedbed of militarism. If anything, football is a fine form of sublimation. It can hardly be said that the last fifteen years, the years of football's ascendancy, have been a high point of American militarism. We did beat Grenada with its squad of Cuban construction workers (in overtime). But when we ran up the score against the Kaiser, Tojo and Hitler, the ruling pastime was the sleepy summer game.

No, football has enough sins. Besides being imperial, it is prosaic. Its action is too complex, too simultaneous for anything other than analysis. Baseball, with its pauses and anticipations, its delicate sequentialism, lends itself to abstraction—and poetry. Roger Angell, baseball's poet laureate, can make baseball sing. Can anyone make music from football?

The only thing troublesome about baseball is its alarming popularity among intellectuals, usually a leading indicator of impending foolishness. When George Will and Yale's Bart Giamatti agree on anything, in this case reverence for baseball, and when Robert Redford concurs (can you imagine *The Natural* about a linebacker?), I worry. No matter. For baseball —against football—one must take risks.

The last out of the World Series, writes Jonathan Yardley, marks the start of a "long, bleak . . . outer darkness" of winter, and, I would add, football. There is one good thing to be said for the Super Bowl. When it's over, it means that dawn is only six weeks away.

The Washington Post, January 25, 1985

Suicide

DEATH OF A PRINCESS

ON JULY 10, 1979, ALONE AND OFF-CAMERA, JO ROMAN, A NEW YORK artist, killed herself with an overdose of sleeping pills. It was not an impulsive act. As early as 1975, she had made up her mind that she would end her life on her own terms, purposefully and "rationally." Several years later, when she learned that she had breast cancer, she moved up the date. She would do it within a year, she decided, and proceeded to tell friends, family, and a TV film crew. Thus began a drama that culminated in a sensational front-page story in the New York *Times* and a harrowing one-hour documentary entitled "Choosing Suicide" that aired June 16, 1980 on PBS.

The documentary is a faithful record of the gatherings Jo held during that year to prepare for her great deed. It records the deliberations of a Greek chorus of chosen literati and hapless family relations drawn into her web as co-conspirators, spectators and participants. At these meetings, all sit in the obligatory circle. Jo, the queen bee, presides. She is quiet, controlled, in command. She is experiencing no pain or disability, but her mind is made up. No one can change her resolve, but all "acknowledge" and "respect" her feelings. There is much touching, hugging, crying and stroking. No one seems distracted by the bobbing microphones and clanking camera stands.

All the while, I am trying to figure out why they are there. The film crew, I suppose, thinks that if she delivers they've got a hot property, and, if it is done with taste, maybe an Emmy. Friends and family must feel the weight of the contemporary obligation to "be there" and share the experience. And how do you turn down an invitation to a suicide?

But what's in it for Jo? Perhaps, like Tom Sawyer, she simply wants to live the fantasy of attending, indeed directing, her own wake. Jo herself invokes loftier motives with more decidedly romantic pretensions: she considers this act a work of art, "the final brush stroke on the canvas of my life." It is a claim taken with utmost seriousness by her friends, who seem to believe that art is anything that artists do (and then proceed to frame). "This is the greatest creative act of your life" gushes one friend. And because it is art, Jo Roman's son can assure her that rational suicide is not something he would recommend for the masses. He has told his friends and co-workers of Jo's plans, he says, but they are all into apple pie, baseball and religion, and they don't understand.

The masses, I infer, could begin to understand the angry crash into the highway abutment, the impulsive leap from the apartment window. They could begin to understand the everyday anguished acts of self-destruction full of killing and pain and suffering. What they would find difficult to understand is the bloodless, careless, motiveless, meaningless art of Jo Roman's rational suicide. Jo's friends, however, are awed by her innovation. After all, one friend comments, we need something more dignified than sidewalk splatter (as passé as action painting, I suppose). And Jo, in a burst of creativity, has given them the ultimate soufflé, the stylish alternative to such crude gaucheries, the artistic way to end it all. She has produced the last word in sophistication: the meticulously orchestrated, thoroughly psychoanalyzed, faithfully filmed, year-long death watch.

Jo has other reasons for suicide besides art. She and her flock coo responsively about how all this has brought them closer together, put them in touch with their own feelings, given them a profound "learning experience." In an interview taped twelve days after Jo's death, husband Mel, looking grave and lost, reflects on how the whole year leading up to Jo's death caused him great pain and suffering. But it has been worthwhile, he says, because he has learned a lot about himself. I found this a particularly sad sight: a grown man in his bereavement seeking solace in the shallowest cliché of adolescent solipsism—the world as an instrument of one's own education. It marked the moment in the show when the banality finally transcended the pathos.

Jo herself occasionally gropes for some deeper philosophic justification for her act. She proclaims suicide as the enricher and clarifier of life. Her friends stroke her hand and nod sagely in the classic group-therapy mode, but I have no idea what she meant. Another group favorite was the idea that Jo is "taking control of her own life," taking responsibility for herself, finishing a job she started. They congratulate Jo for preempting God or cancer and taking her own life. In their preoccupation with the agency of her act, however, they avoid the question of its consequences. And the documentary shows us just what these consequences are: feelings of acute loss for her friends, suffering for her loved ones, bewilderment and self-doubt for her husband. When one of the pernicious seeds of her act begins to flower before her eyes—when her daughter, who also has had cancer, begins to contemplate her own suicide—Jo sees not horror but raised consciousness.

Our usual response to a victim of suicide is, as Pasternak says, to "bow compassionately before [his] suffering" because "what finally makes him kill himself is not the firmness of his resolve, but the unbearable quality of his anguish." Jo Roman, however, denies us our compassion because she denies herself her anguish. She opens the film looking into the camera and calmly proclaiming that her suicide, unlike others, does not involve killing and hurting, but is a reasoned response to her life. But her very coldness persuades us that we are watching not a suicide but a murder. This is why we experience not sorrow but emptiness, why we feel not pity but anger.

The anger is directed both at the murderer and at her mesmerized accomplices. A protesting voice is difficult to find. One friend says to her "I can't understand you. If someone say at age seventy-five said to me 'I have arthritis and I can't type'—O.K. I can understand that, but you . . ." Can't type! What next? Suicide over a lost backhand? A clogged Cuisinart? The anger turns to bewilderment. What happens when these people are threatened by something worse than pain or age or travail? What happens when their children or their values are threatened? Is their reward for sophistication a capacity for self-delusion so prodigious as to turn cowardice into courage, death into creativity and suicide into art?

Not that voluntary death is either new or necessarily eccentric. History contains many acts of voluntary death from Socrates and Christ to the mother who gives up her seat on the lifeboat for her child. But they died for truth or salvation or love. They died for more than a dose of good feelings or artistic conceit. What is most pathetic about Jo Roman's death is that, in her enervated and alienated circle, she died for the illusion that her death would express some transcendent reality. Like the Dadaists, she believed that her life and death were art. But at least the Dadaists were under no illusion. They considered both equally worthless.

"Choosing Suicide" is disturbing because it leaves us with the feeling that the Dadaists were right after all. For all its voguish psychobabble and pseudophilosophic paradoxes, this documentary leaves us with one conviction: that on the altar of her savage household gods—art, growth, feeling, control, creativity—Jo Roman died for nothing.

The New Republic, July 5–12, 1980

III

CONUNDRUMS

Experimentation

THE USING OF BABY FAE

THE PLACING OF A BABOON HEART INTO THE CHEST OF LITTLE BABY FAE caused indignation in many quarters. For some, who might safely be called eccentric, the concern was animal rights. Pickets outside Loma Linda University Medical Center and elsewhere protested the use of baboons as organ factories. Dr. Leonard Bailey, the chief surgeon, was not impressed. "I am a member of the human species," he said. Human babies come first. It was unapologetic speciesism. He did not even have to resort to sociology, to the argument that in a society that eats beef, wears mink and has for some time been implanting pigs' valves in human hearts, the idea of weighing an animal's life equally against a human baby's is bizarre.

Others were concerned less with the integrity of the donor than with the dignity of the recipient. At first, before Baby Fae's televised smile had beguiled skeptics, the word ghoulish was heard: some sacred barrier between species had been broken, some principle of separateness between man and animal violated. Indeed, it is a blow to man's idea of himself to think that a piece of plastic or animal tissue may occupy the seat of the emotions and perform perfectly well (albeit as a pump). It is biological Galileanism, and just as humbling. Nevertheless it is fact. To deny it is sentimentality. And to deny life to a child in order to preserve the fiction of man's biological uniqueness is simple cruelty.

Still others were concerned with the rights of the observing public, and its proxy, the press. For a while, when Baby Fae was doing well, the big issue was made out to be the public's (read: the press's) right to know. There were reiterated complaints about withheld information, vital forms not made public, too few press conferences. It is true that in its first encounter with big-time media Loma Linda proved inept at public relations. But how important can that be? In time the important information will be published and scrutinized in the scientific literature, a more reliable setting for judging this procedure than live television.

Baby Fae brought out defenders of man, beast and press. But who was defending Baby Fae? There *was* something disturbing—subtly, but profoundly disturbing—about the baboon implant. It has nothing to do with animal rights or the Frankenstein factor or full disclosure. It has to do with means and ends.

It turns out that before placing a baboon heart into the chest of Baby Fae, doctors at Loma Linda had not sought a human heart for transplant. That fact betrays their primary aim: to advance a certain line of research. As much as her life became dear to them, Baby Fae was to be their means.

The end—cross-species transplant research—is undoubtedly worthy. Human transplants offer little hope for solving the general problem of children's dying of defective hearts. There simply are not enough human hearts to go around. Baboons grown in captivity offer, in theory, a plausible solution to the problem. To give Baby Fae a human heart would have advanced the cause of children in general very little. But it might have advanced the cause of *this* child more than a baboon's heart, which, given the imperfect state of our knowledge, was more likely to be rejected.

Doctors like to imagine that the therapeutic imperative and the experimental imperative are one and the same. On the contrary. They are almost always in conflict. At the extreme are the notorious cases in which the patient is actually sacrificed on the altar of science: the Tuskegee experiment, in which a group of black men with syphilis were deliberately left untreated for forty years; the Willowbrook experiment, in which retarded children were injected with hepatitis virus; and the Brooklyn study in which elderly patients were injected with live cancer cells. Loma Linda was at the other extreme. Here, far from being at war with the therapeutic, the experimental was almost identical with it. But not quite. The baboon heart was ever so slightly more experimental, more useful to science (or so the doctors thought), more risky for Baby Fae. If it were your child, and you had two hearts available, and you cared not a whit for science (perhaps even if you cared quite a bit for science), you would choose the human heart.

The Loma Linda doctors did not. Hence the unease. One does not have to impute venal motives—a desire for glory or a lust for publicity—to wonder about the ethics of the choice. The motive was science, the research imperative. Priority was accorded to the claims of the future, of children not yet stricken, not yet even born.

Is that wrong?

Civilization hangs on the Kantian principle that human beings are to be treated as ends and not means. So much depends on that principle because there is no crime that cannot be, that has not been, committed in the name of the future against those who inhabit the present. Medical experimentation, which invokes the claims of the future, necessarily turns people into means. That is why the Nuremberg Code on human experimentation (established after World War II in reaction to the ghastly Nazi experiments on prisoners) declares that for research to be ethical the subject must give consent. The person is violated if it is unwillingly—even if only uncomprehendingly—used for the benefit of others.

But not if it volunteers, and thus, in effect, joins the research enterprise. Consent is the crucial event in the transition from therapy to experiment. It turns what would otherwise be technological barbarism into humane science. Consent suspends the Hippocratic injunction "First, do no harm." Moreover, it redeems not only the researcher but the researched. To be used by others is to be degraded; to give oneself to others is to be elevated. Indeed, consciously to make one's life the instrument of some higher purpose is the essence of the idea of service. If Barney Clark decides to dedicate his last days to the service of humanity, then—and only then —may we operate.

Infants, who can decide nothing, are the difficult case. (If Baby Fae had volunteered for her operation, the ethical questions would evaporate.) Since infants are incapable of giving consent, the parents do so on their behalf. In Baby Fae's case what kind of consent did they give? If her parents thought that the operation might save their child (i.e., that it was therapeutic), they were misled. There was no scientific evidence to support that claim. The longest previous human survival with a heart xenograft was three-and-a-half *days*. (Baby Fae lived seventeen more.) The longest *animal* survival in Dr. Bailey's own studies was 165 days.

If, on the other hand, the parents had been told that the purpose was to test a procedure that might help other babies in the future (i.e., that it was experimental), what right did they have to volunteer a child—even their child—to suffer on behalf of humanity?

After Baby Fae died, it was argued, retroactively, that in fact the operation reduced her suffering, that she was pink and breathing instead of blue and gasping. Perhaps. But the cameras were brought in only when she was well. She was not seen when not doing well: enduring respirators, cannulas, injections, stitches, arrhythmias, uremia. Was this really less agonal than a natural death, which would have come mercifully weeks earlier?

No. Baby Fae was a means, a conscripted means, to a noble end. This experiment was undertaken to reduce not her suffering, but, perhaps some day, that of others. But is that really wrong? Don't the suffering babies of the future have any claim on us? How do we reconcile the need to advance our knowledge through research, with the injunction against using innocents for our own ends?

Two serious men have attempted an answer. One is Jonas Salk. "When you inoculate children with a polio vaccine," he said of his early clinical tests, "you don't sleep well for two or three months." So Salk tested the vaccine on himself, his wife and his own children. This is an extraordinary response. It certainly could not have improved his sleep. It did not even solve the ethical dilemma. After all, the Salk children were put at risk, and they were no less innocent than the rest. But by involving his own kin (and himself), Salk arranged to suffer with the others if his science failed. He crossed the line that separates user from used. By joining his fate to the used, he did not so much solve the ethical problem as turn it, heroically, into an existential one.

Princeton philosopher Paul Ramsey offers another version of that response. Ramsey comes from the other side of the great research debate. He argues that children may never be made guinea pigs and that we have no right to "consent" on their behalf. A most stringent Kantian, he would prohibit all experimentation on nonconsenting subjects. But for those of us who see the requirement for research as a moral imperative equal in force to the imperative to respect the individual, he counsels: if you must do it, do it, but do not deny the moral force of the imperative you violate. In a society that grants the future *some* claims, a society that will not countenance the endless destruction of children by polio—or by hypoplastic left-heart syndrome—"research medicine, like politics, [becomes] a realm in which men have to 'sin bravely.' "

Baby Fae lived, and died, in that realm. Only the bravery was missing: no one would admit the violation. Bravery was instead fatuously ascribed to Baby Fae, a creature as incapable of bravery as she was of circulating her own blood. Whether this case was an advance in medical science awaits the examination of the record by the scientific community. That it was an adventure in medical ethics is already clear.

Time, December 3, 1984

Homelessness

ASYLUM

WINTER IS HERE, AND THE HOMELESS WILL BE DYING IN GREATER NUMBERS than normal. Are they dying because of the callousness of urban life? Perhaps. They are certainly dying because of the blindness of current social policy.

Start at the beginning. Who are the homeless? A Boston study published in the current issue of the *American Journal of Psychiatry* attaches numbers to what most of us intuit from looking around: The homeless are drawn mostly from the mentally ill. The Boston study found forty percent of the homeless to be psychotic, thirty percent chronic alcoholics, and twenty percent suffering from other very severe psychiatric disorders.

These numbers may be high. Healthy individuals driven to destitution by calamity—sudden unemployment, family breakup or sheer bad luck—probably account for more than one in ten of the homeless. But not much more. Were our cities not overwhelmed by the mentally ill, the traditional safety nets of social welfare and voluntary charity would be adequate to handle the relatively small number of "new poor" cases.

They once *were* adequate. Twenty years ago there were no armies of grate dwellers. They dwelt elsewhere. Twenty years ago there were about 500,000 people in mental institutions. There are now 130,000. (The number of mental hospital employees, about 200,000, is essentially unchanged. But that, in other contexts known as waste and abuse, is another matter.)

The vast emptying of these institutions, begun in the Kennedy years, was undertaken in the name of the most humane ideals. One was liberty, the simple desire of an era steeped in civil rights to see personal freedom returned to thousands who had been locked away, many against their will.

The other ideal was community, a desire to restore to these people a sociality they had lost by virtue of their illness (and isolation) and that a caring community would help them regain. As President Kennedy said in his 1963 message to Congress that launched the community mental health revolution, "reliance on the cold mercy of custodial isolation will be supplanted by the open warmth of community concern."

It wasn't. Liberty proved a cruel gift for many with only the vaguest attachment to reality. And the idea of community proved simply a mirage. We do have our neighborhoods where people may exchange hellos, perhaps even know each other's names. But the turbulence of modern urban life does not permit anything so organic as the tightly knit community of generations ago. Certainly nothing so organic, it turns out, as to lend protection, let alone "open warmth," to the most difficult and alienated of citizens.

The Kennedy era reformers, of course, cannot be blamed for not seeing all this in advance. We, however, no longer have that excuse. We don't need foresight to see the results of the experiment. A newspaper will do. There now is empirical evidence, encamped on every Main Street from New York to San Francisco. Or in Lafayette Park, in Washington, where Jesse Carpenter, World War II hero, recently froze to death.

What is to be done?

Revolving-door shelters are not the answer. The care they provide is haphazard. As a rule, they are open only at night. Their staffs are rarely trained to deal with severe, disabling illness. Medical, let alone psychiatric, problems go untended. And since the guests are free to drift in and out, no one can keep track of their care anyway.

Shelters, of course, are better than nothing, and in the absence of anything else they must be maintained. There is a better alternative, however, though no one dares speak its name. Asylum. A place where the homeless mentally ill are taken and given food, shelter, hygiene and a sense of order in their lives.

The word asylum, of course, conjures up the snake pit. The fact that the idea was corrupted by periods of pseudoscientific quackery makes for sad history, but it should not paralyze current social policy. The idea of asylum is to provide protection and care. In some historical periods (in the nineteenth century, in particular) the asylum offered just that. It cannot be beyond our wit to redesign humane custodial institutions.

The larger problem facing the idea of asylum, however, is not one of design, but of political will. Asylum means taking people away to be cared for, whether they like it or not. That means taking control, something we can barely bring ourselves to do with children, let alone with recalcitrant adults. (But then again, children are not dying in Lafayette Park.) And that means violating their rights, as currently defined.

The caveat is important. There is nothing sacred (or, as we Americans prefer to say, self-evident) about current definitions. The law has long recognized the principle that people may be committed against their will. What has changed in recent years is the standard justifying commitment. The standard has moved away from a mere incapacity to care for oneself and toward actual dangerousness to oneself and to others.

As the threshold for providing people asylum, against their will if necessary, has risen, so has the price to be paid. It amounts now to an army of broken souls foraging and freezing in the streets.

This is not the result of society's mean-spiritedness, though some advocates for the homeless would have us think so. It comes rather from a curious combination of fatalism, about the lot of the homeless, and sentimentality, about the freedom they are allegedly enjoying. In fact, the homeless mentally ill are abandoned, not free. Nor is their degraded condition at all inevitable. It is the result not of mysterious determining forces, but of a failed, though well-intended, social policy. And social policy can be changed. In this case, it will not be easy. There will be a lot of thundering from civil libertarians. But it certainly can be done.

The Washington Post, January 4, 1985

Abortion

WAR OF THE WORDS

A CURIOUS THING HAS HAPPENED TO THE ABORTION DEBATE. IT REMAINS
politically hot, but it is intellectually spent. Everyone seems to know both
sides of the argument backward and forward. One reason for the exhaustion is that the abortion issue has been—and will be—decided not by the
popular branches of government, Congress or the President, but by the
Supreme Court, our system's concession to aristocracy. When the outcome of a struggle bears little relation to public opinion or practical
politics, debate becomes increasingly autistic. With little prospect of winning converts, both sides in the abortion debate have turned to capturing
words.

Terrorist. Only a few weeks ago it seemed extremely important to
pro-abortionists that those who were bombing abortion clinics be called
"terrorists." The ostensible reason was that using the word would trigger
FBI intervention, although the Bureau of Alcohol, Tobacco and Firearms
appears to have done a fairly good job of rounding up suspects. The larger
aim, of course, was polemical. Everyone hates terrorists. Moreover, anti-
abortionists are generally conservative; conservatives make a big point of
denouncing terrorism; to find terrorists in their midst would be an acute
embarrassment. *Touché.*

Yet last month, on the weekend of the twelfth anniversary of Roe v.
Wade, NOW activists kept overnight vigil in some abortion clinics. The
idea was to deter the bombers by putting people in the buildings after

closing hours. But the very definition of a terrorist is someone who is not deterred by the prospect of harming innocents. In fact, he seeks them out in order to magnify the effect of his violence. To hold a vigil at the U.S. Embassy in Beirut, for example, would be a novel, but imprudent, defense against terrorism.

Abolition. More wordplay, this time on the other side. Everyone would like to borrow some of the glory of the anti-slavery movement. Moreover, for the anti-abortion side it offers a delicious irony. Its opponents tend to be liberals, for whom Abolition (and its twentieth-century successor, the civil rights movement) is the most hallowed of causes. How better to hoist them than by appropriating their cause and portraying them as having betrayed it? Of course, this is all sleight-of-hand. Who is to say whether banning a social behavior constitutes Abolition or Prohibition?

Pro-life and *pro-choice.* Wordplay of a high order. It makes the opponent—against either life or choice—a denier of at least one-third of the promises of the Declaration of Independence. At the same time, these words, like all words that mean everything and nothing, are artfully empty. Pacifists, vegetarians, gun controllers, anti-smokers, Mothers Against Drunk Drivers and the air-bag lobby can equally claim the pro-life slogan. And who is against choice? It is hard to think of a cause that is not pro-choice, from legalizing marijuana to abolishing the income tax (contributions to the government to be voluntary). Suppose you are pro-lynching. Why not call yourself pro-choice? (A fair trial or a lynching: Let the people decide.) Until, that is, you are caught and condemned for a lynching. Not wanting to hang, declare yourself then to be pro-life.

Terminating a pregnancy. When the CIA says "terminate" (with or without extreme prejudice), the euphemism is so outrageous as to be comic. "Terminate a pregnancy," on the other hand, has a medical ring that endows abortion with instant moral neutrality. Yet, one really does not have to believe that abortion is murder to know that "terminating a pregnancy" is a different moral proposition from, say, removing a hangnail.

Pre-born. A favorite of Nellie Gray, leader of the March for Life. Pre-born child is her way, her only way, I gather, of saying fetus. The technique is to make the distinction between a fetus and a child sound like one of packaging. The point is to rig the debate: If what is at stake is a child—differently boxed, perhaps, but a child nonetheless—the entire abortion issue is nicely foreclosed.

Scream. As in *The Silent Scream,* the anti-abortion film shown recently at the White House. The idea, says the film's producer, Dr. Bernard Nathanson, is to "vault over the tired, stalemated, point-counterpoint" debate—to go beyond words—by showing the ultrasound image of an actual abortion. "Scream" refers to a point in the film in which the fetus' mouth appears to open. Neurologists point out that a fetus at twelve weeks is no more capable of a scream than of experiencing pain. "Perhaps the use of the word scream is a little metaphorical," admits Nathanson. "But there is no question this child is grimacing." No matter. Just words.

Things will get worse. In an exhausted debate, all that's left to do is to rework the words. One side plumbs the lexicon of slavery and Dachau; the other speaks medical jargon and clothes its opponents in every variety of political intolerance. There is not the slightest recognition on either side that abortion might be at the limits of our empirical and moral knowledge. The problem starts with an awesome mystery: the transformation of two soulless cells into a living human being. That leads to an insoluble empirical question: How and exactly when does that occur? On that, in turn, hangs the moral issue: What are the claims of the entity undergoing that transformation?

How can we expect such a question to yield answers that are not tentative and indeterminate? So difficult a moral question should command humility, or at least a little old-fashioned tolerance. Instead we get each side claiming truth by linguistic fiat. This is nothing less than a sophisticated form of lying—moral lying perhaps, but lying nonetheless. Well? "Everybody lies," says Stepan in Camus' *The Just Assassins.* "What's important is to lie well." Stepan, by the way, was a terrorist.

The Washington Post, February 15, 1985

Free Will

THE MYTH OF THOMAS SZASZ

LIBERTARIANISM GONE MAD

LIKE THE ATHEIST WHO CANNOT STOP TALKING ABOUT GOD, THOMAS SZASZ cannot stop talking about psychiatry. And as the premier critic of his own profession, he speaks with the familiar animus of the apostate. He is not a theorist. There is no edifice of alternative Szaszian psychology, only a large excavation littered with the debris of classical theory. He did briefly attempt to build "the foundation of a theory of personal conduct," the subtitle of his major work, *The Myth of Mental Illness,* but produced only a rather sterile version of game theory psychology. Szasz seems too preoccupied with demolition to attempt any serious building of his own. This is not to deny his importance; it is merely to define him as the polemicist that he is and sometimes admits to being.

As a polemicist, Szasz has no peer. He has succeeded in focusing attention on the loose and easy quality of psychiatric definitions, on the destructive and indelible stigma that often accompanies psychiatric diagnosis, and on the unique and easily corrupted power that psychiatry has been granted. He has spawned an entire movement of anti-psychiatry, complete with schools, sages and schisms. Ripples from his abolitionist crusade against commitment laws are only now being felt. Self-help groups and legal defense funds for mental patients have sprung up throughout the country. Mental patients' rights recently were upheld and expanded by the Supreme Court, and, only last month, codified by the Senate subcommittee on health in a patients' bill of rights. Szasz deserves much of the credit.

Szasz himself has become a much-sought-after commentator. Having struck gold with mental illness, he has diversified his portfolio and branched out into other areas of social commentary. Hardly a month passes without his gracing the local newsstands with his views on sex-change surgery, drug addiction, the CIA, pornography or what have you.

But what exactly does Szasz say? Without risk of distortion (Szasz himself likes to summarize and number his arguments at the ends of his books), the Szaszian canon can be reduced to two principles; the rest is commentary. First, mental illness is a myth. Corollary: psychiatrists—"maddoctors"—are the state's henchmen who use this myth as a weapon to degrade social deviants. Second, all people, no matter how seemingly "crazy," are equally responsible for their own actions, and equally entitled to liberty. Corollary: no one should be either involuntarily hospitalized or acquitted of crimes on psychiatric grounds. The first proposition is a scientific statement about the nature of disease and derives from a theory of biological determinism. The second is a political statement about the nature of freedom and derives from a theory of radical libertarianism.

The myth-of-mental-illness argument, with its aura of anti-authoritarianism and its promise of demystification, has proven especially appealing. In a decade it has grown from contentious slogan to popular wisdom. But since Szasz is the kind of author no one reads but everyone knows about, few are aware that the entire argument depends on an unusual definition of illness. The only real illness, Szasz says, is a bodily lesion—that is, a structural defect in the body. And to prevent any misunderstanding of his meaning, Szasz provides a clear test to determine what does and does not meet his definition of illness: it's an illness if a dead body can have it. "Every ordinary illness that persons have, cadavers also have," Szasz writes. "Cadavers can have diabetes and syphilis but cannot have depression and schizophrenia."

This, of course, is preposterous. Can a cadaver have a migraine or epilepsy, high blood pressure or a cardiac arrhythmia? Shall we denounce the myth of migraine? The hoax of hypertension? Even a layman might suspect that there is something idiosyncratic, to put it kindly, about this definition of illness. After all, there are many people with bodily lesions whom we would hardly consider ill (a person with no appendix or six toes). At the same time, many of us have gone to a physician in a condition of suffering and disability, only to be told by the doctor, "I can't find anything." On these occasions we think of ourselves not as imposters and fakers, as Szasz would have us believe, but rather as people suffering an illness whose cause is obscure.

Bodily abnormality simply is not the same as illness. Take epilepsy, for example. Many epileptics have no detectable brain lesion or brain wave abnormality. On the other hand many perfectly normal people, when screened, turn out to have abnormal brain waves. According to Szasz's criterion, the former are well, the latter diseased. Szasz's definition of illness confuses screening with diagnosis, knowledge of the cause of an illness with its existence, medical epistemology with ontology.

The rest of Szasz's case is based on a radically Cartesian mind/body dichotomy whose lack of subtlety he makes no effort to disguise. Mind is to body, he states (and in fact repeats in the latest preface to *The Myth of Mental Illness*), as television program is to television set. Just as it makes no sense to attribute bad programming to a defective set, it is "silly, wasteful, and destructive to try to eliminate phobias, obsessions, and delusions . . . by having psychiatrists work on our brains." This is a fallacy, as anyone who has ever been drunk knows. Our minds do indeed receive their programming from the set (brain). This is why alcoholics see pink elephants and syphilitics think they are Napoleon; and it is why Librium can remove the former's hallucinations and penicillin the latter's delusions.

It is one thing to say that for mental illness the connection between mind and body, between brain and behavior, has yet to be elucidated. It is another to say that in principle there can be no connection. The history of psychiatry is full of mental syndromes that were discovered to have an organic basis. If one is to follow Szasz's logic, the mentally ill syphilitics of the 1890s had as fraudulent claim to illness as do present-day schizophrenics. That is, until Wasserman discovered the test for syphilis. It seems curious that this historical accident could instantly transform the sufferers from non-diseased to diseased and make what was only "a problem of living" into a genuine illness.

Perhaps recognizing the philosophic and clinical quagmire that his line of argument leads to, Szasz, in his more recent pronouncements on the myth of mental illness, shows a subtle change of ground. Whereas he previously argued that, in principle, mental illness could not be shown to be illness, he now contends that it could—if and when clinical and laboratory correlates are found. This brings us a long way from "the myth of mental illness." Since, as we have seen, Szasz means by "illness" anything for which a cause is known, schizophrenia and the other classical mental illnesses now are essentially no different from most other medical illnesses, for which the clinical syndrome is well identified but the ultimate cause is still under investigation. Furthermore, with his current claim of only the provisional non-existence of mental illness, Szasz is no longer as blissfully impervious to empirical evidence as he once was. And with recent advances in psychiatric research, his position is becoming increasingly tenuous. To take but one example: there is little better evidence that an illness is "biological" in nature than the demonstration of genetic transmission. The mounting evidence that some mental illness may be hereditary has led one leading researcher, Dr. Seymour Kety of Harvard, to the conclusion that "if schizophrenia is a myth, it is a myth with a substantial genetic component."

If the myth-of-mental-illness shibboleth is put to rest, what happens to part two of the Szaszian canon: his opposition to psychiatric commitment and his insistence on strict moral and legal accountability for the actions of everyone, "mentally ill" or not? If Szasz's opposition to psychiatric commitment depends on his argument that mental illness is a myth, one collapses on top of the other. But Szasz states unequivocally that his primary purpose is to abolish psychiatry's power to commit and acquit. He is not about to let his primary purpose become hostage to a vulnerable scientific theory. He therefore established his abolitionist position on firmly independent and clearly political grounds: that depriving anyone of his liberty in the name of his own better interests or excusing anyone on the grounds of diminished capacity constitutes an affront to the ideal of personal autonomy.

"Autonomy," Szasz declared in a debate, "is my religion." And a devout religionist he is. In fact, only the depth of Szasz's commitment to autonomy can explain the logic of his position on issues such as psychosurgery, Laingian anti-psychiatry, even the myth of mental illness itself. One might have thought, for example, that someone who believes that mental illness is a myth and psychosurgery a brutal fraud would support efforts to ban psychosurgery. Some will be chagrined to learn of Szasz's position:

I am wholly in favor of free trade in psychosurgery between consenting adults. Insofar as other critics of psychosurgery favor banning lobotomy . . . I oppose them just as vehemently as I oppose those who favor banning abortion, heroin, pornography or schizophrenia. . . . Not satisfied with the controls of contract, some critics of psychiatric brutalities seek the remedy in the enemy—the State—for example, advocating the prohibition of lobotomy. . . . Contract and consent suffice to protect those who want to be protected. Any attempt to extend protection beyond this limit makes the "reformers" indistinguishable from the therapeutic totalitarians they oppose.

The melody is classical nineteenth-century libertarianism with lyrics by Adam Smith and John Stuart Mill. Not a note is missing—free trade, consenting adults, contract and consent. The state is the enemy; the contract is the only sacred social institution. Autonomy is the ultimate social value; paternalism is the ultimate sin.

Szasz's libertarian fundamentalism explains his hostility to R. D. Laing's school of anti-psychiatry, which Szasz in many ways helped to create. Laing, the author of *The Politics of Experience*, popularized the view that psychosis is a form of high spiritual achievement in a world of alienation and a creative revolt against, indeed the only truly sane response to, the intolerable conditions of an insanely repressive society. One might have thought Szasz would welcome the views of someone who joined him in proclaiming the myth of mental illness and opposing involuntary hospitalization. But the libertarian in Szasz recoils at the notion of sharing his bed with "a self-declared socialist, communist, or, at least, anti-capitalist or collectivist," particularly one who violates the canons of minimalist government by taking public money and treating his patients without charge, thus forcing one taxpayer to pay for the consequences of another's behavior. What particularly offends Szasz is Laing's view of his "clients" as victims of society on a journey into madness and his view of therapists like himself as protectors and guides. Venerating and cuddling one's "clients," denying them their due as autonomous moral agents, absolving them of responsibility for the consequences of their actions: all this smacks of the paternalism that Szasz finds so repulsive in orthodox psychiatry. Laing blasphemes Szasz's religion of autonomy by denying its central dogma that "human behavior is fundamentally moral behavior," that all action is moral action.

Szasz's mission always has been to uncover the moral dimensions of psychiatric theories. He claims, for example, that schizophrenia was invented to "justify calling psychiatric imprisonment mental hospitalization." This is consistent with his view that ideology and political commitment determine one's scientific beliefs. Szasz himself is a fine illustration of this principle. His central scientific claim, the myth of mental illness, so incomprehensible on scientific grounds, becomes understandable when seen as a product of political ideology. The problem with the concept of mental illness is that "it undermines the principle of personal responsibility, the ground on which all free political institutions rest. . . . [I]t precludes regarding individuals as responsible persons and invites instead treating them as irresponsible patients." In other words, the concept of mental illness fails on political grounds. Even if mental illness does exist, it shouldn't.

Now we can make sense of Szasz's even-handed contempt for psychiatrists ("professional degraders"), Laingian anti-psychiatrists ("base rhetoricians"), ACLU reformers ("a gangster organization"), and the mentally ill themselves ("impersonators," "incompetent, self-absorbed, rejectors of their 'real roles' "). They all deny the patient's responsibility for his or her actions. When Jones says he is Jesus, the psychiatrist says he has a delusion; Laing says he has insight; the ACLU says he has dissident views; Jones knows he has a problem. Dr. Szasz? "I say he is lying."

The consequences of such a radical theory of liberty and responsibility are serious and double-edged. Szasz has performed a service to psychiatry and to medicine by illuminating what has previously remained obscure: the central role of power in psychiatric and medical transactions. Szasz is also correct in identifying a current plague of psychiatric rationalization in which the principle of diminished responsibility is used promiscuously to excuse any action that appears anti-social. If his extremist position has helped to curb this tendency, then he will have done us much good.

But Szasz would not want us to patronize his radical theories by pointing to their salutary effects, or, much worse, to excuse them as a psychological reaction to the current vogue of psychologization itself. He would want to be held to the standards of moral responsibility he demands of others.

Szasz poses the right questions, but his answers are inadequate. His medical theories collapse under the dead weight of the obsolete mind/body dualism he invokes to support them. They can only be viewed coherently when seen as an attempt to distinguish things that "happen to people" from "things that people do." Fundamentally, therefore, "the myth of mental illness" is Szasz's characteristically polemical way of advancing the argument that all action is moral action. It is the scientific gloss on a theory of ethics even more uncompromising than the nineteenth-century libertarianism it sprang from.

When it comes to libertarianism, Szasz is *plus royaliste que le roi.* John Stuart Mill was well aware of the pitiless consequences of unrestrained autonomy, and was prepared to draw the line. In "On Liberty," Mill poses the following dilemma: what should A do when he sees B crossing a bridge that A knows to be unsafe? If there is no time to warn him, Mill concludes, A may forceably seize B and turn him back. "This does not constitute infringement of his liberty for liberty consists of doing what one desires and he does not desire to fall into the river." If there is "only the danger of mischief," and not the certainty, A may not supersede B's right to "judge the sufficiency of the motive that may prompt him to incur the risk." But if B is of diminished capacity ("a child, or delirious or in some state of excitement or absorption incompatible with the full use of their reflecting faculty"), A does have the right to restrain B in B's own interest.

For Szasz, such paternalism is anathema. In a system where "suicide is the greatest human right," diminished capacity is a dangerous and irrelevant doctrine (though Szasz does not hesitate to invoke it for children). Szasz would say that whether or not a person desires to fall into the river is something that no one else can or should ever presume to know. Such relentless and compassionless libertarianism leads Szasz into very dark corners indeed. What *does* Dr. Szasz do when he sees an alcoholic staggering and weaving his way in between cars on the busy highway? Does he bar himself from any interference with the alcoholic's autonomy, or does he grab the drunk and pull him over to the side of the road? And what would Szasz have done in the case of Dr. Frank Olson, the victim of CIA experimentation with LSD, an episode Szasz has so ringingly denounced? Olson, having unknowingly taken LSD, became psychotic and jumped to his death from a tenth-floor hotel room. What would Dr. Szasz have done if he had chanced upon Olson heading for the open window? Recited from *de Tolerantia*? I suspect that if Szasz had been there, he might have attempted a paternalistic (totalitarian?) flying tackle.

And what are *we* to do with the mentally ill—the catatonic, the delirious, the profoundly retarded? Are we to deny them paternalistic care, regard—and, yes, moral and legal extenuation for their actions—until they can prove that they are being "done to" rather than "doing," until they can produce a structural lesion to prove their innocence and achieve absolution?

Szasz is right in believing that any attempt to circumscribe individual autonomy and attenuate individual responsibility, any attempt to draw lines, invites abuse. But that melancholy truth should be a cause for more reasoned and thoughtful line drawing, not for abandoning the enterprise; for offering help to, not heaping abuse on, those (like psychiatrists) whose difficult task it is to draw these lines. Drawing lines, as John Stuart Mill recognized, is one of the characteristics of civilization. It requires care, compassion and balance—qualities difficult to find in the solitary, poor, nasty, brutish world of Thomas Szasz.

The New Republic, December 22, 1979

AIDS

THE POLITICS OF A PLAGUE

THE MORAL MAJORITY, WHICH HERETOFORE HAS BUSIED ITSELF WITH matters spiritual and political, has suddenly taken a deep interest in the nation's blood supply. Jerry Falwell called a July 4 press conference to propose, of all things, ways to protect blood banks from Acquired Immune Deficiency Syndrome. And big-city mayors, who have yet to band together for a national crusade against inner-city tuberculosis, infant mortality or other common medical tragedies, have called for as much (federal) research money as it takes to finance an all-out crusade to stamp out AIDS —now.

There is no more boring political subject than public health, an area normally given over to specialists in screening, sewage and sanitation. But AIDS is no ordinary disease. It fascinates scientists because it is the first transmittable disorder which destroys the body's immune system, the normal defense against cancer and other diseases. It fascinates everybody else because more than seventy percent of its victims are homosexuals. For the press, the story is irresistibly titillating. AIDS has been on every front page from *The Village Voice* to *Moral Majority Reports.* The New York *Post,* the nation's arbiter of what qualifies as the lowest common denominator, accorded AIDS official certification by giving it screaming page one headlines two days running. *Newsweek* gave it its now traditional twice-over Hitler Diary treatment, promoting it in one issue, exposing it in another. Its April 18, 1983, cover warned "AIDS may be the public health threat of the century." Its July 4, 1983, cover deplored "the growing panic over AIDS." But it is politicians and preachers who have evinced a special interest in AIDS. For them, it represents opportunity—opportunity for politicians to score points with homosexuals, and for preachers to score points against them.

For politicians, anti-AIDS pronouncements are the safest possible demonstration of solidarity with gays. Who could be against stopping a killer disease? Elected officials in New York and San Francisco, where large, politically active and increasingly self-conscious homosexual communities represent an important constituency, have led the call for a campaign against AIDS. The Surgeon General has responded by declaring AIDS the nation's "number one health priority" and allocating more than $26 million for AIDS research. Too much, argue critics on the right, who point out that $26 million is more than the combined total spent for Legionnaires' disease and toxic shock syndrome. They conveniently overlook the fact that AIDS is far more virulent: the recovery rate from Legionnaires' disease is 85 percent; from toxic shock syndrome, 97 percent; from AIDS, zero. Too little and too late, say critics on the left, who argue that the Reagan administration is acting only now that it appears that AIDS might be breaking out into the general population. But the fact is that AIDS is *not* breaking out into the general population, as everyone knows who relies on the Center for Disease Control for such information, rather than on the New York *Post* (GRANDMOTHER DIES OF AIDS). Indeed, AIDS may be one of the least communicable of all communicable diseases, remaining for several years confined to very narrowly defined populations of sexually active homosexual men, intravenous drug abusers, Haitians and hemophiliacs.

Nevertheless, one mustn't be too hard on the politicians. They have a self-interest in responding to popular pressure, but they also have a duty to do so. And to say that they are motivated in part by expediency is not to conclude that they have decided the issue wrongly. How much is enough? If balancing the suffering of unemployment against inflation makes for a difficult "fairness" issue, then deciding how much effort society should make against one disease as opposed to another is doubly difficult. Those ready to accuse politicians of either giving too much or too little to AIDS are simply unaware of how capriciously research money for *any* disease is allocated. Congressional appropriations committees have long suffered from a "disease-of-the-month club" syndrome in which they become periodically agitated about a particular disease either because of the power of a lobby (polio, Legionnaires' disease), the fashionableness of the affected constituency (sickle cell anemia, toxic shock syndrome) or the addition of a celebrity to the ranks of the stricken (amyotrophic lateral sclerosis greatly improved its chances in the research funding sweepstakes when it became Lou Gehrig's disease). It is easy to be cynical about the process, but there is simply no morally satisfying way of carrying out the terrible work of triage. And after the push and pull of relatively undirected political forces, a rough justice seems to prevail. Research money by and large is allocated in proportion to number of victims, severity of illness and research opportunities in the field. (I once wrote a scientific paper proposing a mathematical formula for combining these three criteria, as a way of short-circuiting the political bargaining. One reviewer attacked the paper as a case of hopelessly impractical hyperrationality. He was right, of course, as I realized later when I learned that research monies are allocated according to a strikingly similar scheme in France.) On the whole, $26 million seems a reasonable infusion of funds to study a wholly new and deadly disease.

How much of a national scientific effort we devote to fighting an illness is a reflection of the political value we attach to it and to its victims. But that is only the most superficial issue aroused by AIDS. The deeper issue is the moral value we attach to an illness, and on that may hinge the fate of the homosexual movement itself. The initial breakthrough on homosexual rights occurred twenty-five years ago, when private consensual homosexual activity was legalized in Britain. That was a triumph for tolerance —but tolerance implies deviance. The great aim of the homosexual movement in recent years has been to go beyond tolerance to legitimacy. Public acknowledgment of the legitimacy of homosexual life was to take two forms. First, allocation of social—public—space: allowing homosexual gathering places to migrate from the hidden waterfront dive to the downtown homosexual bar, bathhouse and even church. Second, legal recognition of the rights of homosexuals *qua* homosexuals: the addition of "sexual preference" language to antidiscrimination legislation which would, in effect, grant the homosexual community the status of an oppressed minority on a par with blacks and women. These changes would have institutionalized a long historical transformation of homosexuality, which in the last hundred years has traveled the road from criminality, to mere immorality, to illness, and finally to "lifestyle."

Now—just as homosexuality was prepared to take the last step and free itself from the medical mantle which at first protected it and now confines it—comes the "gay plague." Just as society was ready to grant that homosexuality is not illness, it is seized with the idea that homosexuality breeds illness. And that gives those opposed to recent homosexual gains two powerful lines of attack for reversing them.

The first is to challenge on public health grounds the legal recognition and social space accorded homosexuals. It is a lot easier for Patrick Buchanan to call for closing down the gay bathhouses and canceling gay marches because of concern about the spread of AIDS than because he doesn't like what goes on in the bathhouses or what is advocated in the marches. There is one universally recognized exception to the inviolability of civil liberties: during epidemics it is permitted to quarantine individuals and padlock establishments.

Since this epidemic involves gays, and it is they who would be quarantined and padlocked, Jerry Falwell's sudden interest in the nation's blood banks and Patrick Buchanan's concern for the safety of homosexuals reflects a certain disingenuousness. Public health had never been high on the agenda of the Moral Majority, nor had the well-being of homosexuals been of particular concern to right-wing columnists. And since there is no evidence that AIDS is spread other than through intimate contact or the sharing of needles, the alarums raised about a great threat to the general (i.e., nonhomosexual, non-i.v.-drug-addicted) public are exercises in hysteria, and occasionally outright paranoia. *Human Events,* the right-wing weekly, writes that "there has even been speculation"—that convenient formulation that provides license for all kinds of lunatic accusations—"that AIDS victims could deliberately contaminate the blood supply, thus spreading the condition into the general population, as a way to make certain that there is increased pressure on the federal government to find a cure." An old story. "Nothing apparently could be more authentic than the reports that were spread of miscreants who were taken in the act of putting poisonous drugs into the food and drink of the common people," writes Thucydides. Poisoning the wells now has a high-tech version: poisoning the blood.

AIDS does raise a public health issue, but a different one. Although AIDS is not a threat to the general public, it is killing and terrorizing a large number of homosexuals. A study from the U. C. San Francisco Medical Center reports that 1 out of every 333 single males in the Castro area of San Francisco has AIDS. Within the gay community AIDS is a public health emergency, and many gay leaders recognize that the bathhouse is its breeding ground. Faced with the choice between their newly won social space and their health, gay leaders have been bitterly split on the question of abandoning the bathhouse culture they struggled to create. In a Sacramento gay newspaper, two gays with AIDS recently wrote that

the present epidemic of AIDS among promiscuous urban gay males is occurring because of the unprecedented promiscuity of the last ten to fifteen years. The commercialization of promiscuity and the explosion of establishments such as bathhouses, bookstores, and back rooms is unique in Western history. It has been mass participation in this lifestyle that has led to the creation of an increasingly disease-polluted pool of sexual partners.

For other gay leaders the bathhouse culture, as the most extreme and defiant expression of liberated homosexual life, must be defended at all costs. (One gay leader in San Francisco termed the proposals to close the bathhouses "genocidal" and compared them to the Nazi order requiring homosexuals to wear triangular pink shirt patches—an analogy that proved that paranoia and political idiocy are far more contagious than AIDS.)

The fact is that the bathhouse *is* a breeding ground for AIDS and is a menace to the homosexual community. If the bathhouse issue were freed from the political uses to which it has been put by homophobes, and from the political symbolism with which it has been endowed by radical gay activists, it might be easier for the gay community to close the bathhouses to save lives. One would hope that the issue could be de-ideologized and left to the judgment of the affected community. But that is not likely to happen.

The pundits and preachers who want to padlock the bathhouses want to do so not for public health but for political reasons. It is the first step to returning homosexuality to the consensual privacy stage. (And perhaps even further: "Dallas Doctors Against AIDS" wants to recriminalize all homosexuality—on health grounds, of course.) Nevertheless, unless AIDS breaks out in the general population, the public health line of attack is unlikely to succeed. But AIDS presents the opportunity for a second, subtler and more fundamental attack on homosexuality: the suggestion that this disease may be a metaphor for the lifestyle and community from which it springs.

Gays argue that AIDS is not inherent to homosexual life. No one knows the origin of the disease. It might have started in Haiti or with a chance mutation elsewhere, and homosexuals happen to have become its current carriers. One might just as well accuse American Legionnaires of being a breeding ground for the fatal pneumonia that now bears their name. This kind of argument bucks a powerful tide. When Buchanan calls AIDS "nature's revenge," and writes, "The poor homosexuals: they have declared war on nature and nature is exacting an awful retribution," he is appealing to the latent and popular feeling that homosexuality is abnormal. That feeling has lately been overlain by a thin, more liberal, layer of opinion about homosexuality. AIDS could easily sweep it away.

We are notoriously inclined to imbue any illness with meaning.

"Leprous" has entered the lexicon as a synonym for corruption and decay; tuberculosis was transformed by the literary imagination into kind of a gift, a romantic agony that bespoke heightened sensibility and refinement ("When I was young I could not have accepted as a lyrical poet anyone weighing more than ninety-nine pounds," said Théophile Gautier); and cancer is the modern metaphor for malignant, destructive, consumptive evil. Diseases transmitted by taboo behaviors are all the more susceptible to metaphorical interpretation. Early in this century syphilis came to stand for moral degradation, a phenomenon that reached its grotesque apotheosis in Hitler's identification of the disease with his nemesis, the Jews.

AIDS is particularly susceptible to metaphorical interpretation, not only because of its mode of transmission, but because of a recent transformation in what might be called the theory of desires. The notion that illnesses are caused by repression was until recently a very powerful modern myth. By the sixties and seventies even as "physical" a disease as cancer was attributed to sexual and emotional repression (a *reductio ad absurdum* that occasioned Susan Sontag's spirited debunking in *Illness as Metaphor*). That tide has turned. Hysteria, the classical illness of repression, has almost disappeared from clinical practice, to be replaced by the newly fashionable narcissistic neuroses—diseases of *expression*—in which one's troubles stem from quite the opposite problem, enslavement to one's desires. We are recoiling from the liberation of the last few decades (and are more likely now to call it permissiveness); but, as we are still reluctant to express this change of heart in moral terms, we invoke nature as the arbiter. Thus herpes, as benign an infection as one can imagine, became the medical sensation of 1982, nature's way of telling us that sexual liberation had gone too far. AIDS—which doesn't itch, it kills—is an even better metaphor. In an anguished reflection on AIDS published in *The Village Voice,* the gay writer Richard Goldstein acknowledges, and laments, the need for "weighing the odds of contagion against the imperatives of desire, a devastating task." Before Freud that would have been considered a commonplace task. The significance of Goldstein's admission is that after a long historical summer when it was thought that desire *was* health, it is now once again recognized that one may have to choose between the two. And that AIDS may be punishment for the wrong choice.

In reality no one knows whether AIDS is accidentally a homosexual disease or intrinsically so. It seems to me more a theological than an empirical question. Historians still argue whether syphilis, which erupted in Europe in 1494, was brought back by Columbus (perhaps from, of all places, Haiti) or whether it was caused by the mutation of an indigenous European organism. The one empirical fact we know about AIDS is that it is associated with promiscuity. AIDS victims have more than twice as many sexual partners as healthy homosexuals. In that respect AIDS is much like syphilis: any sexual contact is inherently risky, and the more tickets you buy in the lottery the more likely you are to get the prize. And syphilis seems an apt comparison because it illustrates how arbitrary the ascription of meaning to illness can be. When it swept Europe in the late fifteenth and early sixteenth centuries, syphilis was a much more virulent illness than it is today (many died in the secondary stage, which today is rather benign). And yet, writes George Rosen in *A History of Public Health*, "Tolerance in sex matters was generally characteristic of the period from the Renaissance to the eighteenth century, so that there was no stigma attached to the disease." Things changed with the new (Victorian) sexual morality and changed again in the last generation, when antibiotics reduced syphilis to a triviality.

Medical science is not likely to do the same for AIDS soon, and AIDS does not arrive in the permissive context of the sixteenth century, or, for that matter, of the 1960s. In the current revisionist climate, it has come to symbolize, to use Richard Goldstein's words, the identity between contagion and a kind of desire. That metaphorical meaning will pose as great a threat to the homosexual movement as the illness itself poses to its constituents. Gay leaders who are for closing the bathhouses are thinking of saving more than lives. They realize perhaps that their movement might have to yield its most extreme social gains, at least until medicine can do for AIDS what it did for syphilis. At which point they might resume their struggle, without having to wrestle with a metaphorical phantom they cannot defeat.

The New Republic, August 1, 1983

IV

POLITICS

One Cheer for Capitalism

CAPITALISM IS ON A ROLL. FREE MARKET EAST ASIA IS BOOMING. America, under an administration of Coolidgean inclinations (Coolidge was the ultimate hands-off president: when his death was announced, Dorothy Parker asked, "How could they tell?"), is enjoying what the Europeans call the American miracle. American liberals are talking growth and incentives. French socialists have given up redistributionist dreams.

And now—still moving left—Chinese communists have joined the cult of the market. In fact, they have supplied the most resounding empirical support for it. In the six years since market incentives in farming were introduced, China's grain harvest has grown by a third. For the first time in history China is self-sufficient in staple foods. For 1984, a year of further deregulation, as we say here, it reports an astonishing twelve percent growth in national income. Somewhere in heaven a pair of invisible hands is clapping, and they belong to Adam Smith.

Down here, however, many hands are wringing. They belong to steel-workers, farmers and, now, savings-and-loan depositors. The ravaged steel towns, the bankrupt farmers, the locked-out savers evoke Depression images. When seventy-one Ohio S&Ls were closed last week by order of the governor, pointed reference was made to the fact that this is the biggest bank closing since the thirties.

The implied analogy is wrong. These disasters are the product not of capitalism's failure but of its success. In 1984 the American economy grew faster than any time since 1951. The paradox of capitalism is that it is most successful when most dynamic; and when most dynamic, it is most destructive. It is, in Schumpeter's famous phrase, a system of "creative destruction." In its purest form it is Darwinian, and meant to be so.

It is not easy, however, to admit the inherent destructiveness of our economic system. Easier to find villains. Hence, for example, the absurd debate on the farm crisis. David Stockman would like us to believe that the culprits are a bunch of speculators in overalls who bet the farm in the seventies on rising land prices and lost. Hollywood pretends that the problem is a bunch of cold-hearted bankers and bureaucrats who, for the sake of a healthy bottom line, are prepared to torment even Jessica Lange.

The real cause makes neither a good political target nor an attractive movie foil. Forty-five years ago, a quarter of Americans lived on farms. Now ninety percent of them are gone—and we are overproducing food. What made that miracle possible, and is now driving the remaining few off the land, is technology that permits vast economies of scale. When a farm family has to borrow half a million dollars for machinery to keep up with larger operations, it becomes clear that farming on this scale is simply obsolete.

With new crises come new villains. The newest victims of robust capitalism are half a million savings-and-loan depositors. How robust? One bank, the biggest of Ohio's seventy-one privately insured S&Ls, went out and did chancy business with a fraudulent company, lost everything, and thus bankrupted the private insurance that was protecting the other seventy. The S&Ls were shut, and the depositors, not exactly your class of speculator, may never see their savings again.

It seems like a case study in the perils of deregulation. Remove the cap on interest rates and all institutions, even the most staid and old-fashioned S&Ls, will have to compete frantically to pay depositors higher rates. Some will go into more speculative investments. And some will go under. The *Wall Street Journal* scoffs at the suggestion that the problem is caused by deregulation. The cause is simple, says the *Journal:* a foolish bank, a bad deal and a couple of wheeler-dealers, particularly "a prominent citizen named Marvin L. Warner."

But surely the larger point is that capitalism welcomes, indeed invites, foolish bankers and wheeler-dealers to the market. Market entrance requirements are based not on ethics or intelligence, but on what my father calls "Lincoln's recommendation," or that of any other face on the currency. The way to protect the system, the banking system in particular, from too much risk and too many rogues is regulation—i.e., artificial constraints on the market.

It does no good to blame foolish farmers or greedy bankers, if to do so is to assume that without fools and knaves capitalism would be spared its cycles and debacles. The most poignant example is British coal. Arthur Scargill is a Stalinist provocateur, and Margaret Thatcher an iron lady. Both have a high tolerance for other people's pain. But neither will have killed the mining towns that are now to die. They are a victim of energy substitution, foreign competition and environmentalism. Coal is a nineteenth-century fuel, as much as the family farm is a nineteenth-century enterprise. Capitalism writes and, having writ, moves on.

The little saver is shaken by deregulation. The family farm is crushed by mechanization. And industrial workers fall to history and technology. This is capitalism at work.

It is the first system in history to lift the mass of men out of economic misery. But to keep the engine going, it randomly visits misery on selected groups. Instead of searching for villains, it might be more humane for the rest of society, which benefits from that mighty engine, to devote some of its vast surplus to cushioning the fall of its victims.

The Washington Post, March 22, 1985

Whatever Became of the American Center?

THE DEATH OF SENATOR HENRY JACKSON HAS LEFT AN EMPTY STILLNESS at the center of American politics. Jackson was the symbol, and the last great leader, of a political tradition that began with Woodrow Wilson and reached its apogee with John Kennedy, Lyndon Johnson and Hubert Humphrey. That tradition—liberal internationalism—held that if democratic capitalism was to have a human face, it had to have a big heart and a strong hand. At home that meant developing and defending the institutional embodiments of the national conscience: civil rights, Social Security, Medicare, welfare (what ambivalent conservatives, using the language of rescue teams and circuses, call the "safety net"). In foreign affairs it meant an unapologetic preference for democratic pluralism everywhere, and a willingness to "bear any burden" in defense of the cause (what the left now calls "the cold war mentality"). In short: big government for big enterprises, at home and abroad.

In the postwar period that creed gathered such a following and such power that it became the dominant, almost consensual, political tendency in the U.S. Vietnam destroyed that consensus. It did something more. It destroyed the sense of equilibrium that underlay that consensus, and introduced a period of volatility that is with us to this day. Not only is the center fractured, but the political system now oscillates between the remaining extremes. Revulsion with Vietnam pulled the Democratic Party to the left: to McGovern in 1972, and to an abiding distrust of American power and intentions ever since. A countervailing revulsion with growing American weakness—for example, economic prostration before OPEC and national humiliation by Iran—helped pull the Republican Party into the orbit of the Reagan right.

Jackson not only stood his ground, he never lost his equilibrium. He bestrode the center, while others sought refuge from the responsibilities of the Western alliance and the welfare state. He believed, with the Preamble to the Constitution, that the purpose of the Union was to provide for both the common defense and the general welfare. Today the two parties have neatly divvied up those responsibilities between them, Republicans committed to defense ("strength"), Democrats to welfare ("fairness").

Liberal internationalism stands for both. To be sure, it is not the only centrist alternative. Another option is to stand for neither or, more precisely, for as little involvement in either as government can manage. That is the party of small government. Its creed is civilized restraint, and its constituency the brand of Tory that Americans call "moderate Republican" and the British call "wet."

There is a third centrist alternative. It rejects all the foregoing categories. It is aggressively nonideological, neither pro- nor anti-defense, welfare or anything else. It seeks only programs that work: weapons, cars, food programs that are lean, clean and mean. It wants guns that shoot straight; it is not terribly concerned what they shoot at. Most of the world calls these people technocrats; in America nowadays they are called neoliberals.

Of all the varieties of centrist experience, the liberal internationalist is the most significant, and not only because of its pedigree and former dominance. Most centrism is negative: afflicted by on-the-one-hand, on-the-other-hand passivity that searches constantly for the lowest common denominator, that seeks the neutrality of the center as a refuge from the passion of the extremes. Liberal internationalism is a passion for democratic principles, and for bold interventionist government to carry them out. It is a standing challenge, a rebuke, to the rigidities and timidities of the newly dominant right and left. That is perhaps why it commands so large a following among intellectuals, even as it has lost ground among politicians. And lost ground it has. In the end, Jackson stood virtually alone. With his death and the abdication of his heir apparent, Senator Daniel Patrick Moynihan, who has quietly moved to the orthodox liberal fold, the center is now weaker than ever.

But great democracies cannot long tolerate such a void. In stable polities the most powerful forces, those that make for stability in the first place, are centripetal. When the major parties pull apart, the political system, abhorring a vacuum, throws up a centrist alternative. In Britain, when the Tories' heart went hard and Labour's head went soft, a Social Democratic Party was born and quickly achieved remarkable strength. The S.D.P., however, had the advantage of being able to coalesce around the nidus of a small, old, still breathing third party, the Liberals. The U.S. is less hospitable to new forms of political life. Third parties in America gravitate not only to the extremes, but to irrelevance.

If an organic center does not exist, what is to be done? The American answer seems to be: build a synthetic one. The can-do country (its creations include synthetic rubber, artificial flavors and plastic hearts) has come up with a substitute: *ad hoc* centrism. The mechanism is government-by-commission, and unlike the "commission on the future" of years past, today's commission is not meaningless, temporary employment for eminent and idle statesmen. It is an essential political instrument for improvising a center. And it is the political story of 1983.

There have already been three major commissions, each charged with solving an intractable problem, each problem more complex and treacherous than the last. The first of these, the Social Security commission, had the easiest task. It had only to put together a one-shot arrangement, a mathematical compromise between the purely economic demands of various constituencies. When it succeeded in locating a kind of arithmetic mean of the competing claims, its work was done. It packed up and went home.

The Scowcroft commission on strategic forces had a harder task. It had to devise nuclear strategy, an area of constant change not given to final, static compromises. It also had to take into account the moves and countermoves of an unpredictable adversary. (Social Security, a purely domestic problem, brought together players who could all be made to sit at the table and behave.)

Then came the thought: If a commission could mute the rancorous debate on the MX, why not Central America? Why not indeed? Enter the Kissinger commission, charged with solving the Rubik's Cube of Central America. The game here is not a two-sided affair where missiles are shuffled and traded; it is a multisided affair with seven independent countries and innumerable factions at odds, sometimes at war, with each other. Unlike Social Security or nuclear policy, Central America is a living, moving, changing target. A week after the commission's report is delivered, events on the ground may very well have rendered it obsolete.

This is not to say that the Kissinger commission is bound to fail, only that commissions are not the wisest way for a country to make foreign policy. Commissions are at best an expedient. They may be fine in the breach, but, with the collapse of an organic center, our politics is becoming all breach.

What is wrong with government-by-commission? First, finding solutions is only half the job. The other half is building support for them. Centrist politics requires not only that one locate common ground, but that one then encourage people to settle there. Commissions, unfortunately, are designed to issue findings, not create consensus. That is the task of a political party. But at the center there is none, which is why the Scowcroft compromise is so shaky and the Kissinger commission so criticized months before it has pronounced its first official word.

Second, even the most distinguished commission must fold its tent. Kissinger's reports in January, and then what? A new Kissinger commission for the next hot spot? What will the next Democratic President do? Call a Brzezinski commission? No problem, says Thomas J. Watson, Jr., former U.S. ambassador to the Soviet Union. We can improve upon "palliatives such as the Scowcroft and Kissinger commissions," he writes. How? With "a permanent blue-ribbon commission to deal with the central issues and to take our nation's survival out of politics-as-usual." His "National Security Commission" will enjoy more than permanence. It will be given "built-in independence" and "take up only watershed issues of U.S.-Soviet relations, including nuclear weapons." Presumably the rest—fishing rights?—will be left to the President and Congress.

Yet the fundamental problem is not with commissions. It is with a political system so weak at the center that it has grown addicted to them, so paralyzed by ideological conflict that it needs to call on collections of wise men to do the work of government. Republicans stop a Democratic administration from getting arms control through Congress; then Democrats stop a Republican administration from getting its arms (MX) through. A commission (Scowcroft's) is then convened to plead the obvious: that both are linked and must get through together or not at all. A Republican administration wants more aid to El Salvador and a surrogate war in Nicaragua; a Democratic House tries to cut the aid and end the war; both sides prepare to blame the other for a halfway policy that failed. A commission (Kissinger's) is now convened to solve what is at root a domestic political problem.

Henry Jackson was so aware of that problem that he proposed and helped create the Central American commission. He saw imminent danger in an increasingly assertive (bellicose to some) administration policy, proceeding without political support. In the absence of a strong natural constituency—his old constituency—to provide that support, he sought an alternative, however makeshift.

No doubt, *ad hoc* centrism is better than none. But it is at best a temporary and incomplete solution to a structural flaw in American politics. In the meantime, until it is corrected, until the liberal internationalist tradition can rebuild itself into a political force, we can look forward to more oscillatory democracy and, to dampen its abrupt left-right swings, more commissions.

And what happens in the meantime to the old constituency? While the world awaits its renaissance, there are choices to be made and, for the liberal internationalist, unpleasant ones. On the one hand is a Republican Party that obeys the minimal decencies of the welfare state, but is still alien to its ethic, still nibbling at the edges of civil rights, union power and social welfare. On the other hand is a Democratic Party so embarrassed by any assertion of American power that it meets even the Grenada operation with automatic, almost reflexive opposition (that is, until the opinion polls come out, at which point most Democrats neatly reverse field).

Today the liberal internationalist center is without an economic base (what Big Business, for example, is for the Republicans), without institutional support (except for a wing of labor led by Lane Kirkland), and, now that Henry Jackson is gone, without leadership. With little to hold it together, it will likely fracture along existing political fault lines and disappear into the landscape: those most concerned with domestic policy returning to the Democrats, those most concerned with foreign policy casting their lot with the Republicans.

Whatever happened to the American center? It died and left no heirs. A commission has been appointed to look after the estate.

Time, December 19, 1983

America's Holy War

ONE CHARACTERISTIC OF HOLY WAR IS THAT THE PARTICIPANTS WILL persist in disputation even as the world around them is going to pieces. It must certainly strike foreigners, and some Americans too, as strange that at a time of fiscal crisis, war in Central America and declining telephone service, the issue that has aroused the most passion in Congress and among the people is whether children should be praying together in school and whether Christmas crèches should be displayed in public parks.

A reasonable first reaction is to view the whole affair with a mixture of amusement and dismay. Does it really matter whether or not passersby at a public display in Pawtucket, Rhode Island, are to be exposed to a plastic rendition of the Nativity? This country survived one hundred eighty years with school prayer and twenty without; would a minute of mumbled devotion put children on the road to salvation, as some would have it, or on the road to religious tyranny, as others would? Nevertheless, though the immediate stakes appear small, the underlying issue is large. Boundary disputes are inherently conducted over small acreage. Yet the slightest breach in a frontier, especially in a religious war, can be ominous. Moreover, a debate over budgets or foreign policy is an argument about contingencies, about the conditions of national existence. A debate over the relationship between religion and government is about the meaning of our national existence.

My contention is that important as this debate is, it has become impoverished and embittered because it has been wrongly framed, because it has been so dominated by two warring tendencies—one sectarian, the other secular—both of which fundamentally misapprehend the historical role of religion in American public life.

The first of these tendencies is sectarian. Its troops are right-wing fundamentalists; its most visible and forceful agent is the Moral Majority; and its method—which above all alarms its opponents—is to ally itself with political power, in particular with President Reagan and the Republican right, so as to bend government to its ends. These ends are stated unequivocally: to Christianize the nation, that is, make public life and public policy conform as closely as possible to the Gospels. Representative Marjorie Holt said it on the floor of the House during the school-prayer debate: "This is a Christian nation." (To which Representative Barney Frank, who chaired that middle-of-the-night debate at the request of the House leadership and who is Jewish, responded, "If this is a Christian nation, how come some poor Jew has to get up at five-thirty in the morning to preside over the House of Representatives?")

The sectarians intend the "Christian nation" to be not merely a demographic but a legal reality. Hence their vigorous lobbying on such policy issues as homosexual rights (against), abortion (against), and school prayer (for). They deserve the name sectarian and not "religious" because, although ostensibly speaking for religion in the abstract, they are interested primarily in promoting their own particular brand. Their ultimate goal is not theist or monotheist or Judeo-Christian, or even Christian, but Protestant, and—judging from the number of Protestant denominations that oppose this movement (denominations whose interpretation of the Scriptures leads them to diametrically opposed views on homosexuality, abortion and school prayer)—Protestant only in its narrowest fundamentalist form.

The other tendency is secular. Its vanguard is the ACLU, and, because its position understandably elicits less popular enthusiasm, its method is to appeal not to the legislative but to the judicial branch to achieve its ends. These too are stated unequivocally: the secularization of American public life. The secularists are the Grinches who try to steal Christmas crèches. It is the ACLU that sued Pawtucket, Rhode Island, charging that the city's forty-year tradition of sponsoring a public Nativity display at Christmastime violated the First Amendment prohibition against establishment of religion. (Last month the Supreme Court ruled in Pawtucket's favor, five to four.) But the goal of the secularists is not simply to extirpate Christian symbolism from American public life. Their nemesis is religion. Religion is to be kept private. Any public manifestation is to be fought, from school prayer (even a moment of silence, because of its religious connotations) to the national motto. In 1970 the government was sued (though not by the ACLU) for "In God We Trust," and won in the Supreme Court.

Not surprisingly, observers of this holy war—interested observers, since it is their public life that is at stake here—are apt to wish on both sides the sort of fate that has befallen Iraq and Iran. On the one hand are the Bible-thumpers, increasingly resented for their ascending power and pushiness, demonstrated most recently in the enormous pressure they brought on the Senate during the school-prayer debate and in their alliance with the President. They want to make their beliefs the law of the land. Ronald Reagan likes the idea. "I've been told," he recently declared, "that since the beginning of civilization millions and millions of laws have been written. I've even heard someone suggest it was as many as several billion. And, yet, taken together, all those millions and millions of laws have not improved on the Ten Commandments one bit." (Does that mean that Congress should try a quick substitution? Has he read the first four?) On the other hand is a band of zealous relic-hunting secularists, famous for the pettiness of their search-and-destroy missions, bent on excising every last vestige of religious influence from American public life. Not even a forty-year-old plastic baby Jesus is safe.

The whole debate arouses dismay, and not just because of the overreaching claims of both sides. One has an instinctive feeling that religion *has* a place in American public life, and that both sides misunderstand it—that between sectarianism and secularism lies something else.

What is that something else? One answer is pluralism, a pluralism that says, "In public life, religion is proper, but only if all denominations are honored equally." That is precisely the principle animating the "compromise" wording for the proposed (and later defeated) constitutional amendment restoring school prayer, a compromise worked out principally by America's quintessential moderate, Senator Howard Baker. The state would neither compose nor mandate the prayer, which could be silent or spoken. What would that mean in practice? No one is quite sure exactly how the prayers would be generated, but it was generally understood that there would be some sort of rotational system, a kind of ecclesiastical musical chairs for kids, each reciting his or her own very special prayer on different days, even if—in fact, because—it had no meaning to the others. (Otherwise, instituting any single prayer would violate the principle of pluralism.)

This attempt at reasonableness is as absurd as it is earnest. It yields the worst of both worlds. If public prayer has any purpose, it is the bringing together of individuals in common devotion. An arrangement in which the Catholic recites his prayer one day, the Jew on another, the Baptist on the next, is not an exercise in prayer, but in anthropology. It trivializes the whole idea of prayer, while the same time managing to offend almost everyone, since it encourages, if it does not require, children of one faith to join or at least witness the prayer of another.

In his Pawtucket dissent, Justice Brennan elegantly describes the religion clauses of the First Amendment as intending "a benign regime of competitive disorder among all denominations." But not for our *common* public life, and certainly not for the common life of first graders. Religious pluralism in America means a celebration of multiple privacies. It means that any group may establish any church anywhere. It doesn't mean that every sect shall have a chapel in the house of government. Rotational pluralism does not solve the dilemma of religion in our common public life. It mocks it. Its spirit is that of a remark attributed to Eisenhower: "Our government makes no sense unless it is founded in a deeply felt religious faith—and I don't care what it is."

But what if one does care what it is? If not rotational pluralism, where to find an alternative to sectarianism on the one hand and secularism on the other? The answer, I suggest, is this: in two hundred years of American experience. In the authentic and original American public religion that the secularists wish to abolish and the sectarians to narrow. In what Robert Bellah, in an illuminating essay written two decades ago, called the American civil religion.

Civil religion is not an American invention. It appears to have been first described by Rousseau. He distinguished civil religion from three other kinds: private piety; exclusive (i.e., intolerant) national theocracies; and supranational hierarchies, which pervade both private and national life, like the Church of Rome. ("The third kind is so manifestly bad that the pleasure of demonstrating its badness would be a waste of time.") What is unique about Rousseau's civil religion, at least in the Western context, is its nonexclusivity. It can coexist with private belief. It is meant to infuse communal life with a religious dimension. He construed its tenets—a belief in a just Providence, in the sanctity of the social contract, and in tolerance—"not strictly as religious dogmas but as sentiments of sociability." Its purpose was to make of the social contract not merely a convention but a faith.

The American civil religion is not nearly as austere, rationalist or coldly utilitarian. For one thing, it was never planned or decreed by the Founders. One doubts if they were even conscious of it. Yet their vision helped establish it, and for two centuries it has served as the faith—the established religion, if you will—of the American polity.

As elaborated by Bellah, it is not Christianity, though it derives much from it. Nor is it a competitor of Christianity, but a parallel and wholly accommodating faith. It has its own theology. Its God is the God of the (Founding) Fathers: Jefferson's Creator, who endows inalienable rights; Washington's Great Author, who guides the affairs of nations; Lincoln's Lord, whose judgment—even if it be civil war—is true and righteous. He is a deistic God, but with a particular interest in American destiny. Not a set of Newtonian laws, but an embodiment of American Purpose. He threatens no hell, but makes demands of his people nonetheless.

The civil religion has a sacred history: American history. It is perhaps more accurate to say that it consecrates the otherwise profane history of the American people, endowing it with a religious dimension. Accordingly, it has its own calendar. Its supreme holiday is Thanksgiving, a day devoted to thanking Providence for America, and for meditating on its meaning. Other days are set aside, some to honor the saints, Washington, Lincoln and King; others to celebrate the civil virtues as revealed in the American historical experience: liberty (the Fourth of July), sacrifice (Memorial Day), service (Veterans Day). Among its many ceremonies the most important is the Presidential Inauguration. Significantly, every Inaugural Address (with the exception of Washington's perfunctory two-paragraph second) makes reference to the Supreme Being. Equally importantly, none makes reference to Christ or Jesus. (The sole exception, I believe, is an allusion by William Henry Harrison: "like the false Christs whose coming was foretold by the Savior." Thirty days later Harrison was dead from a chill contracted while giving this address. Jefferson's God may be more jealous than advertised.)

The civil religion is a grand American unitarianism, and it has an obvious civil function. As Washington said in his Farewell Address, "Reason and experience both forbid us to expect that national morality can prevail in exclusion of religious principle." Truths may be logically self-evident, but better to root them in the firmer ground of religion. Jefferson is careful to say that the Declaration of Independence derives from the "Laws of Nature and of Nature's God." The civil religion serves as a bridge between positive law and a more secure natural law. The President swears not on the Constitution but on the Bible, to uphold the Constitution.

Yet this unique national faith is not some mumbo jumbo created by the Founders for its utility. They genuinely believed in America's transcendent purpose and in its relation to Providence. Their successors have elaborated the theme, finding echoes of the Exodus in the Revolution, and of Christ and the Resurrection in Lincoln and the Civil War. In our day, Martin Luther King, Jr., was perhaps most attuned to the religious cadences of his own and his country's history ("He's allowed me to go up to the top of the mountain and I've looked over and I've seen the promised land. . . .").

Most Americans believe, though perhaps unconsciously, in the civil religion, and respect its place in public life. Which is why they feel such revulsion for the holy warriors, sectarian and secularist, who neither believe nor respect nor perhaps even understand it. The civil religion establishes a critical distinction in American public life between sectarianism and religion. It forbids the one. It permits, even encourages, the other. Both sides, for opposite reasons, wish to eradicate that distinction.

Among the sectarians, eradicating that line is the project not just of the Moral Majority. In an amicus brief in the Pawtucket case, the Justice Department argued that removing the Christmas crèche "mandates an artificial and undesirable sterility in public life, in which one important and enriching aspect of our history and culture [i.e., religion] is treated as illegitimate. . . . We ask the Court to rule that the First Amendment does not mandate contrived exclusion of religion from public life." Now really. Surely one can ban a municipal crèche as a sectarian symbol (albeit of the majority sect) without being against religion. The event commemorated by the crèche is outside of American history; the religious idea it symbolizes (the Incarnation of the Divinity) is outside of the American civil religion. Though Christmas is designated as a holiday to accommodate the practice of the majority of Americans, the municipal crèche goes beyond accommodation to the (admittedly minor) promotion of one (admittedly major) sectarian religious vision. (Justice Brennan points out just how sectarian celebrating Christmas has been: the Puritans were so opposed to that "Popish" practice that in 1659 it was made punishable by fine in the Massachusetts Bay Colony. As late as 1855 it was not celebrated by Presbyterians, Baptists or Methodists.)

The crèche violates the spirit of the civil religion because it moves beyond religion to sectarianism. More significantly, so does the President. That is why his speech to the convention of Religious Broadcasters created such unease. It is one thing in a public address to invoke—even ostentatiously to ally oneself with—God. Indeed that, minus the ostentation, is in the tradition of the canonical literature of the civil religion. It seems to me equally inoffensive to make religion a political issue. (The whole "hypocrisy gap" charge against Reagan leaves me cold. Tip O'Neill complains that the President hasn't been to church since last June. So what? Tip O'Neill has made a political career of "compassion," meaning helping the needy from the public purse. Who cares whether in private life Tip is generous or a Scrooge? Ronald Reagan's private prayer habits are of interest to his biographer. They are irrelevant to the question of the proper relationship between religion and politics.) But it is seriously overstepping the bounds of the civil religion for the President to announce, as Mr. Reagan did in that speech, that "For God so loved the world, that He gave His only begotten Son, that whosoever believeth in Him should not perish, but have everlasting life." The President then added, "I'm a little self-conscious because I know very well that you all could recite that verse to me." He should be self-conscious: the religious tradition in this country requires that it should have been the other way around.

The secularists are equally disrespectful of the distinction between sectarianism and religion. They are as opposed to "In God We Trust" as they are to the Christmas crèche. This dedication to a rigid secularism and against the slightest trace of religion in public life, derives more from the French Revolution than the American. The Jacobins, deeply anticlerical in a way that the Founders never were, embraced a *civic* religion, a religion of Reason, as jealous and exclusive as the clerical tyranny they overthrew. That branch of Rousseauism, nonaccommodationist and intolerant, has always remained an extreme tendency in America.

But among the secularists it is not just the extremists who miss the distinction between sectarianism and religion. In Justice Brennan's (I believe, correct) minority opinion opposing the crèche, he admitted to some perplexity as to why, if the crèche is impermissible, "In God We Trust," Thanksgiving Day and the opening declaration of each session of his Court ("God save the United States and this Honorable Court") should not also be prohibited. Because, he is forced to argue, they are (today at least) religiously meaningless. Their meaninglessness makes them permissible. The practices of "ceremonial deism" are "protected from Establishment Clause scrutiny chiefly because they have lost through rote repetition any significant religious content." Civil religion is permitted only because it has degenerated into "ceremonial deism."

Has it? Justice Brennan is consoled by the thought that the civil religion is meaningless. Many who care about religion are disturbed by it. For them it is an indictment (and an argument for sectarianism): its God is really no God; when denominational differences are homogenized to yield some kind of neutral Creator, there is little that remains. But American history contradicts that view. The power of the idea of an American Providence is evident in the life and liturgy of the Founders, and, a century later, in Lincoln's deeply religious sense of American destiny. In our day Martin Luther King profoundly grasped the power of the civil religion to move his contemporaries. It is the driving force of his great "I have a dream" speech: ". . . all of God's children, black men and white men, Jews and Gentiles, Protestants and Catholics" will sing ". . . thank God Almighty we're free at last." What God, if not Jefferson's God?

Furthermore, apart from history, there is logic. It is not true that as one widens concentric circles of belief, one necessarily abolishes any content. Take the phrase "Judeo-Christian." Judaism and Christianity disagree over the divinity of Christ, not a trivial matter. Nevertheless, it is certainly not meaningless to speak of a Judeo-Christian tradition. What is agreed upon is important. The American civil religion, emanating from this Judeo-Christian core, enlarges the circle to capture other monotheistic, theistic and even deistic notions. It has content, and power. (Most of the reaction to Reagan's recent speech to the evangelicals focused on his invoking God, not His Son.) The Pledge of Allegiance's "under God" may, as Justice Brennan suggests, be vestigial. What lies behind it is not.

There is one final benefit of the idea of the civil religion. It offers some direction through the minefield of church-state problems. It suggests that the crèche, though a minor matter, lies just beyond the realm of the permissible. On school prayer, it suggests that a common ("civil religious") invocation is perhaps permissible—better certainly than a hodgepodge of rotating sectarian prayers—but that a moment of silent devotion is preferred. The American civil religion is uniquely tolerant, noncoercive and inclusive. It is meant to infuse American life with a sense of transcendence, not to impose a religious order on individuals. Schools are uniquely coercive institutions, because of the vulnerability of children to authority, and the compulsory nature of public education. If adults—say, members of Congress—wish to engage in communal public prayer, there can be no objection; but it would violate the spirit, and the history, of the civil religion to impose a form of worship on the least autonomous members of the community.

Useful as it is, the existence of the American civil religion forces us to face the fact that we do have a kind of established religion in this country —and that for two centuries it has supported, and elevated, the nation. Now it is jeopardized by ignorant armies of secularists and the sectarians who wish to abolish it. Perhaps they fight it so bitterly because it offers a way out of their holy war.

The New Republic, April 9, 1984

The Governor and the Bishops

MARIO CUOMO, GOVERNOR OF NEW YORK AND A CATHOLIC, HAS RECENTLY engaged the hierarchy of his church in a debate on Church and State. The dialogue went something like this: On June 24, the new archbishop of New York, John G. O'Connor, said in a television interview, "I don't see how a Catholic in good conscience can vote for a candidate who explicitly supports abortion." The governor responded, "The church has never been this aggressively involved [in politics]," he said. "Look at what happened in my last legislative session—the Catholic Church killed the E.R.A." And charged Cuomo, "Now you have the archbishop of New York saying that no Catholic can vote for Ed Koch . . . Pat Moynihan or Mario Cuomo —anybody who disagrees with him on abortion." O'Connor returned the serve. He was "surprised" at the governor's statement. He protested that "my sole responsibility is to present as clearly as I can the formal, official teaching of the Catholic church. I leave to those interested in such teachings whether or not the public statements of office-holders and candidates accord with this teaching." And he insisted that he had no "desire to evaluate the qualifications of any individual of any political party for any public office." The governor graciously accepted this "clarification" and expressed pleasure that the archbishop agrees that the church should not tell Catholics how to vote. Deuce. Then, out of the blue, a passing shot from Bishop James W. Malone, president of the National Conference of Catholic Bishops. Cuomo is personally opposed to abortion but does not believe that as a public official he should impose his views on others. Speaking for the United States Catholic Conference, Malone issued a statement saying: "We reject the idea that candidates can satisfy the requirements of rational analysis in saying their personal views should not influence their policy decisions. The implied dichotomy—between personal morality and public policy—is simply not logically tenable." Advantage bishops.

The Reaganite reading of this particular inquiry into the boundary between church and state has been characteristically enlightened. "Shame on you, Mario Cuomo," thundered Senator Paul Laxalt from the podium of the Republican National Convention. "The Democratic governor of New York goes out of his way to attack the Catholic archbishop of New York." There was a time in this country, echoed Reagan at a prayer breakfast the next day, when "a politician who spoke to or of [religious leaders] with a lack of respect would not long survive in the political arena." There was also a time when a lapsed Protestant pretending to be more Catholic than the Pope would have been hooted out of the political arena. But no matter. The President saw a political opening and took it.

Not that either the governor or the bishops are innocent of political motive. Their discourse did not take place in a monastery, but in the New York *Times*. The archbishop's politics are plain: newly installed in New York, he was declaring his intention to pursue a highly active role in political issues he deems important. The governor's politics are more complicated. He spoke up, he told a Washington news conference, because "the whole question of religion in politics is in danger of being co-opted by a single kind of religious group"—meaning the fundamentalists who surround Ronald Reagan. "You have a President who has wrapped himself in religiosity . . . used religion aggressively, as a tool."

And so he has. The President, running for reelection on a platform of peace, prosperity and piety, is pushing "social issues" very hard. At that same Dallas breakfast he said, "Those who are fighting to make sure voluntary prayer is not returned to classrooms [are] intolerant of religion. . . . They refuse to tolerate its importance in our lives." Now, this is a tendentious and dangerous charge. (To say nothing of the language: the use of the peculiar locution "tolerate its importance," to mean "mandate," is Orwellian.) In a pluralist democracy, the charge of religious intolerance should be reserved for the gravest of offenses, of which opposition to "voluntary" school prayer is not one. That position rests on the view that school prayer constitutes state-imposed religion. If Reagan's intent is to promote religion-in-general as opposed to irreligion (a not unreasonable position: see "America's Holy War," p. 99), then he should support silent prayer, which is denominationally neutral. But his intent is to curry favor with the Christian Right, whose expressed aim is to use the cause of religion-in-general as a wedge to promote, using state power whenever possible, its particular brand of Christian fundamentalism.

Reagan's pandering on religion has been a political success. And Cuomo understands why: "brandishing religious values," Reagan is "moving into a vacuum." The usual Democratic response is either to ignore the religious issue or to denounce Mr. Reagan for mixing religion and politics. Secularist appeals, however, don't sell very well. Hence Cuomo's approach, at once more subtle and bold: to pick up the challenge and reclaim religion for liberals by redefining it to include such concerns as peace, compassion and care for the needy. It is a risky strategy. He wants to endow the liberal agenda with religious sanction by advancing liberalism as a fulfillment of the social gospel; but then he has to defend liberalism from religious charges that it offends the rest of the gospel. That's why he confronted the charge at its sharpest point, on the issue that has made liberals look anti-religious: abortion. He claimed first that the church was overstepping the proper First Amendment bounds in its aggressive opposition to abortion. And, second, he claimed his own independence, as a public official, from church teachings on the issue.

So much for the politics of the debate. What of its merits? Unlike the President, Cuomo is serious about his religion. And he has raised two serious questions. What is the proper role of the church in the democratic political arena? And what is the proper role of the believer in that arena?

First, the role of the church. Cuomo criticized O'Connor for going too far—i.e., opposing candidates—in pushing his anti-abortion view; he was careful not to criticize the *principle* of church involvement in political affairs. Others are not so scrupulous. Politicians on both sides of the aisle are constantly declaring themselves shocked—shocked!—to find the church meddling in politics. When the bishops issued their pastoral letter on nuclear weapons, there was much bleating on the right from people who have no trouble with Jerry Falwell's discourses on the dangers of homosexual rights. And vice versa. The protests are selective; they await the church taking a position opposite one's own. If anything, the left, which fancies itself the defender of the First Amendment against right-wing depredations, is more hypocritical. After all, much of the civil rights and anti-Vietnam War movements were *run* out of churches, as was, more recently, the Jackson Presidential campaign. It was when white evangelicals, principally southern whites led by the Moral Majority, began a parallel and, in some ways, reactive involvement in politics that the loudest cries for church-state separation began to be heard. And it won't do to argue that the white evangelicals are trying to dictate to people how to conduct their lives; the civil rights movement brought about a transformation in social life and mores as profound as any in American history.

Nor was there much protest when the high Protestant churches began falling away from their traditional, lofty espousal of strict church-state separation (an economical position for churches whose members once effectively controlled the political system anyway). The left had few complaints when, for example, the National Council of Churches took up its new dispensation of limousine liberation theology.

To his credit, Cuomo seems to accept that there should be one set of rules—namely that in a tolerant, pluralist democratic polity, a church may add its voice to those shaping public policy. But Cuomo draws a line sharply at political partisanship. He agrees with the bishops that the church has the right to teach principles, and even to elucidate policy. But he was scaring them off from endorsing candidates.

It may be a question of nuance, but I think Cuomo has the nuance right. Churches are not quite like democracy's other voluntary associations: one doesn't check into and out of the Catholic Church the way one does, say, the League of Women Voters. For one thing, no one has yet been born into the League. The church is also accorded certain privileges and immunities, like immunity from taxation, in return for which it is reasonable to demand that, beyond principle and policy, it not engage in partisanship, which involves the allocation of power.

Cuomo's parry was salutary. One would again, however, wish for some evenhandedness. On July 14 *The Washington Post* reported that "bishops of the African Methodist Episcopal church at their denomination's quadrennial meeting in Kansas City urged church leaders to organize the church's three million members to help defeat Ronald Reagan this fall." No protest. Asked why an exception should be made for black churches, Father Robert Drinan, president of Americans for Democratic Action, explained that this is "their tradition." True. And what if Reverend Falwell claims that endorsing candidates is part of his? On what grounds, then, to deny him his tax exemption?

Interestingly, some conservative Catholics want the church to stay out of more than just the business of endorsing candidates. They want it out of politics altogether. They wish it to leave politics to the churchgoers. Quentin L. Quade writes in *Catholicism in Crisis*, "Religion achieves its political vitality and its importance through the religionist-as-citizen," and not as a church-in-action. It is also more likely to achieve political success that way. When the church, as church, takes up a cause, like abortion, it gratuitously hands opponents of that cause new ammunition. They can portray anti-abortion as a church-dictated position, fight on constitutional grounds of protecting state from church, and thus be spared having to argue the issue on its merits. Quade calls "the direct intrusion of the Catholic hierarchy, as hierarchy, in the political process [a] case of self-imposed damage to the cause of anti-abortion."

Surely it is no more than a species of anti-religious prejudice to say that those who advocate a public policy position derived from a moral principle which in turn derives from religious belief are violating constitutional norms (mixing church and state), while those who derive their policy choices from moral premises acquired elsewhere (where?) are engaged in legitimate political action. Nonetheless such nonsensical readings of the First Amendment, heard often in the abortion debate, are a fact of political life—and yet another argument for organized churches to speak, if not softly, at least generally.

But what are the political obligations of the believer in a tolerant, religiously pluralist society? That is the other half of the Cuomo-bishops debate, and by far the more complex one. They pose the question this way: Can a believer, Catholic or otherwise, say, "I accept the teaching of my church on abortion, but I refuse to make it into law?"

Does the logic of religious toleration require the subordination of religious beliefs in the public arena? There is an easy answer to that question, and Cuomo does not give it. That answer, offered by John F. Kennedy among others, is: Of course it does. I am a servant of the state first, and am sworn to let nothing supersede that commitment. Cuomo does not say that. Instead, he has publicly said, "I am a governor, I am a Democrat, but I am a Catholic first—my soul is more important to me than my body." This is something Kennedy would not have said because religion for him was more a matter of affiliation than belief.

There is much to be said for Kennedy's way. Undoubtedly, it is to the falling away of belief that we owe much of modern-day religious toleration. Chesterton said, perhaps unkindly, that tolerance is the virtue of people who do not believe anything. But still a virtue. Historian J. W. Allen draws a distinction between two kinds of tolerance. The lesser form, for which he reserves the word toleration, is the "legal indulgence of deviations from established orthodoxy largely because of skeptical indifference to questions of religious belief or worship." We might say: Kennedy's way. It is not Cuomo's. Cuomo is appealing to what Allen calls (true) tolerance: "A mental outlook" based on belief and yet "respectful of all opinion on every subject of thought." Cuomo is not saying: I was born a Catholic, but I will act no differently from an uncommitted, unchurched American. He says that his soul is more important to him than his body, and his soul is Catholic. Can he then at the same time say: I accept church teaching on abortion, but I refuse to make it into law?

No, argues Bishop Malone, it is a logical impossibility. The church teaching on abortion is that abortion is murder, and it is absurd to say, "I am personally against murder, but I will not impose my views on anyone else." (This is not just the position of the clergy. To take only one example among politicians: Joseph Califano, a Catholic and the former Secretary of Health and Human Services, testified vigorously in Congress, in his capacity as Secretary of H.H.S., against federal funding of abortions.)

Is Malone right? The usual refuge is to invoke a distinction between "private" and "public" belief. When Geraldine Ferraro, for example, says she's "personally opposed" to abortion, she means this: I wouldn't have one myself and I wouldn't want my children to have one, but I won't go around telling the people whether to have one or not. Unfortunately, Ferraro is confusing belief with practice. If a person says, "I refuse to own slaves, but I won't go around telling others what to do," it is correct to say that he does not practice slavery, but can one really say he is opposed to it?

Ferraro does not practice abortion, but she is mistaken if she believes that this means she is against it. To say "X is wrong for me" (practice) is not the same as saying "X is categorically wrong" (belief). Belief, unlike practice, must be universal. Furthermore, one minimal test of the sincerity of even a "private" belief on abortion is whether one tries to persuade (not coerce) others *voluntarily* to renounce it. (Ferraro does not pass this test.) But sincerity apart, does not such a belief commit one further—to try to outlaw abortion?

For those like Cuomo who say no, there are several possible defenses. One is based on democratic representational theory. A governor does not always act on his beliefs, religiously derived or otherwise. Often, as a representative of the people, he does what he thinks *they* want, even if he disapproves. A governor may forego the constitutional exercise of a veto, or even of the power of commutation, out of respect for the principle of majoritarianism.

Now, that might explain why, as an executive, Cuomo might legitimately refuse to veto, say, public funding of abortions. It does not explain why he doesn't fight to change the law. Nor can he respond: my restrictive theory of representation extends to legislation, too; a representative is required to faithfully reflect his constituents' views, and not his own; a majority of my constituents, even perhaps a majority of my Catholic constituents, are pro-choice, so I must reflect their views, despite my personal opposition. That still doesn't get Cuomo off the hook, because even on this narrow view, he is still obliged to try democratically to persuade his colleagues and his constituents that they are wrong and that abortion should be outlawed. Democratic theory may have a claim to his vote and his veto, but not his voice.

Which brings us to a second possible line of defense—privacy: One shouldn't even be trying to persuade others to pass such a law, because law is coercive and abortion is a private matter. Note that the privacy in question here is the public's, not the politician's. (A buried "private" belief, if contradicted by public action, is evidence simply of hypocrisy.)

Normally, the privacy claim is powerful. In liberal democratic theory, to find that something is private—as the Supreme Court chose to define (early) abortion—is to make the strongest possible case that it should be outside government control. Not an absolute case, mind you. There is still a large area, from pornography to polygamy ("private morality"), that is often regulated, restricted, sometimes banned by government. Conservatives and liberals argue over whether this category should indeed be regulated. But the church argues that abortion doesn't belong in this category at all. It denies that abortion is in the remotest sense private: if the fetus is a person, abortion is a murder. That turns the abortion debate into, literally, a categorical one. And to those who accept the church's teaching on abortion, it closes the privacy defense. (The privacy defense remains open to some conservatives, who, not holding that the fetus is a person, may want to restrict abortion, as they would other offensive acts of "private morality," but are not committed to banning it.)

If not democratic theory or privacy, then what? I suggest John Courtney Murray's notion of civil peace. In the 1950s Murray presented a conservative Catholic view of religious pluralism in America. He was writing to defend Catholicism from the charge that its universalism and authoritarianism placed it in conflict with American religious pluralism as embodied in the First Amendment. Murray was no great lover of pluralism: "Religious pluralism is against the will of God; but it is the human condition." Yet he argued that, for the American Catholic, it is not only a civic obligation, but a religious duty to separate church and state and respect religious pluralism. He credited Roger Williams with having (despite himself) enunciated the relevant Catholic principle: "It is one thing to command, to conceal, to approve evil," wrote Williams, "and another thing to permit and suffer evil . . . this sufferance of permission of evil is not for its own sake, but for the sake of the good." Murray explained: "The 'good' here is the public peace." Public peace is the highest achievement of the civil law. A civil law which fosters it enjoys not just pragmatic but moral validity, and, ultimately, religious sanction. The First Amendment is not an "an article of faith," but "an article of peace."

Murray was speaking of religious belief and practice; he was explaining why a conscientious Catholic is not required to try to use the instruments of state to spread them to others. He would certainly not approve extending that principle to abortion. Nevertheless, if civil peace is indeed a religious value, then Murray's argument lends religious sanction to policies that work to preserve that peace. Noncoercion on abortion is surely such a policy. One can believe that abortion is murder and at the same time not demand laws outlawing it for everyone. The reason is that whereas normal murder is universally accepted as evil, abortion is not. So many Americans don't believe it to be evil, in fact, so many believe it—however wrongly—to be a *right*, that even if one could muster a majority to ban abortion, that would constitute a grave violation of the civil peace, which both supports and is itself supported by religious pluralism. Reinhold Niebuhr held that the highest form of religious tolerance was based on the humbling belief that "all actual expressions of religious faith are subject to historical contingency and relativity," like Allen's highest form of tolerance—"a mental outlook respectful of all opinion on every subject of thought." Even on what constitutes murder.

I doubt that this line of argument will satisfy Bishop Malone. It may not even satisfy Cuomo. The appeal to civil peace has neither the populist bite of an invocation of majoritarianism, nor the ring of righteousness of an appeal to privacy. Instead, it is a modest, conservative reading of the duty of religous toleration. It resists the anti-abortionist crusade not because that crusade begins in religious belief (a rationale truly deserving of the word "intolerant"), but because it threatens to end in an "appeal to heaven," Locke's term for revolutionary upheaval. Moreover, the appeal to civil peace does not resolve, it pacifies the conflict between religious conscience and political necessity. For zealots on either side it will have no appeal at all.

The New Republic, September 17–24, 1984

Pietygate:
School for Scandal

IF IT TAKES A HINCKLEY TO CHANGE THE INSANITY LAWS AND A DE LOREAN
to curtail sting operations, then the case of Geraldine Ferraro may turn
out to be a first step back from the piety-in-government excursion Americans have been on since Watergate. One day Ms. Ferraro's vice-presidential candidacy, perhaps her political career, hangs in the balance; the next
day, after a tough and gutsy public performance—a Checkers for the '80s
—she is back in gear, leaving us all to wonder if we hadn't lost our heads
for just a moment.

Had we? Ask yourself what exactly she was supposed to have done that
had Washington wondering if she could survive on the ticket—and one
conservative columnist wryly advising Democrats to start warming up
Sargent Shriver in the bullpen?

Not that Geraldine Ferraro is Caesar's wife. There was the illegal campaign loan, the murky Centre Street deal, the questionable exemption
from disclosing her husband's finances. But she insists that she thought the
loan was legal, that she did not know about the deal and that no wife could
satisfy the disclosure law who did not have a good-government partition
in her refrigerator.

As articles of impeachment, the list is not very impressive. In fact, what
most placed her in political jeopardy was not anything she did but something she said she would not do—namely, release her husband's tax returns. It was this affront to post-Watergate morality, by which anything

left private is taken as presumptive evidence of wrongdoing, that turned the flap into a furor.

Finally, to save herself, she relented and produced a mountain of detail that yielded barely a mound of substance. To what end? What were we looking for? What *are* we looking for when we ask politicians to so bare themselves publicly? If we insist that public life be reserved for those whose personal history is pristine, we are not going to get paragons of virtue running our affairs. We will get the very rich, who contract out the messy things in life; the very dull, who have nothing to hide and nothing to show; and the very devious, expert at covering their tracks and ambitious enough to risk their discovery. This is not to say that our current politics does not attract such characters, only that it still manages to attract others as well. A few more Ferrarogates and that pool will be dry.

In some way, candidates like Ferraro unwittingly invite this kind of treatment. She did not get to where she is by dint of a cause, ideology or even issue. Ferraro got to where she is because of who she is: daughter of poor immigrants, teacher, lawyer, mother, prosecutor—political assets she is not shy to exploit. She claims these to be the source of her values, and it was these values and those sources that she displayed so prominently in her acceptance speech in San Francisco. They are, in fact, the only discernible theme of her campaign so far. If you run on your person, it is somewhat disingenuous to be surprised when the world then wants to know, in accountant's detail, exactly what kind of person you really are. The personality candidate, at once so well suited to this age of celebrity, is equally vulnerable to its voracious appetites.

Still, there are limits. The purpose of the disclosure law that Ferraro was suspected of bending is to prevent conflict of interest. There is no evidence that has occurred. Yet the disclosures made and (at first) refused almost destroyed Ferraro. The ethics laws so enthusiastically enacted post-Watergate, so confidently entrusted with protecting the public weal, can also undermine it. And not surprisingly, since they are based on an illusory faith in the redemptive power of institutional arrangements. Owing to their history, Americans suffer from this touching superstition more than most people. After all, the founding fathers did practically invent the separation of powers to prevent the accumulation of tyrannical power. That lucky stroke has predisposed Americans to believe that if they could only find the right law, the right oversight committee, the right disclosure form, they could compensate institutionally for other failings of the human heart. And produce ethics in government, for example.

It may now be time to close the -gate. Ten years is a long time for any political fashion, and it is exactly ten years since the resignation of Richard

Nixon. In that decade we have had Watergate, Koreagate, Lancegate, Billygate and now Ferrarogate, with Meesegate and Debategate on temporary hold. The chronology yields a list in roughly descending order of importance. We have come a long way. From a President resigning for, among other things, organizing a squad of "plumbers" specializing in break-ins, to a vice-presidential candidate arraigned before the bar of the media to answer questions, among others, about her husband's father's buildings' tenants. American political scandal is in sad decline.

Yet too many people still have a stake in its revival: a Watergate-starved generation of investigative reporters who must make do with imitation enemies lists (USIA), imitation graft (Japanese watches) and now imitation laundering (the Centre Street swap); a public so hungry it will accept fiction, if fact is in short supply (Washington politics has been honored with its own seamy TV soap opera); and some vengeful pols, mostly Republicans who suffered for years through the aftermath of Watergate and delight in the chance to do a little Woodward-Bernsteining themselves, now that they smell a smoking Democratic gun.

In the national interest, therefore, why not radical reform? A truce. Sweep the disclosure forms into the White House shredder. Declare, à la Senator George Aiken, the Battle of Watergate won, withdraw the troops and proclaim a general amnesty. After all, we do it for draft dodgers and deserters after a war. We could even do it the way it is done in banana republics: on the President's birthday.

Expect few takers. I broached a modest version of this idea with Patrick Buchanan who had gone through the Watergate affair in the White House: "I'll trade you one Ferraro for one Meese and a future draft choice, and then we call off the whole ethics-in-government thing completely."

"Sure," he answered with a smile. "After the election."

Time, September 10, 1984

We're All
Marxists Now

THE WESTERN PRESS ALMOST INVARIABLY REFERS TO THE SALVADORAN guerrillas as Marxist. So too the regimes in places like Angola and Ethiopia. A generation ago they would have been called Communist. During the Vietnam War that is what we called our enemies. In fact, the use of the word "Communist" in Vietnam helped to discredit it, and rightly so, because it carries the implication of a monolithic world movement and external control from Moscow (or Peking). Another reason the word is rarely heard these days is its use during the McCarthy era as an infinitely elastic category with which to destroy political opponents. Now we speak not of Communists, but of Marxists. It is no improvement. The new term is as deceptively elastic and conveniently vague as the one it was intended to replace.

Of the three patron saints of communism, Stalin is the least popular today, particularly in the West. Since Khrushchev's 1956 speech exposing Stalin's crimes, and the invasion of Hungary, Stalinism has become a term of opprobrium. West of the Urals it is hard to find any Communist, except perhaps a few diehards in Portugal or Albania, with anything good to say about Stalin. Indeed, Stalin has been a useful alibi for Communist apologists for decades. The dismal historical record of Communist rule can always be dismissed as a mere Stalinist perversion of true communism.

True Communists, like Castro, prefer to call themselves Marxist-Leninists. But Lenin, part two of the trinity, has recently suffered setbacks in the West. The latest blow was Susan Sontag's discovery that Leninism is intrinsically tyrannous. She was not just picking off easy (that is, Stalinist) targets like the Soviet Union, but erstwhile third-world paragons of communism like Cuba and Vietnam. She checked the record in "countries in which a Communist—that is, a Leninist—party has taken power and rules," and found that *"every one* of these countries is a tyranny" (her emphasis). The fact that she has been violently denounced for this Galilean discovery by many of the left indicates that there is still some sympathy for Leninism among American radicals. Nevertheless, it seems safe to predict that the Leninist rear guard will end up in the same historical rubbish heap to which the Stalinists repaired after 1956.

That leaves Communists with only one respectable eponym to cling to: Marx. Indeed, it is no accident that a whole unsavory stew of Stalinist and Leninist despots in the world prefers the title Marxist. For obvious reasons. Marxist sounds so bookish: theoretical, critical, humane and, ultimately, optimistic. It conjures up images of afternoon tea, tweeds and elbow patches, professors seeking to change the world, yes, but to understand it first.

Marxist is a term well suited to academia. It is a fine description for a historian who uses the class theory of history, an economist who clings to the labor theory of value or a philosopher beguiled by nineteenth-century dialectics. As followers of a certain philosophic tradition, they have as much right to call themselves Marxists as certain Anglo-Saxon philosophers have to call themselves Benthamites. Both claims are declarations of intellectual genealogy. But just as we would hesitate to say American boys stormed the shores of Anzio in the name of Benthamism, we should hesitate to speak of guerrillas who blow up bridges in preindustrialist and precapitalist El Salvador as Marxists.

When speaking of men of action, those either in power or aspiring to power, the word "Marxist" is either an empty category conveying no information or a confusing one designed to obscure crucial information. I suggest that we abolish it. For it is used to describe two types of social revolutionaries. One type—the vast majority of "Marxist" rulers and guerrillas—practices democratic centralism (meaning authoritarianism) in its own party structure; believes in single-party dictatorship and state control of the means of production; and opposes pluralism—not only in politics, but in art, science and social relations. In other words, this type meets all the operational criteria for Leninism. The other type believes in individual rights against the state, has a concept of limited government that allows a private sector in social and economic life and tolerates democratic forms in government, including a plurality of parties and a rotation of power.

However much they may draw inspiration from Marx, these "Marxists" are, in effect, social democrats or socialists. They may differ from the Socialist International on some points of theology, like their vision of the end of days, but outside of church they look just like Social Democrats.

To call both types of revolutionaries Marxist is simply to obscure distinctions, to confuse two radically different philosophies of power. It allows the social democrats to be tainted by the antidemocratic Leninists, and the Leninists to enjoy borrowed sympathy due the social democrats.

It is incongruous to speak of Marxism when speaking of those in power or those aspiring to it, because Marx had so little to say about what post-revolutionary government would be like. Marx was eloquent in describing capitalism, but cryptic on communism. True, Marx did have contempt for parliamentary forms, individual rights and private economic structures. He did believe in a vanguard party and the dictatorship of the proletariat. But that doesn't make Marx directly responsible for the Gulag. He certainly believed dictatorship to be a temporary expedient, because the proletarian revolution was bound to transform human nature, making the state unnecessary.

Today's "Marxist" revolutionaries are under no illusion that they will wither away after victory. As soon as they seize power, they will need instruction on organizing the secret police, the "committees for defense of the revolution," centralized control of the army, the economy and ultimately the populace. But they will learn little about that from Marx, a lot from Lenin.

For Ethiopia's Colonel Mengistu to succeed in being referred to as a Marxist is surely a triumph of public relations. The universal characterization of the Salvadoran guerrillas as Marxists (even Jesse Helms calls them that) is a veritable PR coup. One imagines the guerrillas sitting around their campfire in their mountain redoubt engaged in responsive reading of *Das Kapital.* The men with the guns—for example, Salvador Cayetano Carpio, the grand old man of the Salvadoran revolution—are proud of the title "Marxist-Leninist." Western observers are not. They find the "Leninist" part too embarrassing to mention. Unfortunately, for Carpio and his men it is the operational clause.

The New Republic, April 7, 1982

The Oil-Bust Panic

TO LISTEN TO THE BANKS, THE OIL COMPANIES AND THE NEW CLASS of petrodollar consultants, you'd never know it was just oil prices that are about to fall. You'd think it was the sky. The doomsayers do not, of course, speak of their own interests. They speak of important-sounding things like orderly markets, price stability and the integrity of the international banking system. And indeed order, stability and integrity are all excellent things. But what we are really talking about here is monopoly control, high prices and the continued flow of interest payments on the almost criminally imprudent loans banks made when they were fat with oil money.

The Saudi oil minister, Sheik Yamani, set the tone for the debate on whether the imminent collapse of the Organization of Petroleum Exporting Countries is good or bad. With characteristic chutzpah he declared: "Everybody needs OPEC, even the consumers, and we read in the various newspapers every day how important OPEC is and [how] important [it is] to keep the price of oil under control." He is right about the newspapers. They've been full of quotes from interested observers who fret about OPEC's health and low oil prices—people like Chemical Bank vice president Gary Smeal ("I don't want to see a drop in oil prices"); Chevron chairman George Keller (he views a sharp decline in prices "with horror"); former Energy Secretary James Schlesinger ("volatility in oil prices may be worse in its impact than high prices"); and oil analyst John Lichtblau (his New York *Times* pitch for moderation came under the headline: OPEC'S HUMBLING COULD BE A PROBLEM). The King James version of this position appeared in the WALL STREET JOURNAL as the lead story just two days before the last OPEC meeting. "CARTEL'S REVIVAL: OPEC NEARS AN ACCORD TO TRIM OIL PRODUCTION TO AVERT PRICE COLLAPSE," went the headline. The story began: "A spectacular collapse in oil prices—an event that many people would applaud at first but, experts say, rue at leisure— apparently has been ruled out for the time being." The story turned out to be mistaken, but it served to alert readers that cheaper oil is something to be rued.

"It is our last chance," Qassem Ahmed Taqi, Iraq's oil minister, said a few days ago. And, in fact, it is the last chance for averting disaster for a lot of people. . . . It's all a bit paradoxical, of course. Talk of lower oil prices stirs visions, in the average motorist's head, of a return to cheap gasoline, and he wonders what's so bad about that. Even on a slightly more sophisticated level, anyone who recalls the trouble caused by the surge in oil prices in the 1970s may wonder why a decline would be so dreadful.

Why, indeed. Let's examine the case. We will start at the "slightly more sophisticated level," looking at the economic problems caused by past oil shocks and the corresponding benefits that everyone agrees would flow from a partial reversal. We will then examine the case for the negative effects of such an event. By establishing how substantial these are, and whether they outweight the benefits, we will be in a position to know whether it is time for some preemptive ruing.

The oil shocks of 1973–74 and 1979–80 acted like a huge excise tax on the economies of all oil-importing nations. It was the worst kind of tax: it not only reduced demand and brought on two recessions by draining two to three percent of GNP from Western economies, it also generated inflation by increasing the cost of oil and all oil-based products. The combination produced a new phenomenon: stagflation. After the second price shock of 1979–80, inflation threatened to get out of hand, so the U.S. government imposed severe restrictions on money supplies, which in turn worsened the recession. The result is relatively stable prices today, but at the cost of the deepest and longest recession since the 1930s.

An oil price collapse therefore would mean tax relief of the best kind: if the price went from the current Saudi benchmark of $34 to $20, it would pump more than $90 billion into the economies of oil-importing nations, increasing purchasing power and demand, and stimulating growth. At the same time, the drop in the price of oil and oil-related goods would be deflationary, and thus would give us what we haven't seen in a decade: noninflationary growth.

The United States alone would receive a stimulus of more than $20 billion a year, almost two-thirds of the income tax cut scheduled for July 1982. Germany and Japan would be even bigger winners, since they are almost totally dependent on external sources of oil. Secondary effects would be felt everywhere. Germany and Japan were the engines of world economic growth in the '60s, until their economies too stalled on inflationary oil prices and the subsequent corrective monetary squeezes. Renewed growth of Western economies would stimulate international trade, and would revive markets for third-world exports. That would improve their balance of payments and reduce their demand for new loans, while improving their ability to repay old ones. And if the moderating effect on inflation was reflected in lowered interest rates, that too would help relieve the burden on third-world countries. For example, for Brazil and Mexico every one percent drop in interest rates would improve their balance of payments position by $700 million to $800 million a year.

But the primary effects on developing countries would be even more dramatic. Their oil bill has gone from $7 billion a year to more than $100 billion in the last decade. Since the second oil shock alone, their indebtedness has risen from $174 billion in the mid-1970s to more than $500 billion today. Debt payment on this enormous sum has gone from fourteen percent of export earnings to more than twenty-two percent. Third-world countries have been particularly hard hit, not only because they had weak economies to start with, but also because, never having been rich enough to afford to waste energy on fripperies, they have been less able than Western countries to cut back on nonessential uses. Lower oil prices means money in their and their creditors' pockets.

That, with numbers added, is the happy vision in the head of the "average motorist" of the benefits of an OPEC price collapse. Those who say that the simple people are wrong respond with two arguments: the Rollover and the Velvet Trap scenarios. The Rollover scenario (named after the Jane Fonda movie in which sudden Arab withdrawals from Western banks lead to a worldwide banking collapse) is simple. Some oil exporters are big lenders. Their losses from a drop in oil prices would decrease the world savings pool, drain the banks, and cause a banking crisis. Similarly, some oil exporters, like Mexico, are big borrowers. They would find it harder to repay their loans, triggering a default and adding to the banking crisis. A corollary is that if oil exporters lose part of their 1970s windfall, they will cut not only their savings but their consumption, too, thus decreasing world demand and inducing economic contraction.

The flaw in this argument is transparent. Say the price of oil drops $10 per barrel tomorrow. That is $10 lost to the Saudis and the Mexicans. But the $10 doesn't disappear into thin air, it is only transferred to the oil importing countries. As one Federal Reserve Board governor put it: "The money would come from all the banks and go to all the banks." The $10 would go, for example, to Brazil, the world's largest debtor, and pump $3.2 billion every year into its economy, which could be used to cut its debt service to the banks almost in half. However Brazil decided to divide its windfall between saving and spending, the result would be a gain in world saving and consumption that would countervail the OPEC loss. Indeed, according to Robert Pindyck of M.I.T., there would be a net *increase* in savings and consumption because of the enormous stimulative effects that the price cuts would have on the world economy.

To claim that the net world savings pool will dry up, one has to resort to an even more sophisticated argument: in the hands of oil exporters that $10 is likely to be saved, while in the hands of oil importers it's likely to be spent. People tend to think of OPEC revenues as a huge savings pool. And it was, for a very short time and for a very few lightly populated states in the Arab world. But no more. OPEC is no longer a net saver; it runs a deficit. The initial rush of oil money in the early 1970s created an enormous appetite for goods and services. The heavily populated countries like Venezuela and Nigeria are running heavy deficits; Saudia Arabia's current account is near balance; the only OPEC countries with surpluses are tiny Kuwait, Qatar and the United Arab Emirates. Furthermore, even if it does turn out that, when transferred to oil-importing countries, the $10 generates less savings than it did in the hands of oil exporters, there is a simple corrective: oil import taxes to soak up part of that $10, taking it away from consumers and putting it in the hands of governments. If, for example, the U.S. taxes half of a $10 price drop, it would instantly create a fund of $7 billion a year. If this money were added to revenues, it would reduce Treasury borrowing needs, and, in effect, increase the pool of world savings by $7 billion.

The shrinking savings pool argument leads analysts into strange territory. According to William Cline of the Institute for International Economics, "non-oil developing countries may tend to be crowded out of international capital markets." The logic of this argument is that it is better for a country like Brazil to pay high prices for oil—so it can then more easily borrow the money back. But certainly it is better for Brazil to keep the $10 at home than to give it to OPEC, have OPEC deposit it in the banks, and then have Brazil borrow it back at fifteen percent interest. Take away the mystification of "recycling"—and recycling always means high interest rates for OPEC lenders and a hefty cut for the banks—and the "crowding out" argument becomes empty.

Some rollover proponents will agree that in the long run the savings pool will not shrink and things will balance out. But, they ask, what about the short run? A precipitous drop in prices could bankrupt oil exporting borrowers like Mexico and bring down the whole banking house of cards. That is why some, like the New York *Times,* who welcome a decline in oil prices, take the "moderate" position of preferring that it be gradual.

The case for moderation hinges on the delicate position of four oil exporters with big populations, big debts and almost total dependence on oil revenues. Mexico, Venezuela, Nigeria and Indonesia make up the Gang of Four, although some analysts like to throw in Canada and Texas, presumably to add a first-world flavor to the stew. But since neither Canada, with a trade surplus of $9.5 billion for the first nine months of 1982, nor Texas, which joined the Union in 1845, is in any danger of defaulting, we can restrict our analysis to the Gang of Four. Imagine that the price of oil drops $10 a barrel overnight. That would cost Venezuela about $7 billion a year, and Indonesia about $4 billion. It would cause hardship to Venezuelans and Indonesians, but it wouldn't break the international banking system. Venezuela has reserves of about $16 billion, Indonesia about $7 billion. (And according to the latest statement of the Bank for International Settlements in Basel, bank exposure on Indonesian loans totals only $5 billion.) In contrast, Nigeria is in terrible shape, having run out of foreign reserves. Yet Western bank exposure on Nigerian loans is only $6 billion, spread among many banks. Furthermore, Nigeria is eligible for almost half of that in I.M.F. loans, if it agrees to tighten its belt (which is what its economy needs anyway to get its wild spending and inflation under control).

So the entire doomsday scenario rests on Mexico. Mexico owes private banks about $60 billion. A $10 drop in oil prices would mean a revenue loss of about $5.5 billion. Assume the worst. Assume that Mexico can increase its exports by only about 200,000 barrels a day (the estimate of the Mexican finance ministry). At the new oil price, that would bring in about $1.5 billion, leaving Mexico with a $4 billion shortfall. Assume that the fall in oil prices does not produce a fall in inflation and a consequent fall in interest rates (which for every 1 percent decrease would bring Mexico $700 million). Does Mexico go under, and with it the entire banking system, for want of $4 billion? Of course not. The international banking system—the Western central banks, the I.M.F., and the U.S. Treasury—would come to the rescue of Mexico today, just as it did six months ago during the peso crisis. It would have all the more reason to help Mexico out of a problem that was not the result of Mexican errors, but of uncontrollable events in the oil market. As Richard Mattione, a Brookings Institution economist, put it, "It is not beyond the wit of man to come up with a plan to bail out those hard hit." Mexico can stretch out its debt, it can be given more I.M.F. support, and, if need be, it can be allowed a moratorium on repayment of principal.

There is a simple way to put the Mexican problem in perspective. Assume the U.S. government decided to capture half the revenue of a $10 drop in oil prices in the form of a $5 per barrel oil import fee. (U.S. government officials already have been considering such a tax to encourage conservation and to keep marginal domestic wells in production.) The fee would create a $7 billion windfall fund for the U.S. government, almost twice the projected Mexican shortfall. Assume that the world banking system, the I.M.F., and all other Western governments froze at the sight of Mexico's peril, and did nothing. The United States alone could take $4 billion out of its windfall fund, and solve the problem: it could give the money to Mexico directly, in return, say, for oil to be delivered at a later date to the strategic petroleum reserve. Mexico would have its money, the banks would collect their debt payments on time, and the United States would have acquired a secure supply of oil for future emergencies—and would still have $3 billion left over for other uses.

If even in the short term the strains on the international banking system are easily managed, why doomsday? We come to the final refuge of the doomsday scenarist: psychology. It is said that any shock to the world financial system makes bankers and traders nervous; any instability can lead to panic. This is the fear itself argument: bankers are jittery people, and if things change too rapidly and they start thinking that bad things are going to happen, they'll, then act so irrationally that they *will*.

This argument is not entirely implausible. But there are two things to be said about it. First, if in fact the real problem is self-fulfilling prophecies not based on fact, then the solution is for people to stop going around prophesying. Second, markets do get jittery and can act irrationally. But not for very long. That is why market economies work. An example of short-term irrationality was the response of the stock market, on January 25, 1983, to the news that the OPEC meeting had broken up and oil prices were headed down. The New York Stock Exchange registered a loss of 23 points. Stocks went down across the board, even in industries like trucking, which benefit from a drop in oil prices. On that same day on the currency markets, the yen dropped against the dollar—another wholly irrational response, in view of the fact that any drop in oil prices will benefit the Japanese economy, which depends totally on imported oil, more than the

U.S. economy, which has a significant oil-producing sector. These market actions made sense only under the assumption that the international financial system faced imminent collapse. In that case, one would not want to be left holding stocks, not even trucking stocks, and one would rather be in dollars than in any other currency. But when the traders woke up the next day to discover that the sky was still overhead, they reverted to a rational economic response to OPEC's disarray. Stocks and the yen recovered dramatically.

The doomsday argument fails, therefore, for the simple reason that if oil falls by $10 a barrel tomorrow, the money doesn't disappear; OPEC simply loses control of it and transfers it to places like the United States, where the $10 can be used to stimulate consumption and thus noninflationary growth, or to increase savings to balance Western budgets, or, if necessary, to support the international banking system.

This brings us to the Velvet Trap scenario, as Chevron chairman George Keller calls it: a sharp drop in oil prices will lead to an increase in oil consumption, a slowdown in energy substitution out of oil and a decrease in marginal production from expensive non-OPEC wells, like those in the Arctic and the North Sea. Increasing world consumption and decreasing non-OPEC production will set the stage for a new oil price shock in the future. This problem is real, but its extent is often exaggerated and the solutions to it usually ignored. Much conservation over the last ten years has been structural and will not be reversed. People are not going to rip the insulation out of their houses, abandon new factories or discard the Boeing 767 because they are too fuel efficient. Many industries are developing multi-use energy generators, so they can switch fuels depending on market conditions. Admittedly, there will be some increase in consumption, and some decrease in switching to alternative energy sources. There will also be some loss of marginal oil production. But the point that is missed is that the extent of these three effects, which up to now has been regulated by OPEC's pricing decisions, will now be controllable by Western governments.

Again, the mechanism is an import fee. Say the price of oil dropped overnight to $20 a barrel. The U.S. government could decide that it did not want the price that consumers pay or domestic producers get to fall below, say, $28. It would impose an $8 per barrel import fee to encourage conservation and keep expensive—though not the most expensive—wells in production. The beauty of a price drop coupled with an import fee is that it allows Americans to set their own price for domestic production and consumption, and it keeps the tax at home.

Those who argue against import fees say that making Americans pay $28 for oil will reduce the economic stimulus of an oil price drop. True, but the sole purpose of an oil import fee is to prop up the *relative* price of energy. Since the $8 is collected by the government, it can be returned to the economy in order to stimulate growth in any number of ways, as long as none rewards oil consumption—for example, a jobs program, or reduced marginal income taxes or an addition to the savings pool (by reducing the budget deficit). In all cases, the money that would otherwise have gone to OPEC producers would end up stimulating the American economy, while keeping energy conservation at whatever level we wish.

Trap theorists must then argue that there is something natural about the current price of oil. *The Washington Post,* for example, tells us that OPEC "never pushed up oil prices, and the collapse of OPEC would not bring prices down." The assumption here is that $34 a barrel is really a kind of market price, and OPEC just a convenient façade created for reasons of third world pride. One's intuitive feeling is that this argument is wrong. In the current issue of *The Public Interest,* Arlon Tussing explains why. True, he says, OPEC didn't push oil prices up in 1973 and 1980. It froze prices at an abnormally high level by moving the contract price to the spot price at the peak of its reaction to the worldwide panics engendered by the 1973 embargo and the overthrow of the Shah. Normally these run-ups in spot prices (which exaggerate real price fluctuations in the market because they deal with such a small percentage of total oil sales) subside when the panic ends. What OPEC did was ratchet up the contract price, and thus lock in higher prices at the top of the swing. In the end, of course, the market worked its will slowly but inexorably. The new monopoly price encouraged conservation, substitution and marginal production: world demand for oil fell by thirteen percent in the last three years alone, and non-OPEC production rose dramatically. The OPEC bench mark is now untenable. Tussing estimates that a free market price for oil would today be between $10 and $18 a barrel. An informal *Fortune* poll places the price somewhere between $18 and $22. But this is not a question for economists or magazines. The market will decide, and the price will undoubtedly fall fast and hard *if* OPEC collapses. Will OPEC collapse? A better question is, will the West let it?

Even those with only mixed feelings about OPEC admit that it is losing its stranglehold on the world economy. "Today, with less than half the world oil market, OPEC may only be able to re-exert control over the price if nonmember producers, like Britain, the United States, and Mexico agree to cooperate with it." So writes Paul Lewis in the New York *Times.* His advice: cooperate, and perhaps guarantee OPEC a price floor of $25 per barrel. Why? The debt problem, conservation, and "political advantages."

"Stable prices would bolster Saudi Arabia and other Gulf states, all relatively firm friends of the West in a particularly volatile region. It would also improve North-South relations." To hear these clichés again is to despair for the West. Precisely these arguments were made in the 1970s to justify Western paralysis in the face of extortionist pricing policies by OPEC. Acquiescing would win friends and influence oil producers, it was said. It did the opposite. It earned their contempt, and, as the 1979–80 price trebling proved, whetted their appetite for imposing more oil taxes on the West. As for the South—the real South like Tanzania and Zaire and Bangladesh—it suffered even more disastrous economic consequences from the fifteenfold increase in its oil bill over the last decade than did the Western countries, because it had so little to start with and so little to fall back on.

Still, the new petroclass persists. Professor Peter Odell, an OPEC expert at Erasmus University in Rotterdam, says that the present situation "offers a golden chance to build new political bridges between North and South." His South (meaning the rich OPEC countries) used the *old* political bridges to cross into the North and cart away a trillion dollars worth of capital, in what Lewis admits was "probably the largest forced transfer of wealth since the Spanish conquistadores plundered the gold of ancient Peru." Now that we have a chance to recoup some of that loss, we are being advised to build new bridges instead. What do we get in return? Lewis again: "a long-term agreement with the major producers for reasonable price increases [increases, mind you] in return for guaranteed supplies and an end to disruptive oil shocks." Guaranteed supplies, at a time when oil producers can't find buyers.

None of this is new. OPEC pulled off one of its first coups of the 1970s with the notorious Tehran agreement, in which OPEC broke existing contracts and raised prices. The State Department urged Western governments to accept: if they offered no resistance, they could at least count on five years' secure supply at stable prices. When the agreement was announced, the State Department called a special press conference to hail it and to say that it now "expected the previously turbulent international oil situation to calm down." That was in February 1971.

Today the petroclass—the bankers, oil companies and consultants—are at it again, defending their interests in the name of yours. If OPEC dies, the businessmen will lose money, and the academics their subject. So they are carrying out a rear-guard action to convince Westerners that high oil prices are good. And they have been doing more than propaganda work. Some are working within OPEC to keep its inherent national and economic contradictions from destroying it. The *Wall Street Journal* reports that in the frantic behind-the-scenes talks among OPEC members to hammer out production and price accords before the Geneva crisis meeting of January 22–24, the chief executive officers of Exxon, Mobil, Texaco, and Chevron joined in the deliberations. The *Journal* continues: "The wide consensus against a continued slide in oil prices—a consensus of oil-producing countries, major oil companies, and international banks—seems to have stilled the chronic political rivalries among the OPEC nations themselves." In fact, it didn't. The petroclass failed in Geneva, but you can be sure that it will keep trying to get Saudi Arabia to lie down with Iran, and to get you to roll over for both of them.

The New Republic, February 21, 1983

The Just Wage

FROM BAD TO WORTH

THE LATEST ENTRY ON THE LIST OF SACRED DEMOCRATIC CAUSES IS comparable worth. According to that doctrine, it is demonstrable that low-paying female-dominated jobs, like nursing, are worth as much (to employers or society) as "comparable" male-dominated jobs, like plumbing, and that therefore by right and by law they should be paid the same. Comparable worth has become not only *the* women's issue of the 1980s, but also the most prominent civil rights issue not specifically directed at blacks. The Democratic Party has warmly embraced it. Every one of its presidential candidates has endorsed it. In the 1984 platform, that sea of well-intended ambiguity and evasion, there are few islands of certainty. Comparable worth is one of them.

Comparable worth is advancing in the courts, too. In 1981 the Supreme Court opened the door a crack by ruling that female prison guards could sue for violation of the equal-pay provisions of the 1964 Civil Rights Act, even though they did not do precisely the same work as the better-paid male prison guards. That narrow ruling was broken open in December 1983 in a sweeping victory for comparable worth in Washington State. A federal district judge found the state guilty of massive discrimination because its female-dominated jobs were paying less than "comparable" male-dominated jobs. He ordered an immediate increase in the women's wages and restitution for past injury. The back pay alone will run into the hundreds of millions of dollars.

Comparable worth may indeed be an idea whose time has come. Where does it come from? When the plumber makes a house call and charges forty dollars an hour to fix a leak, the instinct of most people is to suspect that the plumber is overpaid—the beneficiary of some combination of scarce skills, powerful unions, and dumb luck. The instinct of comparable worth advocates is to see the plumber's wage as a standard of fairness, to conclude that the rest of us (meaning: women) are underpaid, and to identify discrimination as the source of that underpayment. But since overt discrimination on the basis of sex has been legally forbidden for twenty years, to make that charge stick nowadays requires a bit of subtlety.

One claim is that women's wages are depressed today because of a legacy of past discrimination: namely, the "crowding" of women into certain fields (like nursing, teaching, secretarial work), thus artificially depressing their wages. Did sexual stereotyping really "crowd" women into their jobs? Sexual stereotyping worked both ways: it kept women in, but it also kept men out, thus artificially excluding potential wage competition from half the population, and, more important, from about two-thirds to three-quarters of the labor force (because of the higher participation rate of men). Sex-segregation is obviously unfair, but it is hard to see how it caused downward pressure on women's wages when, at the same time, through the socially enforced exclusion of men, it sheltered "women's work" from a vast pool of competitors. Moreover, as the social barriers that kept men and women from entering each other's traditional fields have fallen during the last twenty years, there has been much more movement of women into men's fields than vice versa. "Women's work" is less crowded than ever.

If the crowding argument is weak, then one is forced to resort to the "grand conspiracy" theory. "The system of wages was set up by a grand conspiracy, so to speak, that has held down the wages of women to minimize labor costs," explained the business agent of the union that in 1981 struck for and won a famous comparable-worth settlement in San Jose. But since to minimize labor costs employers try to hold down the wages of everyone, the thrust of the argument must be that there is a particular desire to do so additionally in the case of women. In other words, the market is inherently discriminatory. Women nurses are paid less than they deserve, simply because they are women. How to prove it? Comparing their wages to that of male nurses won't do, since their pay is, by law, equal. So one must compare nurses' wages to that of, say, plumbers, show that nurses make less, and claim that nurses are discriminated against because they deserve—they are worth—the same.

What is the basis of that claim? In San Jose, Washington State, and other comparable worth cases, the basis is a "study." A consultant is called in to set up a committee to rank every job according to certain criteria. In Washington State, the Willis scale gives marks for "knowledge and skills," "mental demands," "accountability," and "working conditions." The committee then awards points in each category to every job, tallies them up, and declares those with equal totals to have—*voilà!*—comparable worth.

There is no need to belabor the absurdity of this system, so I'll stick to the high points. It is, above all, a mandate for arbitrariness: every subjective determination, no matter how whimsically arrived at, is first enshrined in a number to give it an entirely specious solidity, then added to another number no less insubstantial, to yield a total entirely meaningless. (An exercise: compare, with numbers, the "mental demands" on a truck driver and a secretary.) Everything is arbitrary: the categories, the rankings, even the choice of judges. And even if none of this were true, even if every category were ontologically self-evident, every ranking mathematically precise, every judge Solomonic, there remains one factor wholly unaccounted for which permits the system to be skewed in any direction one wishes: the *weight* assigned to each category. In the Willis scale, points for "knowledge and skills" are worth as much as points for "working conditions." But does ten points in knowledge and skills make up for ten points in hazardous working conditions? Who is to say that a secretary's two years of college are equal in worth to—and not half or double the worth of—the trucker's risk of getting killed on the highways? Mr. Willis, that's who.

Conclusions based on such "studies" are not a whit less capricious than the simple assertion, "secretaries are worth as much as truck drivers." Trotting out Willis, of course, allows you to dress up a feeling in scientific trappings. It allows H.R. 4599, Representative Mary Rose Oakar's bill legislating comparable worth in federal employment, to dispose of the arbitrariness problem in the *definitions*. "Job evaluation technique" is defined as "an objective method of determining the comparable value of different jobs." Next problem.

Some advocates of comparable worth, aware of this objectivity conundrum and perhaps less confident that it can be defined out of existence, propose an alternate solution. Instead of ranking the intrinsic worth of the job (by admittedly arbitrary criteria), they propose ranking the worth of the worker. Barbara Bergmann, an economist at the University of Maryland, believes that people with similar qualifications, training and experience should be receiving the same return on their "human capital." Breaking new ground in discrimination theory, she claims that "in a nondiscriminatory setup, identical people should be paid identically." And what makes people identical? Their credentials: qualifications, training, experience. This is not just credentialism gone wild, and highly disadvantageous to non-yuppy workers with poor résumés, who need the help of the women's movement the most; it leads to the logical absurdity that people should be paid not for the actual work they do, but for the work they *could* do. We've gone from equal pay for equal work to equal pay for comparable work, to equal pay for potential work. Summarizing the Bergmann position, the Center for Philosophy in Public Policy at the University of Maryland explains helpfully that "if a nursing supervisor could do the work of a higher-paid hospital purchasing agent, then her wages should be the same as his." But why stop there? What if her credentials are the same as those of the hospital administrator, or her city councillor, or her U.S. Senator? And what about the starving actress, waiting on tables for a living? If she can act as well as Bo Derek (to set a standard anyone can meet), shouldn't she be getting a million dollars a year—that is, if the "setup" is to deserve the adjective "nondiscriminatory"?

Now, even if there were a shred of merit in any of these systems for determining comparable worth, we should be wary of implementing them if only because of the sheer social chaos they would create. The only sure consequence of comparable worth one can foresee was described by the winning attorney in the Washington State case: "This decision . . . should stimulate an avalanche of private litigation on behalf of the victims of discrimination." The judicial and bureaucratic monster comparable worth will call into being—a whole new layer of judges, court-appointed "masters" (there already is one in the Washington State suit), lawyers, and consultants—will not just sit once to fix wages and then retire. The process will be endless. Fairness will require constant readjustment. There will still exist such a thing as supply and demand. Even if comparable worth advocates succeed in abolishing it for women's work (remember, Washington State was found to have broken the law for paying women market wages rather than comparable worth wages), it will still operate for men's wages, the standard by which women's (comparable worth) wages will be set. Now, what if nurses are awarded plumbers' pay, and there develops a housing slowdown and a plumber surplus, and plumbers' wages fall? Will nurses' salaries have to be ratcheted down? And if not, what is to prevent the plumbers from suing, alleging they are underpaid relative to comparably equal nurses?

Which brings us to the equity problem. Almost everyone feels he or she is underpaid. Moreover, even a plumber can point to at least one person or group of persons who are getting more than they are "worth." Why can't he claim that class of people as the equitable standard, and march to court demanding restitution? If comparable worth is simple justice, as its advocates claim, why should only women be entitled to it? Why not comparable worth for everyone?

The whole search for the "just wage," which is what comparable worth is all about, is, like the search for the "just price," inherently elusive in a capitalist system. It is not that justice has nothing to say about wages and prices in a market economy, but that what it does say it says negatively. For example, it declares that whatever the wage, it must be the same for people regardless of sex, race or other characteristics; but it doesn't say what the wage should be. Even the minimum-wage law says merely that a wage may not be below a certain floor. (Even capitalism has a notion of exploitative labor.) Beyond that, the law is silent. The reason it is silent, the reason we decide to let the market decide, is no great mystery. It was first elaborated by Adam Smith, and amplified by the experience of the Soviet Union and other command economies. Market economies are agnostic on the question of a just wage or a just price not simply because of a philosophical belief that the question, if it is a question, is unanswerable, but also because of the belief, and the experience, that attempts to answer it have a habit of leaving everyone worse off than before.

Finally, even granting that women in traditionally female jobs are underpaid, it is not as if we live in a fixed economy which blocks off all avenues of redress. If secretaries are indeed paid less than they are "worth," they have several options. One is suggested by Coleman Young, the mayor of Detroit, a former labor leader and no conservative: "If a painter makes more than a secretary, then let more women be painters. Equal opportunity and affirmative action is how you do that." A woman entering the labor force today has no claim that she has been crowded into low-paying professions because of discrimination. She has choices.

Older women, of course, who have already invested much in their professions, are more constrained. But they have the same avenues open to them—such as organizing—as other similarly constrained (predominantly male) workers who struggle for higher wages in other settings. In Denver, for example, nurses sought comparable worth wage gains in court and lost; they then went on strike and won. True, in some occupations, even strong unions can't raise wages very much. But as the president of the International Ladies Garment Workers Union (85 percent female) explained in objecting to a highfalutin AFL-CIO endorsement of comparable worth, the problem is not discrimination but the market. His workers have low wages because they compete with workers overseas who are paid thirty cents an hour. Comparable worth doctrine may declare that garment workers ought to be making as much as truck drivers. But if the theory ever became practice, garment workers would be free of more than discrimination. They would be free of their jobs.

Why is the obvious about comparable worth so rarely heard? Why is it for Democrats the ultimate motherhood issue? Because here again the party of the big heart identifies a class of people who feel they aren't getting their just due, blames that condition on a single cause (discrimination), then offers a "rational" solution, on whose messy details it prefers not to dwell. But those details add up to a swamp of mindless arbitrariness and bureaucratic inefficiency, shrouded in a fine mist of pseudo-scientific objectivity. And the surest results will be unending litigation and an entirely new generation of inequities. These inequities, moreover, will be frozen in place by force of law, and thus that much more difficult to dislodge.

Comparable worth asks the question: How many nurses would it take to screw in a lightbulb? The joke is that, having not the faintest idea, it demands that a committee invent an answer, that the answer become law and that the law supplant the market. Even Karl Marx, who also had legitimate complaints about the equity of wages set by the market, had a more plausible alternative.

The New Republic, July 30, 1984

Perils of

the Prophet Motive

HAVING PRONOUNCED ON THE BEGINNING OF LIFE (BIRTH CONTROL and abortion) and on the end of life (nuclear weapons), America's Catholic bishops have now turned their attention to life's middle. The subject of their most recent pastoral letter is economics. More specifically, as a committee of lay Catholics (chaired by William Simon and Michael Novak) makes plain in a challenging dissent to the bishops, the subject is capitalism.

The first thing to strike an outsider about this intra-Catholic debate is the language. It takes time before one realizes that "co-creation" is a theological synonym for production (capitalism being, I suppose, the system of private ownership of the means of co-creation). It seems odd to find the Incarnation invoked to shore up the case for federalism. Or to hear one side of a debate on economics talk of the "true sanctity" of "discipleship in the midst of work," and the other to venture the view that "the gate to creativity is narrow and the way strait."

Of course, this is not the first time that an argument about capitalism has been couched in esoteric language. Its original critic (and coiner of the term) embedded his prose in an equally thick fog of German Idealism. But in the end we all learned to translate Marx.

With a similar act of translation, the crux of the disagreement between the bishops and the lay committee becomes clear. It is not quite that one side condemns capitalism while the other celebrates it, although that is the tone of the documents. It is more that the bishops are concerned with the failings of capitalism, and the lay committee with its successes. Given capitalism's historical record, it is not surprising that the laity have the better of it. One need not belabor the point. Few systems of political economy have been able to feed the vast majority of their people or give them liberty. Democratic capitalism has done both. Even according to the bishops' narrow criterion for judging all economic institutions—"the preferential option for the poor"—democratic capitalism has been uniquely successful.

But beyond accounting for capitalism's achievements, the lay letter delicately assigns to any Catholic critique of capitalism a historical, and therefore an ironic, context. After all, the Catholic Church is one of those "privileged concentrations of power, wealth, and income" of which the bishops' letter takes such a dim view. The American Church in particular has achieved that position of wealth and power thanks to the surpluses generated by capitalism, and the liberty to dispose of those surpluses which it bestows on citizens. Moreover, Catholicism's historical record as a frame for economic development is not particularly encouraging. One has only to compare Protestant North America to Catholic South and Central America, or Quebec (before it declericalized itself in the 1960s) to the rest of Canada, to make the point gently. No one has yet accused the Catholic ethic of being a source of economic dynamism.

This is not, of course, to say that Catholicism stands refuted. Religion has other purposes. But it is to say that if a religious hierarchy decides to *make* one of its purposes a prescriptive analysis of how society is to produce and distribute wealth, that hierarchy, mindful of its own history, might proceed with a touch of humility. That quality is difficult to find in the bishops' letter.

Still, the absence of humility would hardly be an issue had the bishops simply delivered a prophetic message about society's responsibility for the widow and the orphan. Isaiah was not a retiring man. A contemporary reiteration of his message, while not particularly novel, would be important, especially in a political economy founded on the principle of self-interest. But in this age of Poland, Chile and liberation theology—an age in which the Church is making history throughout much of the world—the American bishops seem not content with prophecy. They insist on advocacy. They want the word made (or at least given) flesh. Hence the principal undertaking of the bishops' letter: to suggest how prophetic concern for the poor is to be put into practice in a modern industrial economy.

Now, prophets have a certain claim to arrogance. But when the prophetic message is accompanied by a social science analysis and a social program, one should take care that the tone of magisterial righteousness not envelop the entire enterprise. The bishops let that tone trickle down to the most contingent, debatable assertion. Moral philosophy and economic analysis entail radically different epistemologies. One would hardly know it from reading this document.

Enough about tone. What about content? Grant that the bishops refuse to yield the miter when they don economic hats. Thus doubly outfitted, do they have anything to say?

The bishops' mission is not merely to identify the failures of capitalism —unemployment, poverty, homelessness—but to diagnose them. The diagnosis suffers from two shortcomings. First and most obviously, their vision is narrowed by a routine acceptance of liberal assumptions about the causes of social problems. For example, they declare current rates of unemployment "morally unjustified," particularly when compared to the three or four percent that used to prevail at the peak of the business cycle. They discount the possibility that structural changes in the economy, rather than illiberal political choices, may have raised the level of "frictional" unemployment. Among the recent phenomena that might have contributed to this new condition, morally unjustified or not, are the expansion of the labor force with the influx of women; the constraining effect of the safety net—from Social Security to union rules to health and safety regulations—on capitalism's dynamism (and cruelty); and the vast dislocations in Western economies caused by OPEC's excise tax on energy. Which of these do the bishops propose to roll back?

Similarly, in discussing poverty, they note its "feminization," but so scrupulous are they to avoid any hint of blaming the victim that they avoid the question of whether unwed mothers and absent fathers bear some responsibility for their poverty and that of their children. The cause of underclass misery is located variously in sexism, racism, lack of child care —all the usual liberal suspects, save inadequate birth control.

But the poverty of the bishops' analysis derives from more than mere narrowness of vision. It is due most of all to a profound naïveté. And naïveté of a particular kind: a belief in the power of good intentions, and an accompanying obliviousness to the intractability of certain problems, particularly problems that arise from the conflict of competing societal goods. Consider the plight of the homeless. The bishops ascribe this problem (and poverty and unemployment) to a lack of political will and a lack of an adequate theoretical framework. Any solution, they write, "must begin with the formation of a new cultural consensus that *all persons really do have rights in the economic sphere.*" (Emphasis bishops'.)

Must it? Are people sleeping in doorways because "economic rights," unlike political rights, "do not hold [a] privileged position in the cultural and legal traditions of our nation?" In fact, twenty-five years ago economic rights were, if anything, less enshrined than today, and there were no armies of grate-dwellers. There are today, largely as a result of one of the finest reformist impulses of the Kennedy years, the freeing of the mentally ill from the snakepits to which they had been consigned for a century. It was decided to restore liberty to these people. But with liberty necessarily comes a diminution of security. We have an epidemic of homelessness today not because we have yet to accept U.N. declarations on economic rights, but because of a perennial conflict between liberty and security, a conflict most acutely manifest in those people most vulnerable to the ravages of freedom. We can do more for the homeless by forcing them into shelters. We might do still more by forcing them back into institutions. Which shall it be? Perhaps in our reforming zeal we have chosen badly for these people. But choose we must. Even bishops have to choose.

The homeless are the extreme case. But they highlight a chronic dilemma that government faces when trying to help the powerless and the weak. With protection comes dependence. With liberty comes the prospect of failure and, for those who fail, misery. That's the central problem of all welfare policy. If you give money to someone conditioned on his inability to make money on his own, you have created a disincentive to work. And when he begins to work and you at some point cut off his welfare (as you must, or else you are being unfair to other low-paid workers who have never laid claim to welfare), you have created more disincentive. It simply won't do imperiously to proclaim that welfare programs "should encourage rather than penalize gainful employment." Of course they should. But exactly how?

Perhaps there was a time when paradox could be defeated by proclamation. But this is not the age of miracles. And even if it were, an economic document is hardly the place to demand them. The bishops are not daunted: "Efforts to generate employment," they declare, "should be aimed specifically at bringing marginalized persons into the labor force; should give priority to long-term jobs; should produce goods and services needed by society; should be as economically efficient as possible; and should include both the private and public sectors." That would be nice, wouldn't it? In a helpful expansion they urge that "employment programs that generate jobs efficiently without entailing large expense and increased inflation should be emphasized." Another paradox, this time a Keynesian one, is banished. Why, even Jesse Helms would welcome a noninflationary employment policy. The interesting question, to use scientific parlance, is exactly what that policy would be.

The bishops' nontautological remedies are only slightly less disappointing. They amount to more Great Society programs, more foreign aid, and a hint of planning. Where have they been for twenty-five years? We now have a generation of experience with liberal social programs, and the bishops appear to have just discovered them. Not that social generosity has been a failure. Far from it. Its successes are many and of great significance. But the crisis of liberalism—and the consequent search for "new ideas"—comes from the realization that these remedies have reached the limits of their success. The structurally unemployed, the female-headed household, the homeless, the mentally ill—the very kinds of misery that concern the bishops—represent precisely those categories of chronic dependency that have proved resistant to Great Society cures. These are the residue cases. More of the same is not a program that offers much hope.

This is all the more true for the poor of the Third World. Even among the most internationally minded, the zeal for charitable handouts, for the soft-loan window at the World Bank, has waned. Experience has been cruel and unequivocal. Ten years ago to argue that foreign aid was actually retarding development in many Third World countries was eccentric. Today, even at the height of the sub-Saharan famine, one finds such views on the front page of the New York *Times.*

Hunger in the world is not caused by "extractive" Western (or multinational) economic policies. And it will be improved only marginally by more positive assistance from the West. The bishops are surely right that such assistance remains a moral imperative: marginal improvement translates into many starving people saved. But they are wrong to imagine that it will have the slightest effect on the gap between rich and poor nations which they find so disturbing. (The problem, of course, is not the gap. If it were, that could quickly be solved by impoverishing the West—a perhaps not-unintended side effect of the new international economic order the bishops seem to favor. The real problem is how to lift the Ethiopias of the world out of poverty.) These countries are economic disaster areas primarily because of the actions of their elites: destroying indigenous food production with collectivization plans and low food prices designed to serve the city at the expense of the country (e.g., Tanzania); favoring white elephant prestige projects, often undertaken with Western aid; and importing cheap (sometimes free) foreign food that undercuts local farmers. South Africa and Zimbabwe have escaped famine not because white managers are smarter, and not because rain falls preferentially on capitalist econo-

mies, but because economies subject to market discipline are self-correc-
tive in a way that command economies can never be.

The experience of the West, and now of East Asia as well, suggests that
capitalism is the most likely route to rapid development, and thus ultimately, if inconveniently, is *the* preferential option for the poor. But these
are hardly lessons the bishops wish to learn. Capitalism, after all, is a system
based on the vice of acquisitiveness. The bishops prefer to appeal to higher
instincts, the spirit of "discipleship," the more selfless inclinations of man.
This is an excellent basis for a sermon, but not a prudent principle on
which to build an economy.

It is one thing for religious leaders to remind their politicians and
parishioners of the prophetic duty to care for the poor. It is another thing
when these prophets, armed with the authority of technical experts, produce an outline of exactly how that is to be undertaken in a complex
political system. It is even worse when this analysis produces a call for
repeal of the paradoxes of economic life, and for enactment of a spent
political agenda. To have discovered liberalism and to have rediscovered
the poor is perhaps an achievement for any ecclesiastical hierarchy. But
it is no great contribution to American political discourse.

The New Republic, December 24, 1984

V

FACING THE WORLD

Chess and Class War

L'AFFAIRE KARPOV

CAPITALISM'S VICE IS THAT IT TURNS EVERYTHING—EVEN, SAY, a woman's first historic run for the White House—into cash. Communism's vice is that it turns everything—even, say, chess—into politics.

Chess? You may have trouble seeing chess as politics. Americans think chess is a game. The *Great Soviet Encyclopedia,* in one of its few correct entries, defines chess as "an art appearing in the form of a game." And like all art under socialism, it is to be turned into an instrument of the state.

You think I exaggerate. If I quoted you Nikolai Krylenko, commissar of justice, in 1932—"We must finish once and for all with the neutrality of chess. . . . We must organize shock-brigades of chess players, and begin the immediate realization of a Five Year Plan for chess"—you'd say I was dredging the history books for Stalinist lunacies. So I bring you fresh evidence of communism's penchant for politicizing everything, for controlling everything it politicizes, and for letting nothing—shame least of all—jeopardize that control. I bring you *L'affaire* Karpov, a tempest for a teapot.

The story is this. On September 10, 1984, the world chess championship begins in Moscow. It is an all-Soviet final: champion Anatoly Karpov *vs* challenger Gary Kasparov. To win, one must win six games. Draws don't count. After nine games Karpov is ahead 4–0. An astonishing lead.

Kasparov then launches the most relentless war of attrition in the history of championship chess. He deliberately forces draw after draw, at one point 17 in a row, to one purpose: to exhaust the older and frailer champion.

On November 24, Karpov does win a fifth game, but he will not win again. On December 12, Kasparov wins his first. The score is 5–1. Then 14 more draws.

Then something extraordinary happens. Karpov, known for his metronomic logic and unshakable composure, loses game 47, playing "as though in a daze," writes chess master Robert Byrne. Game 48: Karpov loses again. The score is 5–3.

By now, says another expert, Karpov "looks like Chernenko." Chernenko looks bad, but Karpov is 33. He has lost 22 pounds and did not have very many to start with. He is close to collapse. He is about to fall—as Nabokov's fictional champion, Luzhin, fell—into what Nabokov called "the abysmal depths of chess." Kasparov is on the brink of the greatest chess comeback ever.

And on the brink both will stay. Six days later, on February 15, the president of the International Chess Federation, under enormous pressure from Soviet authorities, shows up in Moscow and declares the match a draw—and over. Karpov is saved by the bell, except that here the referee rang it in the middle of a round and at an eight count.

Why? One can understand the Party wanting Karpov to win in 1978 and 1981, when the challenger was Victor Korchnoi—defector, Jew, all-around troublemaker, Trotsky at the chessboard. But Kasparov is not Korchnoi. He is a good Soviet citizen, a party member, and not known for any politics. He is, however, half Armenian, half Jewish. Until age 12, his name was Gary Weinstein. He is no dissident, but he is young (21) and independent. Above all, he is not reliable.

Karpov, a man who needed to be named only once, is reliable. Conqueror of Korchnoi (twice), receiver of the Order of Lenin, ethnically pure (Russian) and politically pliant (a leader of the Soviet Peace Committee), he is the new Soviet man. And he receives the attention fitting so rare a political commodity: he says he was told of the match's cancellation over the phone in his car. Cellular service is not widely available in the Soviet Union.

Now, this is the third time that Soviet authorities have tried to undermine Kasparov's shot at the championship. In 1983 they stopped him from traveling to his quarterfinal match in Pasadena, Calif. The official reason (later pressed into service for the Olympics) was "lack of security." Only a sportsmanlike opponent and accommodating chess officials (they rescheduled the match without penalty) saved Kasparov from defaulting in the candidates' round and losing his chance to challenge Karpov.

But challenge he did. The finals were held in the prestigious Hall of Columns in the House of Unions. That is, until Kasparov's rally in the 47th game. Soviet authorities then suddenly moved the match to the Hotel Sport outside the city center. "Like moving from Carnegie Hall to a gin mill in Poughkeepsie," says Larry Parr, editor of *Chess Life* magazine.

I interpreted the move to mean that Chernenko was about to die, since the Hall of Columns is where Soviet leaders (like Dmitri Ustinov) lie in state. Silly me. I was insufficiently cynical about Soviet behavior. The reason for the move was not to bury Chernenko (he continues to be propped up like a Potemkin villain), but to save Karpov. The move took eight days—eight otherwise illegal days of rest for Karpov.

It didn't help. Karpov was too far gone. Kasparov destroyed him the very next day in the 48th game. Soviet officials then made sure it was the last.

Now do you believe me?

A month ago I would not have believed it myself. (Kasparov still does not believe it.) Fix the biggest chess match in the world? Steal the championship from one Soviet citizen for a marginal propaganda gain? In broad daylight?

Still, we must be careful. An unfortunate episode like this tends to fuel native American paranoia about the Soviets. It encourages the belief that the Soviets are prepared to go to any length in relentless pursuit of even the most speculative political advantage. We must resist such facile reactions. Next thing you know someone will suggest that the KGB got the Bulgarians to hire a Turk to shoot the Pope to pacify Poland.

The Washington Post, March 8, 1985

The New
Isolationism

IT IS A WONDER THAT FOR A CONTINENTAL NATION PROTECTED BY
two oceans and bordered by two weak and friendly neighbors isolationism
should be an epithet. Yet Pearl Harbor made it so, and ever since it has
been mandatory for any serious political actor to deny being isolationist.
Consequently, even those advocating the most radical retrenchment of
American commitments overseas protest that they do not call for isolating
the United States from the world, economically or even diplomatically.
This attempt to retire the word is not very convincing. Isolationism has
never meant total withdrawal from the world. It has always meant *selective*
disengagement from *certain* relationships (alliance, military) in *certain*
parts of the world. Classical nineteenth-century isolationism avoided European entanglements only. As the historian Selig Adler wrote, "Our isolationist barricade had only one wall. We shut only our eastern door." Nor
did classical isolationism mean passivity and neutrality. During its pre-
World War I isolationist heyday, American foreign policy was selectively
active and expansionist, extending American hegemony southward under
the Monroe Doctrine and westward all the way to the Philippines and to
China through the Open Door.

After World War II the United States became the dominant power in
the world, and internationalism became the guiding ideology of its foreign
policy. Internationalism reached its rhetorical high-water mark with John
Kennedy's "bear any burden" inaugural pledge. That was soon put into

practice in Vietnam. Since then there has been a gradual but marked retreat. From the cutoff of aid to Saigon and the Clark amendment (banning U.S. intervention in Angola) to the retreat from Beirut and the Boland amendment (restricting aid to the Nicaraguan *contras*) the United States has selectively, though hardly systematically, sought to reduce its international commitments.

It is debatable whether the decline in America's relative dominance was inevitable. It is not debatable that there have been strong and articulate American voices arguing that such a contraction of America's reach and responsibilities is desirable. Although as explicit an isolationist vision as George McGovern's "Come Home America" is still a rarity, a new isolationism has clearly emerged, picking up the strands of a tradition two hundred years old.

We tend to think of that tradition as a property of the right, since at its apogee on the eve of Pearl Harbor, isolationism had become almost totally identified with anti-New Deal, far right America Firsters. We tend to forget the prewar tradition of left isolationism. It included socialists (such as Norman Thomas), progressives (such as William Borah and Robert LaFollette), and periodically, i.e., when Moscow so instructed, Communists. (Thomas, for example, argued that the cost of foreign commitments would prevent economic reconstruction at home, a familiar argument today on Capitol Hill.) With World War II, both left and right isolationism went into eclipse, not to reemerge until Vietnam.

Today isolationism has regained its voice. It is no longer a philosophy of political eccentrics, as it was from World War II until the mid-sixties. Nor is it, as conservatives now like to charge, the exclusive property of the left. It has reconstituted itself in both parties, finding, as in the prewar era, two distinct forms of expression.

The first of these, left isolationism, has become the ideology of the Democratic Party, not of its ("McGovernite") fringes but of its mainstream. Modern left isolationism is defined by a paradox: its ends remain truly internationalist, but its approved means have turned radically anti-interventionist. There is no retreat from the grand Wilsonian commitment to the spread of American values. These tend now to be called human rights rather than democracy, but the commitment to their success has lost none of its Wilsonian universalism or moral urgency. "The cause of freedom is indivisible," declared Walter Mondale in a major foreign policy address in November 1983. He followed with a *tour d'horizon* of the world's top human rights violators from South Korea to Poland to South Africa. Mondale's detailed interest in what human rights violators rightly call their "internal affairs" is not an isolated burst of Wilsonianism.

Universal human rights has become *the* foreign policy cause of the post-Carter Democratic Party, and for that matter, of post-Vietnam liberalism. This cause is as grandly internationalist in its reach as any since Wilson, FDR and Truman. Only in its means is it novel.

"American restraint on intervention, military action, and covert operations does not mean American indifference," said Gary Hart. "We care about human rights and democratic values and economic development; and we can show our concern in our diplomacy, our aid programs. . . ." Diplomacy. Aid. Something is missing. "You don't bring in democracy at the point of a bayonet," said Daniel Moynihan about Grenada. That idea will come as a surprise to Germans and Japanese (and now Grenadians, too), the beneficiaries of an earlier Democratic internationalism that defined itself (vs. prewar isolationism) precisely by its insistence on the relationship between democracy and bayonets.

Left isolationism is the isolationism of means. And the modern Democratic Party is its home. In the 1984 Democratic campaign, the principal disagreement over Central America was whether the United States should station twenty advisers in Honduras (Walter Mondale's position) or zero (Gary Hart's). On Angola, El Salvador, Grenada, Lebanon and Nicaragua, the Democratic position has involved some variety of disengagement: talks, aid, sanctions, diplomacy—first. In practice this invariably means— only. Force is ruled out, effectively if not explicitly.

Why? Like their prewar socialist and progressive forebears, today's left isolationists consider the international status quo unjust and do not want American power used to preserve it. Walter Lippmann and *The New Republic,* for example, came out against the League of Nations because it meant the United States would have to defend Versailles and the territorial ambitions of the victorious European powers that Versailles sanctioned. Today liberals find the United States the status quo power. And for those on the wrong side of history, as the left likes to say, force is not only wrong, it is futile. "The gravest political and security dangers in the developing world," explains the 1984 Democratic platform, "flow from . . . poverty, repression, and despair. Against adversaries such as these, military force is of limited value." What is of value, then? "Such weapons as economic assistance, economic and political reform, and support for democratic values by, among other steps, funding scholarships to study at U.S. colleges and universities." These must be "the primary instruments of American influence in the developing countries."

What does it mean in practice to rely on cultural, economic and diplomatic tools? No one seriously believes that cultural exchange will secure

American interests anywhere. Its effects are at best diffuse and very long-term. What to use in the meantime? Say, in this century?

Economic aid is always cheap to advocate in the abstract. Giving it is another matter. Congressional Democrats, so emphatic that Central America's root problems are economic and social, gagged on the Kissinger Commission's recommendation of eight billion dollars in aid.

But the problem with economic weapons is not just the sincerity of its advocates. The fact is that poverty in most of the world is endemic and totally unresponsive to any imaginable American economic intervention. To identify poverty as the principal cause of instability—and thus the principal threat to American interests—is to admit that instability is intractable and our interest not defendable.

Economic sanctions are as limited an instrument as economic aid. Experience with South Africa, Russia, Poland and Iran has shown that embargoes fail. Democracies hate to interrupt free trade or to expend taxpayers' money to promote noneconomic ends. The boycotter invariably loses heart and caves in. Jimmy Carter's courageous grain embargo was attacked by everybody, from his presidential opponent to, four years later, his own former running mate. Last week, in criticizing the idea of sanctions against New Zealand for barring U.S. warships, the New York *Times* argued that it would "punish American consumers of lamb at least as much as New Zealand's producers." ANZUS bows before the lamb-eater lobby.

That leaves diplomatic tools. At its most unserious level, this means talk —anywhere, anytime, with anyone. There were even complaints that the Reagan administration had not tried to negotiate with Grenada's Bernard Coard, a little tyrant with whom even Maurice Bishop, considerably more attuned to Coard's thinking, had some difficulty communicating.

There is, however, a serious core to the contemporary Democratic notion of diplomacy as the preeminent foreign policy tool. It is the idea of multilateralism: collective action by peace-loving countries against international malefactors. Multilateralism is the great Democratic defense against the charge of isolationism. "The Republicans have always been unilateralists—go-it-aloners," said Arthur Schlesinger in an interview with Morton Kondracke. "The Democrats are traditional internationalists who believe we can't run the world ourselves." Jimmy Carter's deputy chief of the National Security Council, David Aaron, argued that the isolationist charge "misses the entire thrust of Democratic policy from Truman to John Kennedy to Walter Mondale. What all of them have tried to do is create some sort of stable world order that respects international law and allows for economic development and the spread of prosperity. The Republicans . . . are still unilateralist."

True. For fifty years multilateralism has been central to the internationalist idea. It was to be the principal instrument of world order. In its service were fashioned a host of institutions. Some were global, like the League of Nations, the U.N., and the World Court. Some were regional, like NATO, ANZUS and the OAS. (Remember SEATO? CENTO?) Collective security, which we had failed to implement in the interwar period, was to be the guarantor of peace and stability.

Aren't today's multilateralists the real heirs to FDR and Truman, as Schlesinger claims? Only in form. Multilateralism means something very different today than it did in the immediate postwar period. Then, when the United States was by far the overwhelming power in the world, multilateralism was indeed the preferred means for American action—*and was no real restraint on it.* In 1950 the United States could push through a "Uniting for Peace" resolution in the General Assembly, and in effect, act unilaterally in Korea under multilateral auspices. Kennedy and Johnson could justify intervention in Vietnam by appeal to SEATO obligations and by the presence of "allied" troops from South Korea and Australia. Johnson intervened in the Dominican Republic under cover of the OAS. "For the very strong," says Robert Tucker, "multilateralism . . . does not materially restrict behavior." It is, in fact, "an advantage in that it gives their actions a legitimacy that they might otherwise not possess."

For the strong, multilateralism is a cover for unilateralism. For the rest, it is a cover for inaction. Today the United States is part of the rest. The global multilateral institutions, like the U.N., have been captured by a hostile Third World-Communist majority. The regional institutions are paralyzed by reluctant allies. (The OAS, for example, would never have approved Grenada. That is why we went not to it but to the Association of Eastern Caribbean States, an alliance of dubious existence, to provide the 82nd Airborne with a flag of convenience.) Multilateralism, now a true hindrance to American action, is a synonym—an excuse—for paralysis. It has become what Lippmann once called "the internationalism of the isolationist."

The irony is that classical isolationism opposed multilateral entanglement for fear it would draw America into foreign conflicts. Modern isolationism embraces multilateralism because it keeps America out of foreign conflicts. The reason for the change is a simple reversal in the power relations. In the nineteenth and early twentieth centuries, the United States was a junior partner to the aggressive, imperial powers of Europe. Today the United States is the preeminent, dynamic power. Its allies want nothing more than to tend their vineyards undisturbed. Exquisite concern for their wishes is a guarantee of inaction.

It is also at the heart of Democratic foreign policy. The 1984 platform contains, by my count, no fewer than ten references to multilateralism. Significantly, six are in a single section—the section on the Western Hemisphere, the one area where one might expect the United States, because of tradition, interest and a preponderance of power, to claim a unilateral right to action (what used to be called the Monroe Doctrine).

Listen to Gary Hart's critique of the Reagan administration in his major foreign policy speech of the campaign (Chicago, March 1984): "[It] made no effort to send peace-keeping forces from the U.N. or from neutral nations to Lebanon; to invoke OAS sanctions for Grenada; to back the Contadora government's efforts for a peaceful resolution in El Salvador and Nicaragua. . . . The Reagan administration has turned its back on . . . North–South dialogue between rich and poor nations; turned its back on the World Bank's efforts to offer some opportunity and hope to the world's neediest people; turned its back on United Nations efforts to curb racist rule in South Africa. . . ." The U.N., the OAS, Contadora, North–South dialogue, the World Bank and the U.N. once again: these are to be the vehicles of American foreign policy.

Or listen to Walter Mondale. Immediately after the Grenada invasion, he criticized the President because he failed to "adequately consult with our allies." He noted that Margaret Thatcher opposed the invasion and her advice should have been "fully weighed" because Grenada is a Commonwealth nation. "I understand the French were not consulted at all and have opposed the invasion." The French? "At a time when we are relying on their cooperation and assistance in Lebanon, we should be making every effort to keep their confidence." Oh. Later he charged that "Mr. Reagan ignored the nonintervention provisions of our treaty obligations, as well as opportunities for multilateral action under the OAS charter."

One measure of how far this line of reasoning has penetrated Democratic thinking is a speech given by Senator Moynihan in the 1984 annual meeting of the Coalition for a Democratic Majority. Moynihan takes internationalism very seriously. So much so that he argued that "had the Democratic Party not failed in its foreign policy mission in 1919–20 [to support the League] the world likely could have escaped the Nazis" and World War II. We had a second chance with the U.N., he argued, and we made it work. "Something, however, had changed in the world from the time of Wilson." That was "the rise of totalitarianism." As a result, "the world order Wilson and Roosevelt had envisioned was not really a practical arrangement and perforce we fell back on military alliances, vast rearmament, and eventually a succession of limited wars."

So Moynihan acknowledges that while multilateralism may once have been, it no longer is adequate to meet the new threat to world order. What to do? Continue the forms of American unilateralism (including "limited wars") that we have had to fall back on in the recent past? His answer: "The age of the totalitarian state is waning. . . . The Soviet Union is a declining power." So? "Our grand strategy must be to wait out the Soviets." In other words: between now and then, when the totalitarian threat will wane and permit a Wilsonian internationalism to prevail, there is nothing to be done! While the rest of the party spells out a program of multilateral paralysis, its most serious foreign policy thinker presents wait-ing-it-out as a bold new foreign policy idea. Such is the state of left isolationism.

Left isolationism has received much attention because it has captured the majority party, the party that invented internationalism. However, there is a second species of contemporary isolationist thought, less developed, less noticed, but crucial. These isolationists are weary of, indeed largely indifferent to the world and any dream of reforming it. They call for retreat from Wilsonian goals. They accept Irving Kristol's distinction between foreign policy (the defense of interests) and diplomacy (the maintenance of [the fiction of] an international order). They have little use for the latter.

They have even less use for multilateralism. Schlesinger is right. They are go-it-aloners. They are the classic isolationists of the right: their ends are nationalist, not internationalist; their means uni-, not multilateralist.

Right isolationism has yet to capture a party, but its proponents, still in opposition, are growing in strength and confidence. Kristol, for example, in his essay "Does NATO Exist?" (his answer is no), makes the most radical case for the United States to get out of Europe. Henry Kissinger probes the idea more tentatively with a proposal (in Time, 1984) for cutting U.S. forces in Europe by "perhaps up to half." Owen Harries follows with a proposal to turn from an Atlantic to a "Pacific Community." (There is an echo here. "General MacArthur," wrote Lippmann, "argu[ed] that our interests in Europe are at best an expensive form of philanthropy and that our true destiny is to go it alone in the Pacific and in East Asia.") In Congress, the leader of the effort to cut U.S. troops in Europe is a conservative Democrat, Sam Nunn. Even within an administration that promised a return to a robust internationalism, there is a dissenting column: Caspar Weinberger and the joint chiefs opposed intervention in

Lebanon, only reluctantly went along with Grenada, and are now most wary about involvement in Central America. And the Europeans rightly perceive behind much of the conservative enthusiasm for strategic (Star Wars) defense, the promise of an America that relies exclusively on itself for its own defense—the traditional nationalist-unilateralism of the right.

This is the isolationism of selective disengagement. It is a direct descendant of prewar conservative isolationism: it wants to redraw the American security perimeter, both to reduce the dangers caused by the current imbalance between ends and means, and to restore American freedom of action that is now so constrained by paralyzing alliances.

Administration officials, charged with the day-to-day management of vast overseas commitments, are not as free as conservative intellectuals (or out-of-power Democrats) to indulge their isolationist instincts in public. Which is what makes Weinberger's November 28, 1984, speech, "The Uses of Military Power," despite concurrent and subsequent qualifications, such a remarkable right isolationist text.

It is remarkable because of its insistence on the hallmarks of right isolationism: nationalism and unilateralism. Weinberger first gives ritual nods to "the fulfillment of our responsibilities as a world power." He does not want to frighten half the world to death. He even makes a point of attacking "people [who] are in fact advocating a return to post-World War I isolationism." But interspersed with internationalist boilerplate are references to a much narrower definition of American interests: "We should only engage *our* troops if we must do so as a matter of our *own* vital national interest. We cannot assume for other sovereign nations the responsibility to defend *their* territory—without their strong invitation—when our own freedom is not threatened." (Emphasis Weinberger's.) It is hard to imagine *any* foreign event that can threaten the freedom of a continental power protected by two oceans and possessing 10,000 nuclear warheads. And invitations, no matter how strong, are easily ignored. When Egypt closed the Straits of Tiran in May 1967, Israel asked Britain, France and the United States to honor written guarantees to maintain free passage through the Straits. No one moved a ship.

Weinberger then proceeds to elaborate six conditions for American intervention abroad. Point four is devoted to national interest. "We must continuously keep as a beacon applied before us the basic questions, '*Is this conflict in our national interest?*' 'Does our national interest require us to fight, to use force of arms?' " (His emphasis.) Not a single mention of international law, multilateral action or consulting with allies passes Weinberger's lips. The idea that intervention must be "internationally defensible" and "open to independent scrutiny" (two of Mondale's six conditions in his 1983 speech) is totally alien to right isolationism.

But what is being rejected is not just multilateralism as a means of action. Weinberger is obviously uncomfortable with internationalism as a guide to action. The references to national interest, as opposed to alliance obligations, are reinforced by point five: no intervention without advance assurance of domestic support. This clearly is a policy of prudence (and perhaps a backhanded slap at Secretary of State George Shultz for Lebanon). But it is more than that.

This particular requirement establishes profound limitations on any possible intervention. Domestic opinion, in advance of any intervention, is likely to define national interests very narrowly. "No unpopular war" is almost a prescription for "no wars," certainly for none at the margins of the free world. Domestic support can be counted on (apart from three-day mismatches like Grenada) only for answering direct attacks on the United States: Pearl Harbor and nothing less. This is the *pre-*war standard. Indeed, in January 1938 congressional isolationists went exactly the suggested Weinberger route: they brought to a vote a constitutional amendment to make war, except in response to invasion, subject to a national referendum. It took an extraordinary appeal from President Roosevelt to keep the House from passing what all knew would amount to (again: save direct attack) a guarantee of isolation. To insist on prior domestic support is to reinforce the narrowest nationalist basis for intervention.

Where does nationalist-unilateralism lead? What commitments are to be given up? Right isolationists draw different lines. Weinberger's criteria necessarily exclude from America's defensive perimeter much of the Third World. Some of the old right, like Barry Goldwater, are Monroe doctrinaires. They want to draw a line around this hemisphere. ("Restore the Monroe Doctrine" graces the letterhead of the Conservative Caucus.) About Europe there is great ambivalence. When Owen Harries suggests a turn from an Atlantic to a Pacific Community, he is suggesting more than a tactical ploy to force Europe to defend herself and to permit one form of American disengagement. He is echoing the classic isolationist policy of shutting the eastern door and pursuing American destiny to the west, where American actions have traditionally been less encumbered. Even the logical extreme of the right isolationist view—Fortress America —has its proponents (the most articulate of which was Robert Tucker in his 1972 book, *A New Isolationism*).

Although right isolationists draw different lines, the sentiment animating their efforts is the same: a sense that America has let itself be drawn into commitments that serve not its interests but that of others. From

Washington's farewell address on, that sentiment has always animated classical isolationism, particularly prewar right isolationism. It was never abandoned, not even during the interlude of Vandenbergian internationalism that immediately followed World War II. Even then, the right never fully renounced its nationalist-unilateralist ideology. It did reconsider tactics. Chastened by the interwar failure of the European system, it came to accept the view that American interests could best be served through American-dominated internationalist vehicles. That domination now ended, many conservatives want out. They want to redraw the lines of the American sphere, and withdraw to its unencumbered defense.

The political monopoly enjoyed by postwar internationalism is at an end. It is now faced with a continuing, two-front isolationist challenge. Does internationalism have an adequate defense?

In my view the left isolationist challenge is more easily met. That is because it fails on its own terms. Jesse Jackson's Third World school of American foreign policy, which is not isolationist, is at least coherent. It supports "progressive" (i.e., anti-American) forces abroad and welcomes an encumbering multilateralism and the renunciation of (American) force as the way to further that cause. On the other hand, mainstream Democratic foreign policy, from Hart to Moynihan, professes different goals—the success of the Western idea in the world—but resolutely abjures the means of securing them.

That leads to two results, one dangerous, one merely peculiar. The danger comes from the commitments retained, like the nuclear guarantee for Europe. The enthusiasm on the left for curtailing the military might behind this commitment—the freeze, no-first-use, a moratorium on Pershings, cutting the military budget (which is devoted overwhelmingly to conventional defense)—increases the risk of such commitments. It ensures that were they ever to be challenged and we foolish enough to honor them, the consequences would be catastrophic.

The peculiarity comes from the means renounced. To renounce unpleasant kinds of pressure—those requiring force—is, in effect, to decide for only one kind of intervention: against friends only. The reason is simple. To influence enemies requires the application of means, while to influence friends simply their withdrawal. Hence obsessive Democratic focus on the Philippines, El Salvador, Korea, Taiwan and so on, regimes that do, in fact, violate Wilsonian ideals—not *because* they are friends of the United States, but because, being friends, they are susceptible to the most passive of foreign policy instruments, the only ones left isolationists are prepared to use. To find the origin of this selectivity in a blame-America-first reflex, as does Jeane Kirkpatrick, is to miss the mark. The charge does fit Jesse Jackson but not, for example, Mondale—the choice of San Francisco Democrats—or Hart or Moynihan or Nunn or any other representatives of the party's mainstream. The selectivity of the fervor for reforming the world comes not from anti-Americanism; it is the natural consequence of an incoherent policy that is internationalist in ends but isolationist in means.

Right isolationism is more difficult to refute, not because, in my view, it is any less misguided, but because the argument hinges on a question of values, not logic.

Right isolationist logic is powerful. Arthur Vandenberg is said to have turned internationalist when he saw London fall under German V-rocket attack in 1944. "How can there be any immunity or isolation when men can devise weapons like that?" he said. The opposite lesson, elaborated by Robert Tucker among others, is more compelling: it is precisely the new weaponry, specifically, strategic nuclear weaponry, that permits a return to isolation. It restores the conditions that once made such a policy possible: the unilateral possession of a preponderance of deterrent power. In the interwar period the United States did not have that, and suffered the consequences (World War II) of pretending it did not need it. America needed European allies to create a preponderance of power to deter the enemy (the Axis). No longer. Strategic weaponry has given the United States unilateral possession of that deterrent power. In fact, alliances are a threat to U.S. security. They make the United States risk its own national existence for interests (like Europe) on which its physical security does not depend.

Are American troops in Korea and Berlin there to defend American security? It is not so easy a case to make. South Vietnam fell, and with it all of Indochina. Has that jeopardized the physical security of the United States? Even if all the dominoes fell right up to the Rio Grande, no adversary in his right mind would dare cross it. In terms of a simple calculation of physical danger, to risk our existence on guarantees to weak and exposed allies is the riskiest of all strategies. We are always listening for the sounds of exploding "powder kegs." An isolated America would not have so cocked an ear.

In the nuclear age, alliances are much harder to justify as physical buffers. The counter to the right isolationist argument, therefore, must begin with the question: What is worth fighting for? If America stands only for its defense, if its mission is physical security—if, in other words, its nationalism is like all other nationalisms—then, indeed, why not as narrow a definition of American interests, as tight a circle around our borders as possible? A Finlandized Europe will trade with the United

States. Finland does. And so does the rest of the world, which, from Angola to the Soviet Union, is eager for American commerce.

The ultimate response, therefore, to right isolationism must be the assertion that an alliance of free nations, as the locus and trustee of Western values, is a value in itself. In other words, the answer to right isolationism must be Wilsonian.

Not that freedom is indivisible. That woolly Wilsonian claim is both empirically false and dangerous. It is false because freedom has been lost in half of Europe and Indochina—it can be lost in, say, Afghanistan— without it being lost everywhere, certainly not in the United States. It is dangerous because the belief that freedom is indivisible involved us, among other things, in imprudent defenses of freedom in places like Vietnam.

A new Wilsonianism must argue not that freedom is indivisible, but that it is valuable. A sustained internationalism rests on a large vision of America, an America that stands for an idea. Liberty and democracy are intrinsic to American nationhood as they are not, say, to France or Britain, where the state predates the democratic idea. As Tucker admits, "The price of a new isolationism is that America would have to abandon its aspirations to an order that has become synonymous with the nation's vision of its role in the world." He adds, "Isolationism is opposed, among other reasons, because it is equated with indifference to the fate of others. . . . It undoubtedly is and no useful purpose is served by evasiveness on this point."

And it is exactly on this point that the nationalist and the internationalist part ways. The internationalist may decide not to intervene in particular areas for prudential reasons, but not out of indifference. A wise internationalism and right isolationism differ not on prudence but purpose. It is one thing to admit that we will bear not *any* burden, but only *some* burdens—those within our (relatively) reduced means—for the success of freedom. It is another to say that we will bear burdens only for national interest.

A century ago a foreign policy of such narrow nationalism could be consistent with America's idea of itself. America was weak and could indeed best serve the idea of freedom by preserving itself and through the power of example. Today, as a superpower, that is not enough. Action, sometimes unilateral action, is necessary. It is American power that guarantees the survival of freedom. In Europe, the burden of whose defense has grown too heavy for some, the borders of freedom are defined by a thin line of American soldiers, not by the reach of American example. Czechoslovakians know of the American example.

To disengage in the service of a narrow nationalism is a fine foreign policy for a minor regional power, which the United States once was and which, say, Canada or Sweden are now. For America today it is a betrayal of its idea of itself. Most of all, it seems a curious application of American conservatism, which usually holds liberty to be the highest of political values. Does that idea now stop at the nation's shores?

The New Republic, March 4, 1985

The Tirana Index

NOW THAT THE CAMPAIGN IS OVER AND THE RETURNS ARE IN, ANALYSIS OF the latest Albanian election begins. The facts are clear. The New York *Times* reports that Party chief Enver Hoxha's slate of candidates for Parliament won by the comfortable margin of 1,627,959 to one. The message seems to be: stay the course.

The Party ran well in all regions and among all classes—worker, peasant and apparatchik. It swept the atheist vote. The much ballyhooed gender gap never developed. On the other hand, it failed to make any inroads on opposition support. (In the last Albanian election there was also one vote against.) Some observers had been predicting that opposition support might double, but that prospect dimmed last December when a potential leader of the movement, Prime Minister Mehmet Shehu, committed suicide. At the time Hoxha claimed that Shehu did so "in a moment of nervous crisis." Now Party chairman Hoxha ("himself a successful candidate in the 210th district of Tirana," writes the *Times*) says that Mr. Shehu, whom he described variously as an American agent, a Soviet agent and a Yugoslav agent, had been ordered by Yugoslavia to kill Mr. Hoxha and other Albanian leaders, but finally met his demise when he "broke his head against the unity of the party and the people." (Mr. Hoxha's equivocation recalls the answer that the police captain in *Casablanca* gave to a question about the condition of a prisoner. "We are trying to decide whether he committed suicide or died trying to escape.") Since Albanian election law does not permit absentee ballots, analysts conclude that the one vote against Hoxha could not have been cast by Mr. Shehu. His voice will be missed.

Hoxha's victory margin, though impressive, is not unprecedented. President Assad of Syria won reelection in 1978 with 99.6 percent of the vote. The Soviet Embassy informs us that candidates "always" win more than 99 percent of the vote, usually "around 99.5 percent." Indeed, it seems, anything less than 99 percent is considered a vote of no confidence. Western observers are generally skeptical about these results. Because of their obsession with the authenticity of such elections, they tend to overlook their enormous value as scientific tools. For generations political science has been seeking a way to quantify freedom. Some, like Freedom House, annually classify countries according to their level of political and civil liberty. Others like Morton Kondracke propose the creation of a computerized despot-o-meter to take the guesswork out of such perennially taxing questions as: who's worse, Idi Amin or Roberto d'Aubuisson? The trouble with these pioneering schemes is that they are too complicated. I propose a simpler system, crude, but like all crude instruments, quick, easy to use and blunt. It is the Tirana Index: the higher the vote any government wins in an election the more tyrannous it is. The Tirana Index lends itself to easy rules of thumb. Very bad tyranny (known to some as totalitarian states) usually gets more than 95 percent of the vote, and the more efficient of these, more than 99 percent. Traditional autocracies and military governments (known to some as authoritarian states), such as Turkey and Mexico, can be counted on to clock in somewhere between 80 and 95 percent. (Turkey's last referendum passed by 92.) Well-functioning democracies produce winners who get between 50 and 80 percent of the vote. Countries like Italy, Israel and others where driving is a life-threatening activity regularly produce winning margins of less than 50 percent. They can safely be classified as anarchies.

The New Republic, December 13, 1982

"The Moral
High Ground"

THERE HAS BEEN A LOT OF TALK LATELY ABOUT THE "MORAL HIGH ground" (time is short: call it "mohgro"), that strategic territory the United States apparently ceded to Cuba and the Soviet Union in exchange for Grenada. The loss of this piece of real estate has provoked protests from quarters normally indifferent to the territorial exchanges of the cold war. From the gnashing of teeth and pointing of fingers occasioned by the loss of this former American colony, one would imagine we'd lost another China.

Who lost mohgro? Ronald Reagan, of course. But how exactly did we acquire it in the first place? Robert Kaiser, of *The Washington Post,* explains. He criticizes the President for "squandering the moral high ground the Soviets had granted him by their bad behavior in Poland, Afghanistan and the destruction of Flight 007." So mohgro was won because of "bad behavior" on the part of our adversaries. But wasn't there bad behavior in Grenada, too, shortly before the American invasion? Didn't the military junta assassinate the prime minister, much of his cabinet and a still unknown number of civilians? Exactly. We were in veritable moral orbit then, with all those dead and dying to which we could point with satisfaction and say: "See, that's what happens when you mess with Marxists." Well then, how did we squander our advantage? Answer: By doing something about the thuggery that had granted our side the mohgro in the first place. To be precise, by ending it.

That's the point. When others are bad you can seize the mohgro with a pointed finger and a fine denunciation. On one condition: you do nothing real to help the victims. The denunciation must be impotent. That, after all, is what Afghanistan, Poland and Flight 007 have in common. Not just bad behavior by the Russians, but bad behavior the victims of which we could variously mourn, applaud or pray for, but do nothing to save. Actually raise a finger. Intervene to help the victim, and you run the risk of breaking a rule: for example, violating a frontier, or the OAS Charter, or the sensibilities of 106 members of the General Assembly or the editorial board of the New York *Times*. Then, presto! you become just like the Russians. "Simply put," the *Times* wrote, "the cost [of the Grenada operation] is loss of the moral high ground: a reverberating demonstration to the world that America has no more respect for laws and borders, for the codes of civilization, than the Soviet Union."

Really? Representative Thomas Downey says that in Grenada "we gave up the moral high ground we occupied after the Soviets invaded Afghanistan and shot down the South Korean airliner." Compare Grenada and Afghanistan. Both involved superpower intervention in a neighbor's affairs. The parallel begins and ends there. In Afghanistan, the Russians have been killing people for four years (now with chemical weapons) to keep in power a despised tyranny (an old-fashioned word with the virtue of being acceptable to right and left). In Grenada, the United States got rid of a bunch of thugs (not even the *Times* disputes that characterization) in a three-day operation. And it's not just means but ends that are different. We know what kind of government Babrak Karmal runs. And not even Tom Downey doubts that the United States aims to return Grenada to parliamentary democracy.

My argument is not that because we are a democracy the ends of any American intervention are inherently justified. There are cases—U.S. intervention in Guatemala in 1954, for example—where intervention is undertaken for (correctly or incorrectly calculated) geopolitical advantage at the expense of democracy. However, there are cases where U.S. action serves both its own geopolitical interests and the interests of democracy. Grenada is such a case. The burden of proof is always on those who advocate intervention. But if an extremely limited operation to restore a country from gangsterism to democracy is not justified, then what proof will the critics ever accept? None, I suspect. If you believe that mohgro simply goes to the aggrieved, then you don't bother with moral calculations. You seek instead more grief. It makes for a curious foreign policy.

And it's not just the foreign policy of the mohgro theorists that is curious. So is their language. "Obviously the United States has strategic interests to defend," writes Tad Szulc in the New York *Times*, "but, just as importantly, it must defend its moral high ground." The metaphor is military. And far from being an embarrassment to those making a case against the use of force, it is an asset. The metaphor is pointed: high ground, after all, is not a place to be coveted solely for its pristine air and unobstructed view. It is a place from which to dominate and control. The implication is that occupying the moral high ground confers advantages; losing it is costly—"far more costly than the loss of a dozen soldiers," calculates the New York *Times*. The critics' point is this: staying out of Grenada would not only have been the more moral thing to do; it would have been shrewder. It would have advanced American interests more, left us further ahead than we are now. What we forfeited by going in was so important that, whatever our gains, on balance we lost.

Now, what precisely did we lose? Our moral superiority to the Russians in the eyes of world public opinion. Grenada, explains Walter Mondale, "undermines our ability to effectively criticize what the Soviets have done in their brutal intervention in Afghanistan, in Poland, and elsewhere." Assume that's true. Assume that the invasion of Grenada was, in fact, wrong. And assume further that the three-day Grenada operation was as wrong as the Soviets' four years in Afghanistan and forty in Poland (where one doubts that ninety-one percent of the people, as in Grenada, would tell a pollster that they support the armed intervention of their super-power neighbor). Assume all that and look at the balance sheet.

On the one hand, Cuba has been expelled from Grenada (and on the very next day, domino-style from Surinam), its Caribbean enterprises effectively foreclosed. On the other hand, we lose the ability to criticize the Soviets about Afghanistan and Poland and Flight 007. Now, there are people who think that criticizing the Soviets in areas where we can do absolutely nothing is what foreign policy is all about. For them, the balance sheet is negative. Presumably they also believe that our previous exchanges of moral for strategic territory were positive: the Soviets re-Stalinized Poland, captured Afghanistan (putting them two hundred miles from the Persian Gulf) and ensured that nobody in his right mind will violate their airspace. In return we got to denounce them at the United Nations (though not at all on Poland); and on the KAL disaster our (vetoed) Security Council resolution mustered the barest majority of nine votes. We also got a sixty-day partial ban on flights to the Soviet Union, except that it was called off after twenty-one. Nice bargain.

I am willing to grant that victimhood may be ennobling, but not that it is profitable. Moral victories are things that saints, not statesmen, should covet, and in any case only for themselves. Statesmen, who are entrusted with the safety and liberty of their people, should be concerned first with the strategic high ground. If, in addition, it affords a view of any nearby moral heights, so much the better.

The New Republic, December 12, 1983

The Three Faces of Terror

MUCH OF THE CURRENT DEBATE ABOUT TERRORISM IS CONFOUNDED BY disagreement about what terrorism is. Some of this disagreement is ideological, the desire for the political advantage that comes from painting the other man's freedom fighter as just another terrorist. Some of it, though, derives from the assumption that terrorism is a static or unitary phenomenon. It is not. All terrorism falls under the category of political violence directed against noncombatants. But modern terrorism, born in the postwar world (before World War II, terrorism consisted mainly of political assassination), has undergone a remarkable evolution. At least three distinct types are distinguishable, and each yields a radically different answer to the important questions about terrorism: where it comes from, how serious a threat it is, what should be done about it.

The first type, which might be called classical terrorism, was an extension of war by other means. As practiced by the FLN in Algeria and the NLF in Vietnam, it differed from classical warfare by deliberately targeting civilians. The strategy was to demoralize the population, cause a collapse of public order and hasten the capitulation of the government. The justification was weakness: against a foe superior in technology and power, attacking the defenseless was deemed a military necessity.

Of course, there were bloody-minded philosophers, like Sartre, who defended indiscriminate political murder (by the FLN) with a touch of romance, as *existential* necessity: "To shoot down a European is to kill two birds with one stone, to destroy an oppressor and the man he oppresses at the same time: there remains a dead man and a free man." To which Michael Walzer responded that if Sartre were right and the only way for an Algerian to liberate himself was to kill a European, then the full liberation of Algeria should have required the importation of vast numbers of Frenchmen. By and large, however, except for the occasional Sartrean excursion into sophistry, military necessity—not philosophical authenticity —was the claim of classical terrorism.

By the end of the 1960s, when most of the globe had been decolonized and the wars of liberation won, there emerged an entirely new kind of terrorism: an extension of politics by other means. Its quintessential act was the PLO airplane hijacking, its *reductio ad absurdum* the Moluccan train murders.

This new kind of terrorism differed from its classical forebear in three critical ways. First, *context.* Classical terrorism occurred in the midst of a war; the new kind occurred in the complete absence of real military confrontation. To compensate for that misfortune, the new terrorist often dressed himself up in the trappings of war. Hence, for example, the "communiqué." War was for him, alas, an aspiration only. Second, *objective.* Classical terrorism was designed to panic and demoralize; the new kind aimed to publicize. The PLO seized planes to spread its name and its cause, not fear. In fact, some terrorists—like the Croatians who seized Yugoslav hostages and demanded that newspapers publish their manifesto, and nothing more—sought publicity only. Third, *audience.* In classical terrorism the victim, his class and his kinsmen made up the audience. In the new terrorism there was a radical dissociation between the target of the violence and the target of the message. The PLO hijackings were not addressed to the victims, not even to the enemy (Israel), but to the world. The content of the act was irrelevant. Only the form—violence, sudden and random—mattered. The attack itself lacked even symbolic purpose. It was a mere vehicle: the lure, the entertainment if you will, that earned the terrorist access to the world. This kind of terrorism was, at heart, pure media terrorism.

In this curious incarnation, terrorism became a form of political advertising. Barred from buying television time, the enterprising revolutionary decided to barter for it. Like the early commercial sponsors who produced their own television dramas in order to be able to show their ads, the media terrorists provided irresistible action—kidnapping and murder, live—in return for a chance to air their message.

The message was not lost on others with a cause and no army. In 1975, Moluccan terrorists hijacked a Dutch train and, before the cameras, shot a random traveler and threw his body off the train. In a recent interview with the *Wall Street Journal,* one of the Moluccans explained: "We saw Arafat at the U.N. He was succeeding, and no one even knew about us." To be known: the raison d'être of media terrorism.

By the end of the 1970s, media terrorism was in decline. One reason was simple boredom. There are only so many variations on a theme, no matter how grisly, and it was becoming increasingly difficult to come up with new life-defying feats of derring-do to justify a camera crew.

Furthermore, the major practitioners of the art, and their causes, had by then already achieved international celebrity. Media terrorism had succeeded, but only as far as it could go. Being known doesn't win you anything; it prepares you to win. Arafat, for example, had now to *do* something with his renown. (He tried, in South Lebanon.)

In its place has arisen in the 1980s yet another species: state-sponsored terrorism, an extension now (the echoes are more ancient) of diplomacy by other means. The means are assassination. The 1978 umbrella murder of Georgi Markov by Bulgarian agents in London was considered at the time a deplorable show of excessive zeal on the part of the Bulgarian secret services. It turned out to be target practice. Consider the events of this decade: the Rangoon bombing aimed at the entire political leadership of South Korea; the attempt on the life of the Pope; the attacks on Jordanian envoys on three continents by Syrian agents around the time of the Arafat-Hussein talks of 1983; the assassination of Bashir Gemayel, again by Syrian agents; the Kuwaiti bombings by Iranian agents; the shooting of a British policewoman from the Libyan Embassy. Applying the model of internal repression to foreign policy, state-sponsored terrorism declares the world to be its shooting gallery. Enemies of the people, never safe in the land of tyrants, are now denied asylum anywhere.

The elements of terror have changed again. The objective is neither panic nor publicity, but, purely and simply, the elimination of enemies, preferably enemy leaders. The audience? No audience. State-sponsored terror not only doesn't need journalists, it seeks to hide from them. It does not want the tangled route of plot and subplot to be followed back to national capitals. As for context, we are back to war: a bitter armistice in Korea; a "state of war" (to quote General Jaruzelski) in Poland; a series of wars between Syria and Jordan; Syria's war for Lebanon; an Arab-Persian, Sunni-Shiite war in the Persian Gulf; Libya's war against all. And, in London, cold war.

These are curiously old-fashioned interstate wars. There is no pretense of decolonization or national liberation. The means are old-fashioned, too, a sinister throwback to the prehistory of terrorism, when the speciality was political assassination. But with a critical difference: now it is the work not of revolutionary idealists, but of the most cynical (often hired) thugs, acting in the name of the coldest realpolitik.

The rise of state-sponsored terrorism is worth noting because it radically alters the answers to the important questions about terrorism. First, it puts an end to the endless discussions of the last two decades about origins: hunger, poverty, disease and oppression vs. subversion. For the new terrorism, the origin is a directive; the reason, a reason of state. Second, it provides a short answer to the question of the importance of terrorism: unlike its predecessors, a single act of the new terrorism has the potential to change history. (Consider how much American history was changed by the murder of John F. Kennedy.) And finally, it suggests that the old remedies—from counterinsurgency to land reform—are no longer relevant. The response must be at an international level: sanctions, boycott, quarantine or worse. The new terrorism is war at long distance, and war is an inherently bilateral affair.

The New Republic, August 13–20, 1984

Pro Contras

JUDGING FROM THE MEDIA HOOPLA IN GENEVA, ONE MIGHT HAVE thought it was Anwar Sadat returned to Jerusalem. Yet while the network anchors camped in Geneva, the real story of the week was developing in Managua. The socialist world was gathering for its biggest gala since Ethiopia's $100 million party for Colonel Mengistu. Yesterday, the blessed event: Daniel Ortega was sworn in as Nicaragua's first Leninist president.

Geneva is the place where the United States manages a bilateral relationship of fixed hostility. Managua is the place where another such relationship, this time with a country on the American mainland, is about to be born. For Americans, that is worrying. It means a permanent foreign policy headache. For Nicaraguan democrats it is worse. It means losing their country.

That prospect has become so imminent since Nicaragua's elections last November that the country's most respected opposition leader has made a momentous about-face. In one of the least-appreciated but most important Central American developments of 1984, Arturo Cruz—lifelong anti-Somocist, former junta member and ambassador to the United States—has come out in support of the *contras*.

Cruz had broken with the Sandinistas in 1982, as their rule became increasingly totalitarian. He returned to Nicaragua last year to challenge Ortega for the presidency. He was received by tumultuous crowds, but finally withdrew from the elections when Sandinista harassment convinced him they were designed for show only.

Cruz's conversion is particularly significant because he represents the best of Nicaragua's once vital democratic center. Unlike El Salvador, where constructing a center is like creating life in a test tube, Nicaragua had a developed middle class, widespread commercial activity and an independent peasantry. But the political center, anti-Somocist and anti-Communist, is now being destroyed. Only last week, another democratic leader, Pedro Joaqim Chamorro, editor of the opposition paper, *La Prensa* went into exile.

For Cruz, the final step, support for civil war, was not easy. But after the phony election and the severe repression that followed, he decided that the only remaining obstacle to a Leninist dictatorship was the *contras*. He is now asking Congress not to cut off their aid.

The last Congress did just that. It took its reasons where it could find them. An early charge, that the *contras* are Somocistas, is hardly heard these days. Not just because a man of Cruz's credentials declares they represent "the revolt of Nicaraguans against oppression by other Nicaraguans," but because it is evident that one doesn't raise an army of 10,-000–15,000 peasants with promises of restoring a universally despised dictatorship.

The size of that army blunts a second argument: the *contras* cannot win. So large a force (about twice the size of the Salvadoran guerrilla force, in a country with a bit more than half the population) is a measure of the depth of popular discontent with the repression and economic ruin brought about by the Sandinistas. (The can't-win complaint is doubly curious in that Congress legally forbids the administration to support the overthrow of the Sandinistas, i.e., win.)

A further fear is that the *contras* will draw the United States into war. But as the recent MiG scares show, nothing is more likely to force American military intervention than the consolidation of an aggressive, highly militarized, pro-Soviet regime in the area. The *contras* want to do their own fighting. Cut them off and the only body in the hemisphere able to restrain the Sandinistas will be the U.S. Army.

To deal with this obvious dilemma, congressional Democrats have taken up a chant: Contadora. If it means anything, it means this: Nicaragua's frightened neighbors are to solve for themselves the problem of taming its enormous military. They are to do so with a parchment barrier: The Sandinistas are given free rein within their borders, and in return, they promise not to trespass on anyone else's.

Now, we have experience with Sandinista parchment. In 1979 they pledged to the OAS to establish an open, democratic and pluralistic society. "One can Finlandize a democracy," says a former Sandinista foreign policy adviser. "To think one can Finlandize a totalitarian country is pure fantasy."

The administration, on the other hand, engages in surrealism. It justifies its support of the *contras* on the truly absurd grounds of interdicting arms shipments to El Salvador. After four years and millions of dollars, an army of thousands has yet to produce so much as a smuggled rifle for its efforts. So the administration is gearing up to focus on the Soviet arms buildup, surely an important issue. But not the primary one. To build a case on Soviet weaponry is to make the argument unnecessarily circular: many of those arms are needed to fight the *contras*!

Why can't the administration give it straight? Say it supports the *contras* because there is no other conceivable way to move Ortega's Nicaragua to pluralism. And because a pluralist Nicaragua is the only conceivable guarantor of peace in the region. Is it so hard, at a time when anti-Communist guerrillas are fighting in at least four parts of the world, for Americans, of all people, to develop a theory of legitimate, democratic revolution? And is it so hard to see the connection between a Leninist Nicaragua and chronic instability in Central America?

The objective need not be overthrown. What Cruz and his fellow democrats hope for is an opening for the center. A place, forced if necessary, for democrats in the governance of the country. Cruz calls it national reconciliation. Others call it power sharing. By whatever name, it means genuinely free elections, and a constitution that ensures that power is not monopolized by one party.

That, not Contadora, not a temporary deal with Ortega—that and nothing else short of the Marines—will ensure stability in Central America.

The great moral dilemmas of American foreign policy arise when the pursuit of security and the pursuit of democracy clash. *Contra* aid is not such a case. That is Cruz's message. Is anyone listening?

The Washington Post, January 11, 1985

Four Questions
for President Mubarak

IN THE LAST FEW WEEKS, EGYPT HAS BEEN ALL DIPLOMATIC MOTION, sending secret envoys to Israel and throwing up a variety of peace proposals. Israeli officials, starved for any hint of warmth from Egypt, are required to give any Egyptian gesture the benefit of the doubt. Americans, who are not so desperate, need not be so diplomatic. As partners to Camp David, they have a right to ask questions. The first is: Could there be a connection between this sudden peace offensive and President Mubarak's arrival tomorrow in Washington?

Mubarak comes to Washington to ask for $3.15 billion, plus forgiveness of unpaid interest on Egypt's $4.5 billion military debt. But he will have to mollify Congress, which is in no mood to grant him the money. That is because American largess was our part of the deal at Camp David. For its part, Egypt promised the United States two things: strategic cooperation with the United States and normal relations with Israel.

Congress will ask Question 2: What has happened to strategic cooperation? Its symbol was to be the Ras Banas naval base in southeastern Egypt. Sadat had promised President Carter military facilities at Ras Banas. The United States envisioned it as a staging ground for the Rapid Deployment Force. Mubarak scrapped the whole project. The reason is not sinister. Mubarak simply does not want to be closely associated with the United States, both for domestic and Third World reasons. As Prime Minister Kamal Hassan Ali once said, "We take weapons from the United States, but we are not aligned to the United States." How non-aligned? The United States asked Egypt to allow a Voice of America transmitter on its soil. Mubarak said no even to that. (It will be placed in Israel instead). Fair enough. Egypt is, as we say here, a free country. But if no quid, why our $3 billion quo?

The other half of the Camp David bargain was to be this: Israel gives up Sinai, a buffer zone three times its own size and its only source of oil; Egypt gives normal relations (the verb is strange, but so is the deal) and sends an ambassador to Tel Aviv. Question 3: How are relations and where is the ambassador?

Answer: The ambassador was recalled to Egypt over two years ago, and cultural, commercial and scientific agreements are nearly frozen. As Butros Ghali, Egypt's minister of state for foreign affairs, put it, relations are in a state of "cold peace."

Now, when the United States sponsored Camp David, it did not press Israel to give up all of Sinai for non-belligerency. Israel already had non-belligerency. That was guaranteed not only by the Sinai II disengagement accord of 1975, but by the preponderance of Israel's deterrent power. Israel gave up Sinai for normal relations. Not for the material benefits such relations would bring—they are hardly worth a tenth of the lost oil revenues alone—but because the example of open, routine commerce between Egyptian and Jew might persuade other Arabs to seek coexistence with Israel.

Egypt blames cold peace on the Lebanon war. However convenient an excuse that may once have been—in fact, the freezing of relations began long before Lebanon and accelerated with the Sadat assassination—it rings false now. Israel, under a Labor Prime Minister, is leaving Lebanon. (Likud committed Israel to withdrawing as far back as May 1983, in the treaty negotiated by Secretary of State George Shultz.) Furthermore, Shimon Peres is open to compromise on the West Bank, another "warming" condition recently created by Mubarak.

Well, says Egypt, Israel is still illegally holding Taba. Taba is a dot on the map. In fact, it is in dispute because, when the map was drawn in 1906, the lines were drawn in pencil. All of Taba lies under the width of the pencil mark! Suppose Taba did belong to Egypt. Israel gave up 61,000 square kilometers in Sinai. Taba is less than one.

For returning 99.99 percent of the land, what has Israel gotten? Israel has an embassy in Cairo with an Israeli flag flying over it. But the Israeli mission is totally ostracized by Egyptian society. The ghettoized Israeli Embassy in Cairo mirrors precisely the position of the Israeli state in the larger Arab world: an alien presence in quarantine. If that is what Israel gets for Camp David, then, in fairness, it should have given up Taba and kept the rest of Sinai.

We are now in the midst of a mini-peace enthusiasm. The Mubarak peace offensive, however, is unusually empty, even by Middle East standards. He asks the United States to start a "peace process" by negotiating with a Jordanian-PLO delegation. This is a transparent attempt to get the United States to deal with the PLO, without the PLO's renouncing terror and recognizing Israel (America's longstanding condition for such talks). It is also a way to get Hussein off the hook of direct talks with Israel.

If the "process" is nothing more than maneuver, what of the "peace"? The peace everyone will be talking about next week is ultimately to be brought about, all will agree, by the "land for peace" formula. Well, land for peace is not just theory. It now has a history. That history—Camp David—suggests a final question, not only for Mubarak but for others eager to press Israel into new and riskier concessions: We can all see the land. Mubarak has Sinai. Where is the peace?

The Washington Post, March 8, 1985

Chernenko: Soul on Ice

THERE HAVE BEEN MANY ARGUMENTS MADE AGAINST ATHEISM. THE medieval philosophers divined a variety of proofs of God's existence. Aquinas had five. But the argument from Motion or the argument from Contingency is not the kind of thing we moderns talk about anymore. So for the definitive modern case against atheism, I suggest a radically modern experience: watch a Soviet funeral.

I do it all the time. As Soviet state funerals have become regular events —Chernenko's was the third revival in twenty-eight months of Death of a Helmsman—I have become a regular viewer. They mesmerize me, in a horrible sort of way. It is not just the music, the numbing repetition of Chopin's funeral march, but the massive, stone-cold setting. The Lenin Mausoleum, the focus of the ceremonies, is a model of socialist brutalist architecture. Cathedrals also remind us of the smallness of man, but poignantly, by comparing him to God. The Lenin Mausoleum has nothing to compare man to but its own squat vastness. The comparison is mocking.

Then there are the speeches, a jangle of empty phrases. Chernenko was eulogized for his "links to the masses," his "party principledness," his achievements in the fields of "ideology and propaganda." Was there a man behind—underneath—all this socialist realism? If so, not a word about him. The utter effacement of the person by the party reminded me of a response spokesman Vladimir Posner gave a few weeks ago to an American's question about Chernenko's health. "In this country," he said, annoyed, "the private lives of the leadership . . . are not subject to discussion." It was as if he had been asked to confirm Chernenko's sexual preferences, not his existence.

Finally, and to me most chilling, was the open casket displaying Chernenko's (and Andropov's and Brezhnev's) powdered body afloat in a sea of fresh flowers. The open bier is a mere variation on a Communist theme: the mummification of the great leader. In believing cultures, where there is some sense of a surviving soul, this pathetic attachment to the body is unnecessary. In fact, it is discouraged. In the great monotheistic religions, the redeemer—Moses, Jesus, Mohammed—has no earthly resting place at all. In the great materialist religions, Soviet and Chinese communism, the resting place of the redeemer, indeed his frozen body, becomes a shrine. The result is the ultimate grotesquerie: after death, a fantastic assertion of the final primacy of man, even after he has become nothing more than embalmer's clay.

It turns out I'm not the only one to have been chilled by the barrenness of the Soviet way of death. Shortly after his return from Brezhnev's funeral, George Bush talked about what had struck him the most. He mentioned the austere pageantry, the goose-stepping soldiers, the music, "the body being drawn through Red Square—not, incidentally, by horses, but behind an armored personnel carrier. But what struck me most . . . was the fact that from start to finish there was not one mention of —God."

Why should that matter? you ask. After all, many of us are as tepid in our belief as the proverbial Unitarian who believes that there is, at most, one God. What is wrong with a society that believes in none? The usual answer follows the lines of an observation by Arthur Schlesinger (and many others) that "the declining faith in the supernatural has been accompanied by the rise of the monstrous totalitarian creeds of the 20th century." Or as Chesterton put it, "The trouble when people stop believing in God is not that they thereafter believe in nothing; it is that they thereafter believe in anything." In this century, "anything" has included Hitler, Stalin and Mao, authors of the great genocidal madnesses of our time.

However, as the robotic orderliness of Chernenko's funeral demonstrates, the Soviet system is not anything but mad. The "monstrous creeds" have changed. Totalitarianism was once a truly crusading faith: messianic, hopeful, mobilized and marching. Now it is dead, burnt out. Classical totalitarianism has been replaced by what philosopher Michael Walzer calls "failed totalitarianism," the cold empty shell of the old madness: the zeal, the energy, the purpose are gone; only bureaucracy and cynicism remain. Today the Soviet system, the greatest of all the failed totalitarianisms, no longer believes in "anything." It now believes in nothing. A nothing on eerie display at Chernenko's funeral.

Chesterton's case against atheism is that even if it is (God forbid) true, it is dangerous. Three hours of watching Chernenko placed in the Kremlin wall convinces me otherwise. The case against a public life bereft of all spirituality rests less on its danger than on its utter desolation.

The Washington Post, March 15, 1985

The Reagan Doctrine

We must not break faith with those who are risking their
lives on every continent from Afghanistan to Nicaragua to
defy Soviet-supported aggression and secure rights which
have been ours from birth . . . Support for freedom fighters
is self-defense.

PRESIDENT REAGAN,
The State of the Union address, February 1985

RONALD REAGAN IS THE MASTER OF THE NEW IDEA, AND HAS BUILT THE
most successful political career in a half century, launching one after
another. His list of credits includes small government (Barry Goldwater
having tried, and failed, with it first), supplyside economics and strategic
defense (Star Wars). These radically changed the terms of debate on the
welfare state, economic theory and nuclear strategy. All that was left for
him to turn on its head was accepted thinking on geopolitics. Now he has
done that too. He has produced the Reagan Doctrine.

You may not have noticed. Doctrines, like submarines, tend to be
launched with fanfare. The Monroe Doctrine was instantly recognized, on
both sides of the Atlantic, as a historic declaration; the Truman Doctrine
was unveiled in a dramatic address to a joint session of Congress; and when
President Carter announced a new aggressive Persian Gulf policy on Janu-

ary 23, 1980, by the next morning the New York *Times* had dubbed it "the Carter Doctrine." President Reagan saw fit to bury his doctrine in his 1985 State of the Union address beneath the balanced budget amendment, school prayer and the line-item veto. That he decided to make his a footnote is as much a tribute to Mr. Reagan's prudence as to his modesty. Truly new ideas—what Democrats lie awake at night dreaming of—are as risky as they are rare. This one has already precipitated a storm.

The Reagan Doctrine proclaims overt and unashamed American support for anti-Communist revolution. The grounds are justice, necessity and democratic tradition. Justice, said the President in his February 16 radio address, because these revolutionaries are "fighting for an end to tyranny." Necessity, said Secretary of State George Shultz in a subsequent address in San Francisco, because if these "freedom fighters" are defeated, their countries will be irrevocably lost behind an Iron Curtain of Soviet domination. And democratic tradition, said the President, because to support "our brothers" in revolution is to continue—"in Afghanistan, in Ethiopia, Cambodia, Angola . . . [and] Nicaragua"—200 years of American support for "Simón Bolívar . . . the Polish patriots, the French Resistance and others seeking freedom."

That tradition ended abruptly with Vietnam. It is true that President Carter sent arms to the Afghan rebels and that Congress concurred. Congress has also gone along with economic aid to the non-Communist resistance in Cambodia. However, since the Clark Amendment of 1976 prohibiting aid to anti-Marxist fighters in Angola, Congress has refused to support war against indigenous Communist dictatorships, no matter how heavily supported by the Soviet Union or its proxies. President Reagan's program of CIA support for the Nicaraguan *contras,* who are not fighting foreign occupation, broke post-Vietnam precedent. At first, and for three long years, that new policy was given the flimsiest of justifications: interdicting supplies to the Salvadoran guerrillas. The Reagan Doctrine drops the fig leaf. It is intended to establish a new, firmer—a doctrinal—foundation for such support by declaring equally worthy all armed resistance to communism, whether foreign or indigenously imposed.

To interpret the Reagan Doctrine as merely a puffed-up rationale for Nicaraguan policy is like calling the Truman Doctrine a cover for a new Greek and Turkish policy. In both cases, the principles established have a much more profound implication.

The Truman Doctrine set out the basic foreign policy axiom of the postwar era: containment. With J.F.K.'s pledge to "bear any burden . . . to assure . . . the success of liberty," the idea of containment reached its most expansive and consensually accepted stage. With Vietnam, the consensus and the expansiveness collapsed. Since then the U.S. has oscillated, at times erratically, between different approaches—different doctrines—for defending its ideals and its interests.

The Reagan Doctrine is the third such attempt since Vietnam. The first was the Nixon Doctrine: relying on friendly regimes to police their regions. Unfortunately, the jewel in the crown of this theory was the Shah of Iran. Like him, it was retired in 1979 to a small Panamanian island. Next came the Carter Doctrine, declaring a return to unilateral American action, if necessary, in defense of Western interests. That doctrine rested on the emergence of a rapid deployment force. Unfortunately, the force turned out neither rapid nor deployable. It enjoys a vigorous theoretical existence in southern Florida, whence it is poorly situated to repel the Red Army.

If regional powers prove unstable, and projected American power unreliable, what then? It is a precious irony that the answer to that question has been suggested to Americans by a band of fanatical Islamic warriors in Afghanistan. Unaware of their historic contribution to the theory of containment, they took on the Soviet army, made it bleed and slowed its march to the more coveted goal, the warm waters of the Persian Gulf.

This insurgency, and those in Cambodia, Angola and Nicaragua, pointed to a new form of containment, a kind of ex post facto containment: harassment of Soviet expansionism at the limits of empire. There is an echo here of the old 1950s right-wing idea of "rolling back" communism. But with a difference. This is not the reckless—and toothless—call for reclaiming the core Soviet possessions in Eastern Europe, which the Soviets claim for self-defense and, more important, which they are prepared to use the most extreme means to retain. This is a challenge to the peripheral acquisitions of empire.

The Brezhnev Doctrine proclaimed in 1968 that the Soviet sphere only expands. The Reagan Doctrine is meant as its antithesis. It declares that the U.S. will work at the periphery to reverse that expansion. How? Like the Nixon Doctrine, it turns to proxies. Unlike the Nixon Doctrine, it supports not the status quo but revolution.

And that makes it so hard for both left and right to digest. For the left it seems all quite paradoxical, and hypocritical: the administration denounces Salvadoran guerrillas for blowing up power stations and attacking villages, while at the same time it supports Nicaraguan guerrillas who are doing the same thing only a few miles away. But the idea that intellectual honesty requires one to be for or against all revolution is absurd. You judge a revolution, as you do any other political phenomenon, by what it stands for. Suppose you believe that justice was on the side of the central government in the American Civil War. Does that commit you to oppose the

Paris Commune of 1870 or the Hungarian revolution of 1956? In Salvador, the rebels want to overthrow the President, a Christian Democrat. In Nicaragua, the rebels want to overthrow the President, a Marxist-Leninist. To judge rebels by who they are and what they fight for, and against, is not a political morality of convenience. It is simple logic.

On the right, the idea of supporting revolution is equally hard to accept, though for different reasons. Conservatives may find it easier to support revolution in practice than in theory. This is already obvious from their choice of words. Reagan finds it hard to call the good guys rebels. Instead, he insists on calling them "freedom fighters," a heavy, inconvenient term, with an unmistakable socialist-realist ring. "Freedom fighters" practically announces itself as a term of bias. Rebels, Mr. President. With practice, it will get easier to say.

Language, however, is the easier problem facing the Reagan Doctrine. Morality poses thornier ones. By what right does the U.S. take sides in foreign civil wars? What about sovereignty? What about international law?

The President may be revolutionary, but he is not reckless. To ensure that he does not stray too far from current thinking, he appends a reference to international law: "Support for freedom fighters is self-defense and totally consistent with the OAS and U.N. charters."

This, it must be admitted, is stretching things. There are two difficulties. How can one plausibly argue that the success of Islamic rebels in Afghanistan is a form of self-defense of the U.S.? The Nicaraguan *contras,* perhaps, might qualify under a generous interpretation of collective security. But Cambodian rebels? Angolans? Eritreans?

The second problem is that if international law stands for anything, it stands for the idea that sovereignty is sacred. Rebels, by definition, do not have it. The governments they fight, no matter how tyrannous, do. How, ask congressional critics, can one justify violating the sovereignty of other countries by helping overthrow the legitimate government?

The answer must begin with cases. Consider Uganda under Idi Amin. Amin was the legitimate ruler when Tanzania invaded and overthrew him. The Tanzanians might say that this was in response to Ugandan border incursions, but Amin had ordered his troops withdrawn more than a month before Tanzania's action. In any case, if repelling a trespass at the border was the problem, Tanzania should have stopped there. It hardly had to drive to Kampala and install the leader of its choice. Tanzania's action was a violation of Ugandan sovereignty. Yet it is hard to see how ridding the world of Amin can be said to be wrong.

Morally speaking—and congressional critics of the Reagan Doctrine are speaking morally, above all—sovereignty cannot be absolute. Indeed, it is not a moral category at all. Why must it be accorded respect, moral respect, in cases where it protects truly awful regimes? The Nazis were the legitimate government of Germany. That does not mean that one is justified in overthrowing any government one does not like. It does mean that one has to face the crucial question: How awful must a government be before it forfeits the moral protection of sovereignty and before justice permits its violent removal?

In Congress today there is almost no opposition to supporting Afghan and (non-Communist) Cambodian rebels. There is a consensus that resistance to invasion warrants support. But by what logic should support be denied to those fighting indigenous tyranny? It seems curious to decide the morality of a cause on the basis of the address of its chief oppressors.

There are more relevant criteria. First, the nature of the oppression and the purposes of those fighting it. The difference between El Salvador and Nicaragua is that, in Salvador, a fledgling democracy is under attack from avowed Marxist-Leninists. In Nicaragua, a fledgling totalitarianism is under attack by a mixture of forces, most of which not only are pledged to democracy and pluralism but fought for just those goals in the original revolution against Somoza.

A second important distinction is whether the insurgency is an authentic popular movement or a proxy force cobbled together by a great power for reasons of realpolitik. In both Salvador and Nicaragua, the governments say their opponents are puppets of different imperialisms. In neither case does the charge stick. Consider Nicaragua. As no less a democrat than Arturo Cruz, leader of the (nonviolent) opposition, writes, the *contras* now represent an authentic "social movement." Indeed, they are more than 12,000 strong and growing, even after the cutoff of American aid.

If a revolution is both popular and democratic, it is hard to see the moral objection to extending it support. But there is a practical objection: if every country decided for itself which revolutions to support, there would be chaos. What about the prudential reasons for respecting sovereignty and international law?

This argument has the virtue of recognizing that international law is not moral law but an arrangement of convenience: like the social contract in civil society, it is a way to keep the peace. This argument has the vice, however, of ignoring the fact that, unlike the domestic social contract, international law lacks an enforcer. It depends on reciprocal observance. If one country breaks the rules at will, then later claims its protection, what —apart from habit and cowardice—can possibly oblige other countries to honor that claim?

The idea that international law must be a reciprocal arrangement or none at all is not new. As Churchill said to Parliament in 1940, "Germany is to gain one set of advantages by breaking all the [neutrality] rules [upon the seas] . . . and then go on and gain another set of advantages through insisting, whenever it suits her, upon the strictest interpretation of the international code she has torn to pieces." He added, "It is not at all odd that His Majesty's government are getting rather tired of it. I am getting rather tired of it myself."

So is today's American government. There is something faintly comical about Nicaragua going to the World Court to accuse the U.S. of fomenting revolution and interfering in its affairs, when for years the Salvadoran revolution was quite openly headquartered in Managua—and not for a shortage of housing in the Salvadoran jungles.

The Reagan Doctrine is more radical than it pretends to be. It pretends that support for democratic rebels is "self-defense" and sanctioned by international law. That case is weak. The real case rests instead on other premises: that to be constrained from supporting freedom by an excessive concern for sovereignty (and a unilateral concern, at that) is neither especially moral nor prudent. The West, of late, has taken to hiding behind parchment barriers as an excuse for inaction when oppressed democrats beg for help. The Reagan Doctrine, while still hiding a bit, announces an end to inaction.

Only a few months ago, a Nicaraguan friend, an ex-Sandinista who still speaks their language, said in near despair that the struggle of democrats around the world was doomed by the absence in the West of what he called "democratic militance." The Reagan Doctrine represents a first step toward its restoration.

Time, April 1, 1985

VI

DETERRENCE
AND
ITS ENEMIES

In Defense
of Deterrence

"SAFETY WILL BE THE STURDY CHILD OF TERROR, AND SURVIVAL THE TWIN brother of annihilation." That was Winston Churchill's description of what he called "the balance of terror." Each superpower has the ability to incinerate the defenseless population of the other many times over; each refrains from attacking because it fears retaliation in kind; each knows that aggression is tantamount to suicide. That is deterrence. And deterrence has prevented the outbreak of nuclear war, indeed any war, between the United States and the Soviet Union for a generation.

Living in a world of deterrence is very uncomfortable. Every American and Soviet city dweller knows that he is targeted for destruction by nuclear weapons five thousand miles away. But the physical danger is only part of the problem. The world of deterrence is a world of paradoxes. Weapons are built in order never to be used. Weapons purely for defense of helpless populations, like the antiballistic missile systems, can become a threat to peace. Weapons aimed at people lessen the risk of war; weapons aimed at weapons increase it.

The strains of living in such a world are enormous. A vast antinuclear movement is now rising in the U.S., animated principally by weariness and revulsion with this arrangement. Why now? Ronald Reagan is much of the answer. He helped defeat the SALT II treaty before his election, and has been reluctant to engage the Soviets in strategic arms talks since. For the first time in more than a decade, the U.S. and the Soviet Union are not engaged in negotiations to control strategic nuclear weapons. Worse, Mr. Reagan and some of his advisers have spoken in frighteningly offhand ways about "limited nuclear war" and nuclear warning shots. The Carter administration's mobile MX plan played a part, too. It appeared such an enormously cumbersome and expensive contrivance that people began to wonder if the experts had not lost touch with reality. So millions of Americans have decided it is time for them to take the problem into their own hands, and an antinuclear grass-roots crusade has emerged.

Like all crusades, it has its bible: Jonathan Schell's just published *The Fate of the Earth*; and its banner: the freeze. Recently it even acquired an auxiliary brigade, four members of the American foreign policy establishment who opened a wholly new front by calling for a U.S. renunciation of any first use of nuclear weapons. The bible, the banner and the brigade approach the nuclear dilemma from different directions, but they all challenge the established doctrines of deterrence. The brigade wants to limit deterrence; the freeze proponents want to ignore it; and Jonathan Schell wants to abolish it. Each deserves the closest scrutiny.

Jonathan Schell flatly rejects deterrence. That is the source of his originality. Otherwise his three-part thesis is unremarkable. Part I restates, albeit elegantly, the awful details of a nuclear holocaust, and concludes that it would lead to the extinction of the human race. (That is the view of some scientists, though not of the National Academy of Sciences' study which Schell used in reaching many of his conclusions.)

Part II, an interminable rumination on the meaning of human extinction, comes to the unsurprising conclusion that extinction would be monstrous. "From the foregoing, it follows," Schell writes, after delivering his message in a reiterative style that constitutes its own kind of overkill, "that there can be no justification for extinguishing mankind."

The real interest in Schell's book lies in Part III, "The Choice." Here he argues that traditional approaches to nuclear peril, like strategic arms limitation treaties, are mere gestures, aspirin given to a dying patient. He argues that deterrence is a logical fraud because the leaders of a country that had sustained a first strike would have no reason to retaliate—indeed, no country in whose name to retaliate.

What Schell refuses to acknowledge is that any potential aggressor would be deterred—and for over thirty years has been deterred—from striking first because he must anticipate not only the logical responses of the victim, but all possible human responses. Revenge, for example, is one motive to launch a second strike. Paul Warnke, President Carter's arms control chief, gives another. He argues that "our moral commitment" would "require that the leaders who had perpetrated this enormity not be allowed to inherit the earth and bend its people to their will." Soviet leaders reading Warnke (a nuclear dove and a supporter of the freeze) are highly unlikely to calculate that a first strike would meet with no response because that would be "illogical." Furthermore, no one knows what would happen in the confused, unimaginably strained atmosphere of a nuclear crisis. To act—to attack—under the assumption that the other side is constrained to follow purely "logical" courses of action is itself totally illogical. It is precisely because of these calculations that nuclear deterrence has succeeded in preventing nuclear war. That is not to say that deterrence can never fail, but the argument from history is a powerful one. An even more powerful one is the absence of an alternative.

Not that Schell shies away from providing one: a world graced by total disarmament (nuclear and conventional), the abolition of violence, the eradication of national boundaries, the renunciation of sovereignty, and the founding of a new world political order for the peaceful settlement of international disputes. How does he propose to bring this about? That is a detail he could not work into his 231-page treatise. "I have left to others those awesome, urgent tasks."

Although he does not explain how we are to bring about a lion-and-lamb scenario which even Isaiah had the audacity only to predict and not to mandate, he does give us a clue as to what the operating principle of his post-messianic world will be. Here we come directly to the critical center of Schell's thinking, to the force that not only underlies his passion today but will save mankind tomorrow—fear. In his world, Schell writes, "Fear would no longer dictate particular decisions, such as whether or not the Soviet Union might place missiles in Cuba; rather, it would be a moving force behind the establishment of a new system by which every decision was made. And, having dictated the foundation of the system, it would stand guard over it forever after, guaranteeing that the species did not slide back toward anarchy and doom." I have my doubts.

Fear is not just the saving principle of Schell's new world order; it is the animating force behind a new mass movement—the freeze campaign. The movement demands a mutual halt in the development, production, and deployment of all nuclear weapons, "because," as the campaign slogan puts it, "no one wants a nuclear war." Like Schell, freeze proponents are deeply concerned, and rightly so, about the prospect of living in a world in which we have the capacity to blow ourselves to bits at any moment. The freeze crusade has enlisted hundreds of thousands of Americans by showing what happens if the sword of Damocles ever drops. Schell recognizes that removing this sword requires renunciation not just of overkill, but of minimal deterrence, of the simple capacity to destroy the other side *once.* But very few freeze proponents advocate reducing levels below "sufficiency," because they recognize that in a pre-messianic world this would destabilize the nuclear balance and increase the chances of war. Under a freeze—indeed, under even the most radical of arms proposals, such as former Ambassador George Kennan's proposal to cut nuclear levels in half—the superpowers would still retain the capacity for the total destruction of the other society. Insofar as people support the freeze because they can't stand the thought of being a target for Soviet missiles, they have joined the wrong movement. The freeze offers no solution to that problem. They should be with Jonathan Schell's total disarmament movement, working on the "awesome, urgent task" of remaking human nature.

Some might argue that there is another way, short of universal brotherhood, to remove the sword of Damocles. That is unilateral disarmament. But quite apart from the fact that such a move would mean the surrender of our values, it would do little to secure our survival. The historical record does not support the proposition that helplessness is a guarantee of safety. There has been one nuclear war on record; in it a nonnuclear Japan lost Hiroshima and Nagasaki. So far there has been only one biological war, the one going on today in Laos and Cambodia. These weapons, now used against helpless tribesmen, were never used against American troops fighting the same Vietnamese forces in the same place. The Hmong, unlike the Americans, lack the capacity to retaliate in kind.

The freeze is not unilateralist, nor do many of its advocates reject deterrence. They say they reject overkill. "Enough is enough," they say. "Why waste billions on useless weapons if all they will do, as Churchill said, is to make the rubble bounce?" (It is sometimes also argued, somewhat anomalously, that having useless, rubble-bouncing weapons is at the same time dangerous.)

The problem is that in their zeal to curb overkill, freeze advocates ignore the requirements of deterrence and, in particular, the requirement for survivability of the deterrent. Our weapons must be able to withstand a first strike and penetrate Soviet defenses in a retaliatory strike (and vice versa). If either side finds the survivability of its weapons systems declining, the world becomes less safe. In an international crisis, each side, particularly the more vulnerable side, has incentive to strike first: the invulnerable side to use its advantage, the vulnerable side to strike before it is too late.

What would happen under a freeze? The U.S. retaliatory capacity depends on the three legs of its strategic triad: the land-based ICBMS the bomber force and submarines. Because of the increasing accuracy, power and numbers of Soviet missiles, the U.S. land-based missile force will soon become vulnerable to a first strike. (It is precisely to eliminate that vulnerability that President Carter proposed hiding the MX in multiple shelters, a scheme now abandoned.) That leaves the bomber and submarine forces. The bomber force consists of aging B-52s that are increasingly vulnerable to attack while still on the ground, and to being shot down while trying to penetrate Soviet air space. Hence President Carter's decision to deploy air-launched cruise missiles, which would be better able to penetrate Soviet defenses and would allow the B-52s to remain outside Soviet air space. The freeze proposal would prevent deployment of these missiles. It would also prevent production and development of a new bomber, either the B-1 or the Stealth, which would be better able to elude destruction on the ground and Soviet defenses in the air. Note that the B-1 or the Stealth would not be any more destructive than the B-52. They would not make the rubble bounce any higher. They would simply be more likely to get to the target, and therefore present the Soviets with a very good reason never to launch a first strike.

That leaves the submarine force, which the United States is now in the process of modernizing to make more survivable. The new Tridents are quieter than existing subs, and because they have longer-range missiles they can hide in larger areas of the ocean. The freeze would stop their deployment.

The freeze, a proposal devised for its simplicity, does not deal very well with paradox. It is one of the paradoxes of deterrence that defensive weapons (the ABM, for example) can be more destabilizing and therefore more dangerous to peace than offensive weapons. The freeze fixates on nuclear weapons because they appear more terrible than others. And indeed they are. But they are not necessarily more destabilizing. As former Under Secretary of the Navy James Woolsey points out, the freeze does nothing to prevent nonnuclear antisubmarine and antiaircraft advances, which weaken deterrence. But it does prevent modernization of nuclear systems designed for survivability, which enhances deterrence.

What exactly does it mean to say that if survivability declines, war becomes more likely? One quick fix for a vulnerable deterrent is to adopt a policy of launch-on-warning: as soon as we detect enemy missiles leaving their silos, we launch our missiles before they can be destroyed. (Some officials unsuccessfully urged President Carter to adopt launch-on-warning as an alternative to building the mobile MX.) But this creates a hair-trigger situation, where the time for the world's most important decision is not a matter of minutes but of seconds, too short to check out a faulty radar reading or a misinterpretation of data. That's the price of ignoring deterrence.

This analysis looks simply at what would happen if the freeze were already a reality. But however fervently American citizens may wish it, they cannot vote a "mutual verifiable freeze" into existence. Unfortunately, that must be negotiated with the Soviets. And bad as a freeze would be as an end point, it would be worse as a U.S. negotiating position—which is exactly what it would be if, say, the Kennedy-Hatfield amendment were adopted. First, it is certain to delay other arms control initiatives. The freeze appeals to American voters because of its simplicity, but a mutual freeze would involve complex negotiations with the Soviets. What exactly would be frozen? At what stage? How would it be verified? The production, stockpiling and qualitative upgrading of nuclear weapons cannot be detected by satellite, and the Russians have always refused on-site inspection. That problem alone turns the freeze into either a nonstarter or a source of interminable negotiation.

Ironically, there does exist an arms control proposal which, though very complicated, poorly understood by the American people and unsuited for two-hour ratification by town meetings, is very well understood by the Soviets: SALT II. They have already signed it. If the aim of the freeze movement is a quick, simple, bold move in arms control that would allow us to proceed to real reductions, then the answer is not a freeze, but SALT II. Representative Les Aspin has already pointed out with dismay the American penchant for reinventing the arms control wheel every four years. In 1977 President Carter rejected the Vladivostok Accords negotiated by President Ford and proposed drastic reductions instead. The Soviets rejected his proposal out of hand. It took more than two years to renegotiate SALT II on the original lines of Vladivostok. President Reagan in turn rejected SALT II and called for as yet unspecified START talks. The freeze proponents are doing precisely the same thing. It simply makes no sense to propose a freeze that would require years of negotiations when SALT II is at hand, has already been approved by the Soviets and could be adjusted in small details and ratified quickly. Of course, SALT is not as catchy a slogan as the freeze. But it is certainly a better, quicker and more serious path to arms control.

Another aim of the freeze campaign is to move to real reductions. But to arm a U.S. negotiating team with a freeze offer is to ensure that it will have no leverage with which to bargain the Soviets into reductions. We will have unilaterally announced our willingness to forgo all our modernization programs, like the Trident, the cruise missile and the Stealth bomber. The theory is that this gesture will elicit from the Soviets a more conciliatory negotiating position. The theory is in conflict with history. The Soviets do not have a good record of responding to unilateral gestures. At the Glassboro Summit in 1967, President Johnson tried to interest Premier Kosygin in ABM negotiations. Kosygin demurred. A year later, the Senate defeated an amendment to deny funds for an American ABM system. Three days later, Soviet Foreign Minister Andrei Gromyko announced the Soviets' willingness to negotiate arms control. Eventually they agreed to an almost total ban on ABMS. We are using the same strategy today in Geneva, offering systems that we propose to build as bargaining chips. We offer to forgo deployment of the Pershing II and ground-launched cruise missiles in Europe if the Soviets dismantle their SS-20s. Under a freeze, our position in Geneva would collapse and the SS-20s would remain in place. (Brezhnev calls *that* arrangement a freeze.) In strategic arms talks, any attempts on our part to, say, bargain away one of our new systems against the Soviets' destabilizing silo-killing ICBMs would fail.

The freeze is not a plan; it is a sentiment. (Montana's proposed freeze resolution, for example, opposes, "the production, development and deployment of nuclear weapons by any nation." It will unfortunately not be binding on President Zia of Pakistan.) The freeze reflects the deeply felt and wholly laudable wish of millions of Americans that something be done to control nuclear weapons. But when taken seriously as a plan, the freeze continually fails on its own terms. It seeks safety, but would jeopardize deterrence; it seeks quick action, but would delay arms control; it seeks real reductions, but removes any leverage we might have to bring them about.

Finally, it mistakes the most likely cause of an outbreak of nuclear war. In its fixation on numbers, the freeze assumes that somehow high weapons levels *in themselves* make war more likely. True, an uncontrolled arms race breeds suspicion between the superpowers and can increase the risk of war; but arms control measures (like SALT I or II) can allow higher levels, and still decrease the risk by building confidence on both sides and letting each know precisely what the other is doing. If nuclear war ever comes, it most likely will be not because the weapons fire themselves, but because some national leader, in order to preserve some national interest, orders them fired. When did we come closest to nuclear war in the last thirty-six years? In October 1962, when President Kennedy decided to threaten Khrushchev with war unless he obeyed our ultimatum on the Cuban missiles. In 1962 the level of nuclear arms was much lower than it is today. And when was the chance of nuclear war smallest? Probably at the height of detente, during the Apollo-Soyuz love fest, when U.S.-Soviet relations were good, even though each side had the capacity for multiple overkill.

The absolute level of nuclear weapons is only one factor, and a relatively small one at that, in determining the likelihood of nuclear war breaking out. (It is certainly less important than the balance of vulnerabilities on each side, i.e., the stability of deterrence.) The most likely source of nuclear war is from a regional conflict between the superpowers, where one or the other has important interests, but finds itself at a conventional disadvantage. That is the American situation today in Europe and in the Persian Gulf. To prevent the Soviets from taking advantage of their superiority in conventional arms, the U.S. has reserved the option of using nuclear weapons to respond to a nonnuclear Soviet attack. This policy of extending nuclear deterrence to conventional conflicts has kept the peace. But it is dangerous. It blurs the line between conventional and nuclear war, and by threatening "limited" nuclear war it opens the door to a nuclear holocaust, since no one knows whether a limited nuclear war can be kept limited. The most effective way to eliminate that danger, and thus eliminate the greatest existing risk of nuclear war, is to make this kind of extended deterrence unnecessary: to right the conventional balance by radically bolstering allied forces, particularly on the West European frontier. NATO could then deter a conventional attack without having to threaten to wage nuclear war.

One of Schell's dictums is that compared to the peril of a nuclear holocaust, all other human values pale into insignificance, indeed, lose their meaning because they lose their context. If the antinuclear crusaders really believe that, they should be clamoring for increased conventional forces to reduce the European imbalance. They aren't. The reason is that the freeze crusade, which springs from deeply felt antiwar and antiarmament sentiments, is not comfortable with the thought that preventing nuclear war may require a radically enlarged conventional defense. Furthermore, one of the major appeals of the antinuclear movement is the promise to halt the economic drain caused by "useless" nuclear weapons and to redirect resources to human needs. But a shift away from strategic to conventional weapons would be very expensive. Our reliance on nuclear weapons—and the current conventional balance in Europe—results in large part from a desire to *reduce* defense spending. In the 1950s we decided to buy defense in Europe on the cheap. Rather than match the vast armies and tank forces of the Warsaw Pact, we decided to go nuclear, because, as John Foster Dulles put it, it offered "more bang for the buck."

But the European defense balance has become more unstable since Dulles's day. In the 1950s the U.S. threatened "massive retaliation." If the Soviets crossed into Western Europe, we would attack the Russian homeland with a strategic nuclear strike. When the Russians acquired the same capacity against the U.S., that threat lost its credibility. The Kennedy administration adopted a new policy of "flexible response," a euphemism for a limited nuclear war. Under the new doctrine, the U.S. reserved the right to use theater nuclear weapons on the battlefield to thwart a conventional Soviet attack. That has been our policy ever since. (Ronald Reagan did not invent it, although he has the habit of throwing it around more casually and publicly than other Presidents.) This doctrine has troubled many Americans, but as long as the U.S. was not prepared to challenge the Soviet conventional superiority in Europe, nor prepared to abandon its European allies, there seemed no other choice.

Enter the auxiliary brigade of the antinuclear movement: four former high administration officials, two of whom, under President Kennedy, gave us "limited nuclear war" (Robert McNamara and McGeorge Bundy); one of whom gave us "containment" (George Kennan); and one of whom gave us SALT I (Gerard Smith). Two weeks ago they opened an entirely new front in the crusade. They called for the adoption of a "no-first-use" policy on nuclear weapons. It was a renunciation of "flexible response" and of "extended deterrence." (They would retain extended deterrence in one restricted sense: as a retaliation for a Soviet *nuclear* attack on Western Europe, an unlikely possibility since the Soviets are prepared to renounce first use, and since with their conventional advantage they have no reason to attack with nuclear weapons.)

The problem with folding our nuclear umbrella, as the four wise men themselves acknowledged, is that, unaccompanied by conventional rearmament, it means the end of the Western alliance and the abandonment in particular of West Germany to Soviet intimidation and blackmail. The other problem with a no-first-use policy is that it might paradoxically increase the chances of nuclear war. Today a war between the U.S. and the Soviets is deterred at its origin: since even the slightest conventional conflict between them carries the threat of escalating into a nuclear one, neither happens. The no-first-use policy moves the "firebreak" from the line dividing war from peace to the line dividing conventional war from nuclear war. It trades the increased chance of conventional war (because now less dangerous and more "thinkable") for a decreased chance of such a war becoming nuclear. But no one can guarantee that *in extremis*, faced with a massive Soviet invasion of Western Europe, the U.S. would stick to its no-first-use pledge. Thus, by making a European war thinkable, this policy could, whatever its intentions, lead to a nuclear war.

Unless, that is, we have the conventional forces to preserve the original firebreak between war and peace. Thus, to prevent both political and (possibly) nuclear calamity, a no-first-use pledge must be accompanied, indeed preceded, by a serious conventional buildup of Western forces on the European frontier. The problem with McNamara et al. is that although they acknowledge this need, they treat it very casually—certainly with nothing like the urgency with which they call for abandoning extended deterrence. They speak only vaguely of the need for "review" and "study" of conventional military needs, of whether the political will exists in the West for such a buildup, and of "whether we Americans have a durable and effective answer to our military manpower needs in the present all-volunteer active and reserve forces." (They cannot quite bring themselves to say the word "draft.") Their eagerness to be the first off the blocks with a no-first-use policy is obvious. Their reluctance to urge on their antinuclear allies the only responsible and safe (and costly) means of achieving it is lamentable. The result of their highly publicized, grossly unbalanced proposal is predictable: another support in the complex and high vulnerable structure of deterrence has been weakened. The world will be no safer for it.

Despite the prophesies of Schell, the pandering of the freeze-riding politicians and the posturing of the four wise men—and the good intentions of millions of concerned Americans caught up in the antinuclear maelstrom—there is no need to reinvent nuclear policy. There *is* a need for arms control: SALT II is the best transition to real reductions. There *is* a need to avoid limited nuclear war: rebuilding our conventional strength and perhaps reintroducing the draft would reduce that risk. These proposals are neither new nor exciting. Unlike Schell's crusade, they don't promise to restore "the wholeness and meaning of life." They don't suggest that "the passion and will that we need to save ourselves would flood into our lives. Then the walls of indifference, inertia, and coldness that now isolate each of us from others, and all of us from the past and future generations, would melt, like snow in spring." They don't promise to set right "our disordered instinctual life." That is because working to reduce the chances of nuclear war is not an exercise in psychotherapy. It is not a romance. It is mundane work in pursuit of mundane objectives: a modest program of nuclear modernization, SALT II, and a bigger conventional defense. These measures will not cure anomie, but will help to maintain deterrence, that difficult abstraction on which our values and our safety depend.

The New Republic, April 28, 1982

Will Star Wars Kill Arms Control?

IT IS NOT DIFFICULT TO MAKE THE CASE THAT PRESIDENT REAGAN'S Star Wars plan aimed at making "nuclear weapons impotent and obsolete" is an illusion, and that the promise it holds out, of repealing deterrence, is a fraud. Deterrence can be abolished only by a leakproof population defense. As early as the Pentagon-commissioned Hoffman report of October 1983, serious strategists concluded that such a defense is simply not on the horizon. And even if such a miraculous ballistic missile defense were possible, the American people would remain vulnerable to nuclear retaliation—deterrence—by cruise missile or bomber.

A somewhat harder case to make is that even if Star Wars could work, arms control is better. Star Wars has great intuitive appeal. A "defensive transition" would make the world safer, it seems. Perhaps, but not safer, not more stable, than an offensive transition by mutual agreement.

Consider two near-ideal scenarios. In scenario A, the dream of arms control advocates (like the Scowcroft Commission), both the United States and the Soviets have revised their offensive weaponry, banned multiple warhead missiles (known as MIRVs) and gone to a regime of single warhead (Midgetman) missiles. Neither has a defensive shield. In scenario B, the near ideal of strategic defense advocates, both the United States and Soviets have established elaborate, say ninety-nine percent effective, defenses against ballistic missiles. They have also continued improving the quantity, accuracy and MIRVing capacity of their offensive weapons. Which regime is more stable?

The strategic stability of regime A is based on the fact that both sides are deprived of any incentive ever to strike first. Since it takes roughly two warheads to destroy one enemy silo, an attacker must expend two of his missiles to destroy one of the enemy's. A first strike disarms the attacker. The aggressor ends up worse off than the aggressed. Moreover, in scenario A, the equilibrium is stable: to disrupt it, or, as the experts say, to break out, would require rebuilding a MIRVed missile force. And that would take years and hundreds of billions of dollars, and be easily observable.

Regime B also achieves equilibrium, but an unstable one. Regime B is based on a system of defensive shields that are extremely complicated and delicate. They are inherently subject to sudden breakdown, as we see, for example, in the far less sophisticated space shuttle program. A faulty valve or switch or computer could let down either shield. Furthermore, the shields are vulnerable to attack. In a crisis, if one side decides to strike first (remember: it has kept perfecting the offensive weapons to do so), it will surely begin by attacking the space-based defense, which itself is highly vulnerable to disruption or destruction. Thus under regime B breakdown or breakout can occur at any moment.

It seems to me, therefore, that arms control based on revision of offensive weaponry offers the hope of a less fragile nuclear balance than one based on exotic defenses. For all arms control advocates, however, the question is how to get there from here.

In the intervening months, the Soviets have provided a somewhat ironic answer to that question: Star Wars. Or more precisely, the threat of a certain kind of American strategic defense.

Ever since the President managed to turn his Star Wars idea into a $26 billion program, the Soviets have been positively desperate to stop it. So anxious are they, that they have returned to the Geneva talks which they had abandoned a year ago, without any of their conditions for returning having been met. Their principal objective, stated quite openly, is to stop the arms race in space. ("Militarization of space," they call it, as if the vast majority of their hundreds of Cosmos satellites are not military.) They are particularly anxious to stop American testing of antisatellite (ASAT) weapons scheduled for this spring. Last summer they tried to make a moratorium on such testing a condition for a resumption of arms control talks in Vienna. They also insisted that these talks deal exclusively with space weapons. When the United States insisted that offensive weapons be included on the agenda, plans for the talks collapsed. After the election, the Soviets accepted the American position. "Umbrella" talks begin January 7 in Geneva.

Something that scares the daylights out of Chernenko & Co. is not automatically to be embraced. But it does merit attention. Kremlin behavior in the face of the possibility of American space weapons raises an important question. If Star Wars is as useless a system as it seems, why are the Russians so afraid?

One theory is that, like Americans who understandably would like to close their eyes and wish upon a star that American ingenuity will somehow pop an impermeable astrodome over the United States, the Russians believe that American defensive technology will triumph, leaving the Soviet Union disarmed. I can't believe the Russians believe it. The Russians may be paranoid, but they're not stupid. They can read our technical journals as well as we can. And the overwhelming evidence from studies inside and outside the government is that a population defense, which must be perfect, is out of the question.

What scares the Kremlin is another prospect: an imperfect American strategic defense. It is possible, and it could perform an important function. It could defend weapons.

The elements of such a strategic defense are easy to imagine. (I shift terminology from Star Wars to strategic defense, not to favor one side or the other, but because the partial defense I'll be talking about is built mainly on existing technology and needs few space-based elements.) It is basically the kind of "intermediate" defense advocated in the Hoffman report: the "lower tiers" of a multilayered system, the upper tiers of which are left to the future. "Lower tiers" stop incoming missiles at the last stages of flight, as they approach American targets. Most important is what is called "terminal defense," antimissile missiles that ring American military targets (like missile bases or command and control centers) and shoot incoming warheads out of the sky. This is not as crackpot an idea as it sounds. The Army successfully tested such a "bullet hitting a bullet" last June. This is essentially a modern version of the old Sentinel and Safeguard ABM idea that the United States considered, then abandoned in the sixties and seventies. Except that the modern system works. (It is also similar to the existing ABM system that defends Moscow.)

The technology for such a defense exists today. And to accomplish the mission of defending weapons, it probably does not even require the addition of more exotic defensive layers, namely, mid-course and boost-phase interception. However, even imperfect versions of these latter systems would improve the effectiveness of any terminal defense. And the United States is about to test a sophisticated ASAT system, which could be useful in mid-course interception of orbiting warheads. (The highest defense layer, "boost-phase" defense which attacks enemy missiles as they leave their silos, is far in the future.)

Now, any such system is bound to be imperfect. For a city defense, that makes for failure. If one bomb gets through, that means the city is destroyed. In defending military targets, and missile bases in particular, that's not true. If only a sizable proportion of incoming warheads are destroyed, the defense is successful.

This is how. Suppose A launches a first strike, composed of missiles each carrying eight warheads. Since it takes two of A's warheads to destroy one of B's missiles, every A missile can potentially destroy four B missiles. Against a defense that is only seventy-five percent effective (that would take out six of every eight warheads), every A missile takes out one B missile. A gains no advantage from launching a preemptive attack. (Note that to allow twenty-five percent of incoming warheads to leak through a city defense is catastrophic.) Seventy-five percent efficiency will no doubt be difficult to attain, but it's not pie in the sky. And unlike a heavily space-based defense, terminal defense is deployed on the American land mass. Therefore, unlike an exotic Star Wars system, it could be deployed without Soviet acquiescence.

That would have two major effects on the Soviets. In the strategic nuclear balance, the United States has clear advantages in submarines, in penetrating aircraft, and in cruise missiles. The one area where the Soviets have a countervailing advantage is land-based missiles. The SS-18s and -19s, heavy and MIRved, are accurate enough to pose a serious threat to the American military targets. A partial American defense around such targets, even a leaky one, would, in effect and unilaterally, degrade this Soviet arsenal. It would close the famous window of vulnerability proclaimed by Ronald Reagan and others in the 1970s. (Mention of which was discreetly dropped by Mr. Reagan when he could do nothing about it as President in the 1980s.) It would largely destroy the value of the Soviets' greatest military asset.

But that's not the worst of it. If coupled with a continuing American buildup of offensive weapons—particularly highly MIRved, accurate missiles like the MX, and the D5 to be deployed on submarines in the next decade—it would have, from the Soviets' point of view, a second, even more alarming effect. It would give the United States a credible first strike capacity. The tables will have been reversed. The United States will have achieved what Ronald Reagan promised in 1980: strategic superiority.

That is what is driving the Soviets to Geneva. Star Wars is a particularly good bargaining chip. Most bargaining chips work only when traded away.

The MX, for example, does not solve American vulnerability to SS-18s. It simply creates a parallel (and, we hope, intolerable) vulnerability for the Soviets. An imperfect Star Wars works by thinning the Soviet SS-18 and -19 force whether they deal or not. It places the Soviets in the position where either they can see their offensive weapons degraded unilaterally, getting nothing in return, or they can reduce them bilaterally and get a reduction in American defensive (and perhaps offensive) deployments as well. It forces the Soviets, as it were, to negotiate on warning: use it (to deal) or lose it.

The warning has already concentrated Kremlin minds on the wisdom of dealing. While in London last month, Mikhail Gorbachev announced that the Soviets were prepared to negotiate deep reductions in offensive systems, once Star Wars was disposed of. And Gromyko is on his way to the Geneva umbrella talks.

Ironically, in this country the idea of strategic defense as a road to arms control is quite unpopular. Those who want strategic defense tend to care little for arms control, and those who want arms control tend to care even less for strategic defense.

The President heads the first school. In fact, he sees Star Wars as a means to transcend deterrence, a more lofty goal than mere arms control. Last month he again opined that any nuclear policy based on killing millions of people—i.e., his policy today—is immoral. In this he is joined by Secretary of Defense Weinberger, who in a recent speech denounced the system by which "our safety is based only on the threat of avenging aggression." (Which, by the way, is the rationale for our *conventional* forces: what else are our boys doing in Korea and Germany?)

Most of the President's men no longer sing that tune. In 1983 the President's science adviser, George Keyworth, was touting Star Wars as a way "of getting off the runaway horse of massive retaliation." By December 1984 he was defending "an initial ballistic missile defense," as a way to "return us to an era when ballistic missiles represented a retaliatory deterrent, not a preemptive strike," an era for which he had previously evinced little nostalgia. Under Secretary of Defense Fred Iklé used to urge Americans to "reject the permanent nightmare" of deterrence. Now he talks of "intermediate" deployments—exactly the term used by the Hoffman report to describe largely "terminal" defenses for silo, not people, protection. And last month the National Security Adviser, Robert McFarlane, was talking about a strategic defense "60, 70, or more percent" effective that would make the Soviets realize that an attack on the United States would not succeed. Which, of course, is a definition of deterrence.

But even these advisers, who now see strategic defense as a way to enhance, not overthrow, deterrence, do not seem to agree that defense should be bargained away for arms control. In fact, the administration's position heading into the Geneva talks with Gromyko seems to be that Star Wars will not be given up. Leaking this position to the New York *Times* is certainly good gamesmanship. Better to make Gromyko work hard—and give up much—to restrain an American defense. But if the current hard line proves to be not a tactic but a fixed position, the administration will have missed a historic opportunity.

The severest critics of Star Wars, on the other hand, prefer to forfeit this historic opportunity in advance. They want strategic defense killed in the crib, by Congress if necessary. I refer here to the school headed by the Gang of Four ex-strategists (George Kennan, McGeorge Bundy, Gerard Smith and Robert McNamara), by now the establishment's permanent opposition on things nuclear. They deny that strategic defense is a road to anything except danger. In an article in *Foreign Affairs* titled "The President's Choice: Star Wars or Arms Control," they argue that strategic defense will destroy arms control.

On the face of it, this seems a curious proposition, coming just weeks before the Soviets' return to the bargaining table, principally to stop space weapons. What they mean, however, is that a defensive system would sink the ABM treaty.

Now, the ABM treaty is certainly an achievement, indeed *the* achievement of the SALT era. But treaties are not ends in themselves. Stability is. The purpose of the ABM treaty is to stabilize the strategic balance. Banning defenses does not automatically do that. Other conditions must hold. The ABM treaty does not protect stability if offensive innovations permit one side or both to acquire first strike capacities against the other's retaliatory forces. Which is exactly what happened in the last decade with the development of MIRVing technology. Subsequent arms control did not control MIRVS. SALT I limited launchers, not warheads; SALT II capped MIRVS, but at very high levels.

How to restore stability? One way is to protect those retaliatory forces. Permit defenses that protect weapons and command centers, though not populations. That is what an "intermediate" strategic defense would do. The ABM treaty did not ban all defenses: it permitted protection of two sites in each country. That was later revised down to one. Why should it be beyond the capacity of American and Soviet negotiators to revise the number up? Because, write the Four, "even a tightly limited and partially effective local defense of missile fields . . . would require radical amendment or repudiation of the ABM treaty and would create such interacting fears of expanding defenses that we strongly believe that it should be avoided." And yet "tightly limited and partially effective local defense of missile fields" would be highly stabilizing. It is making a fetish of the treaty to prefer it in its present form over stability.

There is even more compelling evidence of the Four's making arms control an end in itself. The Soviets are building a phased array radar station in Krasnoyarsk in central Siberia, "a violation of the express language of the [ABM] treaty," they say. (No such radar is permitted except on each country's periphery.) In view of this violation, the Four urge Congress to urge the administration to urge the Russians to respect the ABM treaty. Krasnoyarsk "does raise exactly the kinds of questions of intentional violation which are highly destructive in this country to public confidence in arms control," they write. Note: the problem with this violation is not what it does to U.S. security (it is of "marginal importance," they say), or what it reveals about Soviet trustworthiness, but what it might do to American confidence in arms control!

The Four don't stop there. While they can't blame Star Wars for the existence of the Krasnoyarsk station (it was started before the thought of Star Wars ever entered Mr. Reagan's head), they blame Star Wars for making it impossible to complain about the violation. "No such sensitive discussions will be possible while Star Wars remains a non-negotiable centerpiece of American strategic policy." Why a clear violation of an existing treaty cannot be discussed with the Soviets because of an American policy which postdates the violation and is within the terms of the treaty (it permits research) is a mystery to me.

In fact, if the United States wanted the crudest possible justification for Star Wars it could simply claim that, given the Soviets' own research in defensive technologies and their overt violation of the ABM treaty, prudence dictates that the United States conduct defensive research as a hedge against a Soviet breakout from the ABM treaty. But the United States need not say that. We need only say that we are thinking about Star Wars because MIRVing has gotten out of hand and dangerous. "Intermediate" strategic defense protecting silos is one antidote to MIRV. Better still —if the Soviets will join us—is a grand strategic compromise: we curb defense if they curb offense and negotiate a transition away from MIRV to single-warhead stability.

Is it possible? It has already been done. "In 1970," as David Holloway tells it in *The Soviet Union and the Arms Race*, "the Soviet Union proposed that a treaty be concluded on ABM systems alone, thus showing concern about the prospect of a race in defensive systems. The United States insisted, however, that offensive systems be covered too, since one of the main American aims at SALT was to obtain limitations on the deployment of the heavy SS-9 ICBM, which, it was feared, would pose a threat to American ICBM silos. The ABM Treaty and the Interim Agreement on Offensive Missiles were signed in Moscow in May 1972."

In arms control, ends (safety, parity, stability) are often obvious, and mutually, even sincerely, agreed upon. Means are the problem. Star Wars is a means. The Kremlin sees that point very well. The pity is that in the United States the most important advocates and the most important critics of strategic defense miss that point completely.

The New Republic, January 21, 1985

On Nuclear Morality

THE CONTEMPORARY ANTINUCLEAR ARGUMENT TAKES TWO FORMS. THERE is, first, the prudential argument that the nuclear balance is inherently unstable and unsustainable over time, doomed to breakdown and to taking us with it. The animating sentiment here is fear, a fear that the antinuclear campaign of the 1980s has fanned with great skill. One of the antinuclear movement's major innovations has been its insistence on a technique of graphic depiction, a kind of nuclear neorealism, as a way of mobilizing mass support for its aims. The graphics include slide shows of devastated Hiroshima and the concentrically circular maps showing where and when one will die in every hometown.

There are, however, limitations to this approach. The law of diminishing returns applies even to repeated presentations of the apocalypse. Ground Zero Day can be celebrated, as it were, once or perhaps twice, but it soon begins to lose its effectiveness. The numbing effect of detail, as well as the simple inability of any movement to sustain indefinitely a sense of high crisis and imminent calamity, have led to the current decline in popularity of the pragmatic antinuclear case.

Consequently there has been a subtle shift in emphasis to a second line of attack, from a concern about what nuclear weapons might do to our bodies to a concern about what they are doing to our souls. Medical lectures on "the last epidemic" have been replaced by a sharper, and more elevated, debate about the ethics of possessing, building and threatening to use nuclear weapons. (The most recent documents on the subject are the Pastoral Letter of the U.S. Bishops on War and Peace and Michael Novak's response, *Moral Clarity in the Nuclear Age.*)

The moral antinuclear argument is based on the view that deterrence, the central strategic doctrine of the nuclear age, is ethically impermissible. That doctrine holds that a nuclear aggressor will not act if faced with a threat of retaliation in kind. It rests, therefore, on the willingness to use nuclear weapons in response to attack. The moral critique of deterrence holds that the actual use of such weapons, even in retaliation, is never justified. As the bishops put it, simply, one is morally obliged to "say no to nuclear war." But the issues are not so simple. There are different kinds of retaliation, and different arguments (often advanced by different proponents) for the inadmissibility of each.

The popularly accepted notion of deterrence (often mistakenly assumed to be the only kind) is "countervalue" retaliation—an attack on industrial and population centers aimed at destroying the society of the aggressor. The threat to launch such retaliation is the basis of the doctrine of "mutual assured destruction," also known as MAD, massive retaliation, or the balance of terror.

For the bishops—and others, including nonpacifists like Albert Wohlstetter, who advocate "counterforce" deterrence—MAD is unequivocally bad. Deliberate attacks on "soft targets" grossly violate the just-war doctrine of discrimination. They are inadmissible under any circumstance because they make no distinction between combatants and noncombatants; indeed, they are aimed primarily at innocent bystanders.

The bishops, however, reject not just a countervalue strategy, but also a counterforce strategy of striking military targets. Since military targets are often interspersed with civilian population centers, such an attack would kill millions of innocents and thus violate the principle of proportionality, by which the suffering inflicted in a war must not outweigh the possible gains of conducting such a war. "It would be a perverted political policy or moral casuistry," write the bishops, "which tried to justify using a weapon which 'indirectly' or 'unintentionally' killed a million innocent people because they happened to live near a 'militarily significant target.' " The bishops also reject, in a second sense, the idea that a counterforce war would be limited. They share the widespread conviction that limited nuclear war is a fiction—that counterforce attacks must inevitably degenerate into countervalue warfare, and thus bring us full circle back to the moral objections to MAD and all-out nuclear war.

That doesn't leave very much. If a countervalue strategy is rejected for violating the principle of discrimination, and a counterforce strategy is rejected for violating the principle of proportionality (and also for leading back to total war), one runs out of ways of targeting nuclear weapons. That suits the bishops: they make a point of insisting that their doctrine is "no-use-ever." The logic, and quite transparent objective, of such a position is to reject deterrence *in toto*.

However, the bishops suffer from one constraint: Vatican policy seems to contradict this position. Pope John Paul has declared that "in current conditions 'deterrence' based on balance, certainly not as an end in itself but as a step on the way toward a progressive disarmament, may still be judged morally acceptable." What to do? The bishops settle for the unhappy compromise of opposing not deterrence in itself, but simply what it takes to make deterrence work. Accordingly, they do not in principle oppose the possession of nuclear weapons when its sole intention is to deter an adversary from using his; they oppose only any plan, intent or strategy to use these weapons in the act of retaliation. You may keep the weapons, but you may not use them. In sum, the only moral nuclear policy is nuclear bluff.

It is a sorry compromise, neither coherent nor convincing. It is not coherent because it requires the bishops to support a policy—deterrence —that their entire argument is designed to undermine. And it is not convincing because the kind of deterrence they approve is no deterrence at all. Deterrence is not inherent in the weapons. It results from a combination of possession and the will to use them. If one side renounces, for moral or other reasons, the intent of ever actually using nuclear weapons, deterrence ceases to exist.

Pacifists unencumbered by papal pronouncements are able more openly to oppose deterrence. To take only the most celebrated recent example, in *The Fate of the Earth* Jonathan Schell makes the case the bishops would like to make, stripped of any theological trappings. In its secular version the argument goes like this: biological existence is the ultimate value; all other values are conditional upon it; there can be neither liberty nor democracy nor any other value in defense of which Western nuclear weapons are deployed, if mankind itself is destroyed; and after nuclear war the earth will be "a republic of insects and grass." (Schell too rejects the possibility of limited nuclear war.) Therefore nothing can justify using nuclear weapons. Deterrence is more than a hoax; it is a crime.

Schell's argument enjoys a coherence that the bishops' case lacks, but it is still unsatisfying. Judged on its own terms—of finding a policy that best serves the ultimate and overriding value of biological survival—it fails.

For one thing, it willfully ignores history. Deterrence has a track record. For the entire postwar period it has maintained the peace between the two superpowers, preventing not only nuclear but conventional war as well. Under the logic of deterrence, proxy and brushfire wars are permitted, but not wars between the major powers. As a result, Europe, the central confrontation line between the two superpowers, has enjoyed its longest period of uninterrupted peace in a century. And the United States and the Soviet Union, the two most powerful nations in history, locked in ideological antagonism and engaged in a global struggle as profound as any in history, have not exchanged so much as small-arms fire for a generation.

This is not to say that deterrence cannot in principle breakdown. It is to say that when a system that has kept the peace for a generation is to be rejected, one is morally obliged to come up with a better alternative. It makes no sense to reject deterrence simply because it may not be infallible; it makes sense to reject it only if it proves more dangerous than the alternatives.

The breakdown of deterrence would lead to a catastrophic increase in the probability of precisely the inadmissible outcome its critics seek to avoid. The bishops unwittingly concede that point in a subsidiary argument against counterforce when they speak of such a strategy "making deterrence unstable in a crisis and war more likely."

The critics argue that no ends can justify such disproportionate and nondiscriminatory means as the use of nuclear weapons. That would be true if the ends of such use were territory, domination or victory. But they are not. The sole end is to prevent a war from coming into existence in the first place. That the threat of retaliation is the best available this-world guarantee against such a war is a paradox the bishops and other pacifists are unwilling to face.

Nevertheless, moral debate does not end with the acceptance of the necessity, and thus the morality, of deterrence. Not everything is then permitted. There is a major argument between proponents of countervalue and counterforce deterrence. The former claim that counterforce threats lower the nuclear threshold and make nuclear war more likely because it becomes "more thinkable." The latter argue that to retaliate against defenseless populations is not only disproportionate and nondiscriminatory but dangerous as well, since it is not credible and thus actually lowers the nuclear threshold. Note that the debate among nonpacifists is over the relative merits of different kinds of retaliation, and not, as is sometimes pretended, between a "party of deterrence" and a "war-fighting party." The latter distinction is empty: all deterrence rests on the threat of nuclear retaliation, i.e., "war fighting"; and all retaliatory (i.e., nonlunatic) war-fighting strategies from McNamara to today are designed to prevent attack in the first place, i.e., for deterrence. The distinction between these two "parties" has to do with candor, not strategy: the "war fighters" are willing to spell out the retaliatory steps that the "deterrers" rely on to prevent war but prefer not to discuss in public.

Whichever side of the intramural debate among deterrence advocates one takes, it seems to me that deterrence wins the debate with its opponents simply because it is a better means of achieving the ultimate moral aim of both sides—survival.

There is another argument in favor of deterrence, though in my view it carries less weight. It appeals not to survival but to other values. It holds that (1) there are values more important than survival, and (2) nuclear weapons are necessary to protect them. The second proposition is, of course, true. The West is the guarantor of such fragile historic achievements as democracy and political liberty; a whole constellation of ideals and values ultimately rests on its ability to deter those who reject these values and have a history of destroying them wherever they dominate. To reject deterrence unilaterally is to surrender these values in the name of survival.

The rub comes with the first proposition. Are there values more important than survival? Sidney Hook was surely right when he once said that when a person makes survival the highest value, he has declared that there is nothing he will not betray. But for a civilization, self-sacrifice is senseless, since there are no survivors to give meaning to the sacrificial act. For a civilization, survival may be worth betrayal. If indeed this highly abstract choice were the only one, it would be hard to meet Schell's point that since all values hinge on biological survival, to forfeit that is to forfeit everything. It is thus simply not enough to say (rightly) that nuclear weapons, given the world as it is today, keep us free; one must couple that statement with another, equally true: they keep us safe. A nuclear policy—like unilateralism—that forces us to choose between being dead or Red is morally dubious. A nuclear policy—like deterrence—that protects us from both calamities is morally compelling.

Nuclear weapons are useful only to the extent that they are never used. But they are more likely to fulfill their purpose, and never be used, if one's adversary believes that one indeed has the will to use them in retaliation for attack. That will to use them is what the moralists find unacceptable. But it is precisely on that will to use them that the structure of deterrence rests. And it is on the structure of deterrence that rest not only the "secondary" values of Western civilization but also the primary value of survival in the nuclear age.

Commentary, October 1983

VII

MEMORY

Collective Guilt, Collective Responsibility

NO MATTER WHICH SIDE OF THE BITBURG DEBATE PEOPLE ARE ON—SHOULD President Reagan lay a wreath at a German World War II cemetery or shouldn't he?—everyone from Helmut Kohl to Elie Wiesel seems to agree that there is, or ought to be, no such thing as collective responsibility. As Wiesel said in his White House address, "I do not believe in collective guilt nor in collective responsibility. Only the killers are guilty."

Can that be true? To start with, it is not the view of the common law. If you rob a bank and shoot the teller, you are not the only person guilty of murder. Your unarmed accomplice is, too. And the driver of the getaway car. In short, anyone who knowingly joined the criminal enterprise. The law spreads wide the net of guilt in order to express a moral truth: When you join a killing enterprise your private moral scruples do not limit your guilt. *You* may not be a killer, but if you sign up with killers, you are party to the deed.

In fact, Wiesel's own argument against the Bitburg visit rests (correctly) on the idea of collective guilt. Wiesel implored the President not to go because of "the presence of SS graves." He did not inquire into the individual deeds of these SS men. He did not need to. To be a member of the SS is enough. Did any of these men pull the trigger at Malmé, where the *Waffen* SS murdered 71 American POWs? Or at Oradour, where they murdered 642 Frenchmen? Or was it their comrades? It hardly matters. These crimes simply compound the guilt; to be a member of the SS establishes it. When you join the most monstrous of killing organizations, when you carry its seal, you become responsible for its crimes.

The collective guilt of the German Army is of a different order. The SS was designed to kill; the Wehrmacht, to defend the killers and conquer at their command. This does not make the ordinary German soldier a mass murderer. But that said, he does not become the moral equivalent of, say, an American soldier. Between mass murder and ordinary soldierhood lies a vast moral no man's land, and in that no man's land lies Bitburg. Soldiers who die defending a regime of incomprehensible criminality are not criminals, but they bear—let us be charitable—a taint. (Which is why, even without the SS, Bitburg's dead are far down any list of those deserving to be graced by the presence of an American president.) A soldier cannot totally divorce himself from his cause.

When Lord Mountbatten died, he left instructions that the Japanese not be invited to his funeral. He could not forgive the way they had treated his men as prisoners in Southeast Asia during the war. Now, certainly only those Japanese who tortured his men were torturers. But, just as certainly, the nation that produced these torturers and produced the war in which the tortures took place, bears some taint. Not enough, by any means, to warrant a trial. But enough, certainly, to warrant exclusion from a funeral.

We apply the same logic of collective guilt and measured response to white South Africans. Why, after all, are they banned from civilized international life (like sports), if not for the feeling that by acquiescing to apartheid, they bear some guilt—for which ostracism is not too disproportionate a penalty?

But what about those with no conceivable connection to an historical crime? Two thirds of Germans today, Chancellor Kohl likes to remind us, are too young to remember the war. Surely they do not bear collective responsibility for Germany's past.

Surely they do. They bear, of course, no guilt. But they bear responsibility. The distinction is important.

Ask yourself: None of us was around when treaties were made and broken with the Indians a hundred years ago; we bear no guilt; are we absolved of responsibility to make redress today for the sins of our fathers?

I wasn't born when Japanese-Americans were interned during World War II. If Congress decides to apologize or to compensate the victims with my tax dollars (Senator Matsunaga introduced the resolution yesterday), will I have suffered an injustice?

I think not. The point is this. There is such a thing as a corporate identity. My American identity entitles me to certain corporate privileges: life, liberty, happiness pursued, columns uncensored. These benefits I receive wholly undeserved. They are mine by accident of birth. So are America's debts. I cannot claim one and disdain the other.

During the centuries of slavery in America, my ancestors were being chased by unfriendly authorities across Eastern Europe. I feel, and bear, no guilt for the plight of blacks. But America's life is longer than mine. America has a history, and obligations that flow from that history. To be American today is to share in those obligations.

Or are my children going to default on Treasury bonds issued today on the grounds that they were not yet born when these collective obligations were incurred?

It is good politics around VE-Day to deny the notion of collective responsibility. Only, it is nonsense. Collective responsibility is an elementary principle of national life. It is not just that without that principle there would be no national apologies (like that proposed by Senator Matsunaga) or war reparations (like those given by democratic Germany to Nazi Germany's victims). There would be no bond market.

The Washington Post, May 3, 1985

The Bitburg Fiasco

WHEN PRESIDENT REAGAN AND CHANCELLOR KOHL OF WEST GERMANY first discussed the idea, it seemed like a good one: a V-E Day visit by the President to a cemetery in Germany where American and German soldiers lie side by side. It would be a ceremony of friendship and reconciliation.

It has, of course, become a disaster. It turned out that no American dead from World War II are buried in Germany. It would have to be a purely German cemetery. And it turned out that Bitburg, the one suggested by Chancellor Kohl, contained the graves of forty-seven members of the SS.

But even before the unraveling, and the storm that followed, was there anything wrong with the original scenario? Just a few months ago, after all, did not Kohl and President Mitterrand of France hold a moving reconciliation at the World War I battlefield at Verdun? When Kohl raised with Reagan the idea of a cemetery visit, he cited the Verdun ceremony as the model.

The analogy does not hold, and that Kohl and Reagan could miss the point is at the heart of the Bitburg fiasco. World War II was unlike World War I, or any other war. It was unique because Nazism was unique. Nazi Germany was not just another belligerent; it was a criminal state. Even that term is inadequate.

This does not make the eighteen-year-old who died defending the Nazi regime a criminal. Nor does it lessen the grief of his mother. But it does lessen the honor due him from the President of the United States. Even among the dead, we are required to make distinctions. It is not just grotesquely wrong to say, as the President said last week, that German soldiers are as much victims as those whom the Germans tortured and murdered. There is also a distinction to be drawn between Hitler's soldiers and the Kaiser's. Mitterrand's choice of Verdun, the awful symbol of World War I, shows a grasp of that distinction. The choice of Bitburg does not.

If the distinction seems subtle, after the discovery of *Waffen* SS graves the need for subtlety vanishes. Even if one claims that the ordinary German soldier fought for Germany and not for Hitler, that cannot be said of the *Waffen* SS. Hitler's 1938 edict declared them to be "a standing armed unit exclusively at my disposal." A further directive in 1940 elaborated their future role. After the war the Third Reich would be expected to contain many non-Germanic nationalities. The *Waffen* SS would be the special state police force to keep order among these unruly elements. They proved themselves during the war: forty miles from Bitburg, the *Waffen* SS murdered seventy-one American POWs.

Of all the cemeteries of World War II, one containing such men is the most unworthy of a visit by an American president. The most worthy— the graves of Allied liberators or of the Nazis' victims—were originally excluded from President Reagan's agenda. After the furor, the administration hastily scheduled a trip to a concentration camp. It believes it has balanced things.

For the Jews, a camp; for Kohl, Bitburg; and for American vets, perhaps a sonorous speech. The picture now contains all the right elements. But the elements do not sit well on the canvas. They mock one another. What can it mean to honor the murdered if one also honors the murderers and their Praetorian Guard? This is photo opportunity morality, and so transparent that it will convince no one, offend everyone.

Peter Boenisch, a Bonn government spokesman, complaining about the uproar in the United States over the Bitburg visit, said, "We can't start denazification of the cemeteries." Exactly. That's the reason to stay away.

The President's lapse is not just moral but historical. At first, he declared that he would put the past behind him: reopen no wounds, apportion no blame, visit no death camp. But one cannot pretend that the world began on V-E Day 1945. One has to ask the question: Where did the new Germany come from? Some concession had to be made to history. The President decided to make it. And he chose precisely the wrong history.

V-E Day separates two German histories. The moral rebirth of Germany after the war was, and is, premised on a radical discontinuity with the Nazi past. The new Germany is built around the thin strand of decency, symbolized by people like Adenauer and Brandt, that reaches back to the pre-Nazi era. If history is what the President wants to acknowledge, it is this German history that deserves remembrance. For Kohl and Reagan to lay a wreath at Bitburg is to subvert, however thoughtlessly, the discontinuity that is the moral foundation of the new Germany.

It is a Soviet propagandist's delight. The Soviets play the Nazi–West Germany theme night and day. It is false. West Germany's honorable history is its refutation. Why then a visit that cannot fail symbolically to affirm the lie?

This is not just bad history, but terrible politics. It is all the more ironic because the only conceivable reason for the Bitburg visit in the first place is politics: alliance politics. Kohl had a problem. His exclusion from D-day ceremonies last year gave ammunition to those who complain that Germany bears equally the burdens of the Western alliance but is denied equal respect. Reagan wanted to use this ceremony to help Kohl.

Now, strengthening democratic and pro-NATO forces in Germany is a laudable end, particularly in light of domestic and Soviet pressures on Germany over Euromissile deployment. But surely there are less delicate instruments than V-E Day for reinforcing NATO. And surely there are limits to alliance politics. At this point President Reagan is reluctant to change his plans because of the acute embarrassment it would cause the German government. But that injury is certain to be more transient than the injury to memory that would result from sticking to his plans.

The Bitburg fiasco is a mess, but even messes have a logic. This incident is a compound of some of the worst tendencies of the Reagan presidency: a weakness for theater, a neglect of history and a narrowly conceived politics.

Commemorating victory over radical evil demands more than theater, history or politics. Among the purposes of remembrance are pedagogy (for those who were not there) and solace (for those too much there). But the highest aim of remembrance (for us, here) is redemption. The President and the Chancellor did indeed want this V-E Day to bring some good from evil. But for that to happen at Bitburg will require more than two politicians. It will require an act of grace, and that is not for politicians—or other mortals—to dispense.

It is perhaps just as difficult to find redemption at Bergen-Belsen, but there is a difference. There the blood of Abel cries out from the ground. We cannot answer that cry, but listening for it is in itself a redemptive act. To imagine that one can do the same over the tomb of Cain is sad illusion.

Time, April 29, 1985

CHARLES KRAUTHAMMER was born in 1950 in New York City and raised in Montreal. He was educated at McGill University (B.A. in Political Science and Economics, 1970), Oxford University (Commonwealth Scholar in politics at Balliol College, 1970–71) and Harvard (M.D., 1975). He practiced medicine for three years as a Resident and then Chief Resident in Psychiatry at the Massachusetts General Hospital. During that time he published several papers on manic-depressive illness, for which he received the Edward Dunlop Award.

In 1978 he left medical practice, came to Washington to direct planning in psychiatric research for the Carter administration and began contributing articles to *The New Republic.* He served as assistant and speechwriter to Vice-President Walter Mondale during the presidential campaign of 1980. After the campaign, he joined *The New Republic* as a writer and editor. In 1983 he began contributing a monthly essay to *Time* magazine. He also writes a nationally syndicated weekly column for *The Washington Post.*

In 1984 he won the National Magazine Award for Essays and Criticism. He has also been honored with a Champion Tuck Media Award for Economic Understanding, and the First Amendment Award of People for the American Way.

He lives in Washington, D.C. with his wife, Robyn, an artist, and son, Daniel.